Passagemaking
Handbook

Passagemaking Handbook

A Guide *for* Delivery Skippers *and* Boat Owners

John Rains and Patricia Miller

Seven Seas Press
Camden, Maine

Published by Seven Seas Press/International Marine Publishing Company

10 9 8 7 6 5 4 3 2 1

Library of Congress Cataloging-in-Publication Data

Miller, Patricia (Patricia Helen)
  Passagemaking handbook : a guide for delivery skippers and boat owners / Patricia Miller and John Rains.
    p. cm.
  Includes bibliographical references.
  ISBN 0-915160-99-4
  1. Yachts and yachting.   I. Rains, John. II. Title. III. Title:
Guide for delivery skippers and boat owners.
GV811.M48   1989
623.88—dc20   89-37283
                                     CIP

Seven Seas Press offers software for sale. For information and a catalog, please contact TAB Software Department, Blue Ridge Summit, PA 17294-0850.

Questions regarding the content of this book should be addressed to:

Seven Seas Press
Division of TAB Books, Inc.
P.O. Box 220
Camden, ME 04843

Typeset by Graphic Composition, Inc., Athens, GA
Printed by Fairfield Graphics, Fairfield, PA
Design by Faith Hague/Watermark Design, Camden, ME
Edited by Elizabeth Holman

CONTENTS

DEDICATION

To all of you who have entrusted us to deliver your beloved boats. Without you this book could never have been written.

ACKNOWLEDGMENTS

We would like to extend our thanks to Mara Mattia for her illustrations, Larry Serra for his contract editing and encouragement, and Janis Ward for her help with the seagoing exercises.

Thanks to those faithful magazine editors who waited patiently for promised articles while we labored at this book.

And thanks to all our friends and relatives for dragging us to the surface when we disappeared inside our computers for weeks on end.

INTRODUCTION

As we travel in our business around the watery portions of the world, people we meet invariably ask three questions:

1 "So, you deliver these luxurious yachts *for a living*?"
2 "Need any crew?"
3 "How can I do what you're doing?"

The answer to the first two questions is yes. We do make an honest, decent living by moving other people's power and sailing yachts for them, and we've been doing it full-time for 12 years with never an insurance claim. Yes, we frequently hire crewmembers and even refer our excess business to other delivery captains.

Because we've been successful at what we do, we're willing and qualified to answer the third question. Three kinds of people ask it:

1 Boat owners making their first serious voyage from Point A to Point B who hope to learn the hard-won secrets of the professionals so they can either do it themselves or hire a good captain;
2 Sailors preparing for their first extended cruise and seeking advice on such diverse topics as readying their boats for sea, provisioning, offshore seamanship, and recommended routes along the U.S. East and West Coasts and through the Caribbean;

3 Experienced sailors who want to turn their seamanship talents into professional, money-making skills, perhaps so they can throw over the traces of the nine-to-five world and make a living at sea instead.

We wrote this book for all three groups. One reason is that we got started in yacht delivery from these exact situations. We both were boat owners who needed solid answers to a zillion slippery "how-to" questions—answers normally gleaned from years of trial and error—and we were extremely reluctant to proceed with only the well-intentioned advice of nonprofessionals. There weren't any books available then that put it all together as we've done here. And later, we built on our years of experience in recreational boating, enabling both of us to migrate from more constricting jobs directly into yacht delivery.

The best place to start a new adventure is with good information. Memorizing a book full of facts can never substitute for the knowledge you gain from personal experience. But we feel that if you're first armed with the straight scoop about yacht delivery, you're better able to make informed choices, whether you're choosing a new Satnav, screening prospective crewmembers, or deciding what to do first, bail or call "Mayday."

We divided this book into four parts: Preparing Yourself, Preparing the Boat, Underway, and The Yacht Delivery Business. Using this book as a reference, you can meander through the pages, guided by the index to locate answers to such questions as: "How would I know how much food to buy for four crew for a 30-day trip?" "Who pays for the food?" "What sort of watch system should we use?" Or you can refer to the chapter headings to find successful solutions to challenges you already may have encountered.

Part I shows you how to set up your own program of self-teaching to quickly develop the skills you'll need, whether you just want to move your own boat, go cruising forever, or enter the yacht delivery business.

Part II shows you how to prepare any boat—even an unfamiliar one—for a major passage. This section serves as an elaborate checklist, detailing each step from surveying the boat and drawing up a spares list to provisioning and performing the sea trial. It covers both sail and power boats. Powerboat owners should find this section particularly useful since most cruising manuals on the market today give only scant treatment of "the noise maker." Veteran cruisers might assume such preparations are identical to those required for a long-range cruise, but we'll show you how to streamline the preparation of an unfamiliar vessel quickly and inexpensively, without sacrificing safety. What normally takes experienced cruisers a few months to do, you'll learn how to do in a few days.

In Part III you move off to sea, as if you were actually underway and making a long-range delivery with some coastal hops and stops in foreign countries. You'll establish life patterns aboard with round-the-clock watches, night orders, log books, and healthy ship-keeping habits. Between exotic foreign port calls for fuel and supplemental provisions, you'll learn how to use the radios to monitor weather and how to navigate coastal waters and offshore, with and without electronics. You'll even encounter hurricanes.

Though not intended as a comprehensive seamanship manual, Part III is loaded with tips about life underway that might otherwise take a lifetime of cruising to discover.

Part IV is a complete and concise miniguide for setting yourself up in the business of yacht delivery. It includes everything from organizing office procedures to handing over the boat keys. We've indicated who your strongest sales contacts and best-paying clients are likely to be, and we've shown you how to start developing them now. With samples of our own successful contracts, you'll find out what your legal responsibilities are, and how to write your own contracts. We've hired hundreds of temporary crewmembers over the past decade, and our hiring guide will help you avoid the common mistakes. There's also a chapter for boat owners who are looking for a good delivery captain. The miniguide to starting your own business simply codifies the business practices of yacht delivery, and is aimed at continually raising your level of professionalism within the industry.

There also are four appendices: The Ideal Boat, Planning those Meals, Weather and Routing from Florida to California via Panama, and Suggested Reading.

While writing this book our stickiest problem was deciding who should be the author of which parts, and then which voice to use—John's, Pat's, or both. We solved it by merging our very distinct writing styles and by using the ubiquitous *we,* except where confusing or misleading to the reader. Each time squall lines arose between us over whose personal version would stand in print, we resolved it in a manner befitting a couple of professional captains in the same boat. We fought tooth and nail, and then we compromised.

May your berth always be comfortable and dry.

John Rains and Pat Miller

PART I
PREPARING YOURSELF

CHAPTER 1
ADVICE TO BOAT OWNERS

Many aspiring cruisers spend years working on their boats, getting them ready for a big trip. Every spare moment is filled redoing the varnish, installing a roller-furling system, rebuilding the generator. The list is endless. The aspiring cruisers dream and dream about their big adventure, but seldom do they get underway. Finally the big day comes, the boat is all ready and they take off, often finding out in short order that they really don't know what they are doing "out there."

The problem is that they have gotten the boat ready, but they haven't readied themselves, because in all that time they have very seldom left the dock. The knowledge and experience of a boat operator are just as crucial to a successful voyage as the condition of the vessel.

For the aspiring yacht deliverer the big problem is: How can I ever get myself into a position where a boat owner will pay me to deliver his boat? It will never happen until you gain enough experience at running a boat successfully to distinguish yourself from the enormous crowd of yachtsmen.

For amateurs and aspiring professionals alike, self-preparation requires a concentrated, two-pronged effort involving study and practice underway.

Veteran cruiser Hal Roth puts it this way in *After 50,000 Miles:*

You can learn the fundamentals quickly, but half a lifetime seems scarcely enough to perfect your techniques. A good sailor is always studying and learning and asking questions. People who travel and work on the sea tend to be literate souls who often write books. There is an astounding library of nautical volumes that you can digest bit by bit to hurry your learning process. But in spite of the help to be got from books, you must learn about sailing at first hand. You do not become a seaman by reading. You need practice. You need to get your hands dirty.

If you own your own cruising boat, you already have the perfect vehicle for training yourself. Even a small pocket cruiser requires the same basic skills as running a larger vessel, except for docking and other close-quarters maneuvering.

Start by establishing your own stringent, self-teaching program that will get you immediately on the proper heading to become a competent cruiser or a professional boat mover. Your training should combine classroom learning with time at sea, plus lessons on maintaining your own boat as if it were someone else's. You may have a lot of fun in the process of self-education, but always take your lessons seriously.

Start by enrolling in all the basic seamanship and navigation classes available to you. The U.S. Coast Guard Auxiliary and the U.S. Power Squadron both offer such courses as a public service. The cost is minimal, just enough to cover registration and course materials. Generally available are classes on safety and boat handling, Rules of the Road, sailing dynamics, coastal piloting, celestial navigation, marine diesel maintenance, and boating equipment.

Start your classwork with a basic piloting course, often called Coastal Navigation, then move up to more advanced piloting. Don't rush into a celestial navigation course until you've truly mastered piloting. Coastal piloting requires closer attention to detail, and the consequences of error are more immediate, possibly resulting in grounding or worse. If piloting is at all mysterious to you, celestial navigation will be meaningless. Once you're an accomplished coastal navigator, move into the celestial realm.

Celestial navigation separates the seals from the sea lions. It's amazing how many delivery skippers know only coastal navigation. By not learning celestial, they are very much limiting the number of delivery jobs they can handle. This is another area of expertise where you can forge ahead of the pack. And if you are an amateur planning an offshore trip, you must learn celestial whether your vessel is Satnav-equipped or not. What would you do if the machine quit in midocean?

Buy a good sextant. It's an investment in your future that you can start enjoying immediately. It will also help you learn celestial navigation faster and more thoroughly. Practice just offshore from your homeport to see how accurate you are. Then move increasingly farther offshore during your overnight practices.

Weather is another subject in which even professional mariners have little academic background. If you live in a maritime community, special courses tailored to the sailor's needs should be available. If not, check your local colleges or adult education programs. Weather knowledge pays great dividends in planning a voyage and may also give you the basis for interpreting weather reports while underway, so you can decide whether to seek the shelter of port or change course to avoid a brewing storm.

Take your boat out as often as possible to practice what you are learning in the classroom.

Study and practice are complementary. Study is very important but it's not enough by itself. You must have the practical experience of going to sea. On the other hand, seatime alone isn't enough either, when you aren't practicing what you've learned in class. We recommend a combination—a concerted effort of learning by doing, trial and error, and learning from your mistakes.

We've known many boaters who grew up on the waterfront and have owned or lived aboard boats for years, yet barely know enough to take a Sunday afternoon sail around the bay. That's fine if they never want to venture farther, but preparing for a long cruise requires serious additional study.

Start with the basics. Practice dead reckoning in familiar waters by laying out complex courses. Then practice fixing your position by taking bearings on known objects. If you're used to eyeballing your way around in familiar waters, you may discover that these exercises require more concentration than you think.

Take longer and longer trips on your boat as often as possible. First cruise locally, spending your nights at anchor. The simple principles of anchoring can be learned from a book, but you have to feel many slow drags and solid sets before you know you've got it right. Anchoring is one area in which most yachtsmen could stand to improve their technique.

When John first started boating, he learned the hard way. He recalls:

I went on a weekend trip on a friend's 36-foot sloop. We sailed 55 miles west from San Diego out to San Clemente Island. The spot where the captain chose to anchor was quite deep for the amount of anchor and rode he had aboard. In about 60 feet of water he put the anchor down with 80 feet of rode and declared us set for the night. Even as a novice I knew that your scope should be a bare minimum of three to one, ranging up to seven to one for storm conditions. The captain had out less than two to one.

However, I kept my mouth shut. He was the captain. In the middle of the night we heard a banging on the hull. One of the neighboring boaters had rowed over to inform us that we were dragging. Indeed, with the current running as it was, we would have been on the rocks within minutes. So in the middle of the night we moved to shallower water and set the anchor with the proper amount of scope, and had no more trouble.

As a novice, Pat set out to teach herself the ways of a boat. She explains:

I started by completing every U.S. Coast Guard Auxiliary course offered in San Diego for two years.

When I got my own little sailboat in Mexico, I began to practice anchoring, navigating, and repairing outboards in the privacy of remote coves and uninhabited islands. I supported myself with freelance writing, which gave me the time to learn and practice. I was my own boss, my own captain. I was hooked.

Before bringing my boat back to the U.S., I singlehandedly rerigged her, rewired her, and installed plumbing and a new steering system. The day I restepped the mast, I had about forty helpers, including the Mexican Navy. During this learning period I made several long coastal and offshore passages, accompanying other cruisers on their boats.

The next step in gaining experience is staying out all night—underway, not anchored. If you have a full-time job, use your vacations and long weekends to take these longer trips. Or plan overnights in which you don't reach your anchorage until after sunrise. Or rest up all day Saturday, sail up and down the coast or around in a big circle all night long, and come back in to your home port Sunday.

Nighttime navigation requires particularly close attention because of background lights and the lack of other visual references. Many people fear night sailing for this reason, but such fears can be overcome as you gain experience and build confidence. In John's training days, he used to spend a weekend sailing a triangular course overnight. He would tack straight upwind and out to sea for several hours, then go on a reach for several hours, returning to port during daylight on a broad reach. With no electronics other than a depth sounder, this was a very practical oceangoing exercise.

Quickly get yourself into the routine of standing night watches. Learn to take bearings on lighthouses and conspicuous landmarks. If you have radar, learn to take bearings on invisible points of land that are only seen as radar targets.

On your longer vacations, seek out cruising grounds far enough away to give you good practice. In Southern California, we use the Channel Islands off Santa Barbara. These are beautiful, primitive islands with a variety of anchorages. Very few of the anchorages are all-weather, so you must be able to pick up and move when the wind and current change, and you must know where to move. Getting to islands and back is good training in coastal navigation.

Every area of the U.S. offers a different type of cruising ground, so plan your trips to include offshore legs to new destinations. Constant practice in sheltered waters can lull you into a false sense of security about your abilities. In South Florida, the Keys are beautiful for cruising, but they seldom force you to venture into open waters. The nearby Gulf Stream is as good a proving ground as you'll find anywhere. Consider crossing to the Bahamas. You'll encounter a strong current and possible exposure to heavy winds and seas.

Owning a boat is the best course in yacht maintenance. It can teach you the basics of keeping most boats running well and looking good. Some of the lesson headings might be: Maintaining Gelcoat; The Varnish/Humidity Factor; Elementary Raw Water Impeller Replacement and Gasket Fabrication; Electrical Panel Anatomy; and How Fast-Setting Is a Truly Hot Batch of Resin?

If your own boat is not a shining example of your maintenance skills, you are probably weak in these areas and need to concentrate on improving them. The aspiring yacht deliverer should keep his or her own boat "shipshape and Bristol fashion," because it is a billboard constantly advertising his personal skills. Owners who pay others to do their work expect perfection.

You are fortunate if you have a natural mechanical aptitude, because many aspects of yacht delivery depend on it. The cruiser must have basic mechanical skills as a matter of self-sufficiency. When the engine dies in midocean

because the fuel filters are clogged, he can't call up a dockside mechanic to come out, change the filter, bleed the engine, and get it started again.

As your skills increase, plan more challenging trips for yourself. John describes his "graduation exercise":

Just before my first professional delivery, I sailed my own boat to Guadalupe Island, about 220 miles south of San Diego and 150 miles offshore. In a way, this trip was a graduation exercise, because it was the culmination of many courses along my route of self-directed study. I needed to complete this trip to gain enough confidence in my nautical abilities to start this new career.

Choosing Guadalupe as a destination meant I'd have to clear in and out of a foreign port (Ensenada), sail an offshore Pacific passage, and make a successful landfall on a small island using celestial navigation. If I couldn't do all that, I needed more training, I told myself.

We had a rough trip down with Force 6 winds on the beam. It was harder than I imagined to take celestial sights from the small, bouncing boat, especially with my cheap plastic sextant. Despite its 4,000-foot peak, tiny Guadalupe Island is shrouded in fog and remains invisible until you're practically within the surf line. I successfully made the landfall, but the first thing I did on my return was to buy a good metal sextant.

THE BIG TRIP

After a few vacation-length cruises, many boat owners dream of spending a lifetime visiting idyllic tropical paradises. Some save up their money, maybe sell a house or business, quit a job, and take off to pursue their dream.

On the East Coast, they might winter in the Bahamas or Caribbean. On the West Coast, it's Mexico, Costa Rica, or Hawaii. Often, these trips prove to be a watershed in cruisers' lives. For every cruiser whose plans are fulfilled, there are others whose dreams turn to nightmares because they lack necessary skills or because their boats aren't prepared.

Many who set out well prepared find they have an aptitude for the cruising lifestyle, and if they have the financial resources, they might spend the rest of their lives doing it. Other successful cruisers, lacking a big bank account, yearn to support themselves in their chosen lifestyle. Yacht delivery is a good way for such people to make a living at sea.

CHAPTER 2
LEARNING BY CREWING

If you don't own a boat, you can gain experience by crewing for others. If you learn your lessons quickly and well, this route to cruising competence or professional yacht delivery can be less expensive and faster than owning a boat.

Begin by seeking a regular crew position for bay sailing, and move ahead by crewing without pay or expenses on longer cruises. As your skills increase, so too will your chances of being paid to crew on better and better vessels sailing to more interesting destinations. You might crew for professional yacht delivery captains, for example. Once you're being paid, you can work your way from crew to mate and, ultimately, to captain.

Climbing the ladder like this is the most time-honored route to becoming a competent skipper. Since all you have to pay for is your travel (at first) and your personal expenses, this is the cheapest road to the captain's seat.

Landing a crew position ahead of other aspirants requires some study. You must be able to offer at least one valuable skill that may be lacking aboard a cruising boat. Take the courses we previously recommended for boat owners. Not only will you learn the skills, but you will be taking classes with boat owners and may develop the contacts you need.

Many of the cruising skills you need aren't exclusively nautical and could be picked up in a classroom in the middle of Kansas: diesel- and small-engine mechanics; celestial naviga-tion (for airplane pilots); cooking classes; Spanish, French, German, or any foreign language; amateur radio operation; electrical or electronics repair; scuba diving; canvas sewing; welding; or emergency medical training.

If you have practical experience and an aptitude for onboard mechanics, or proficiency in the previously mentioned skills, you'll be welcomed aboard a cruising boat, especially one in which these skills are lacking. This is probably the quickest route to a paid crew position even if you have no previous seagoing experience.

It is possible to learn navigation from classroom work and study, especially using exercises that simulate a cruise. Though practice underway is essential to becoming a full-fledged navigator, you might be able to find a crew slot as backup navigator. This is particularly true if you know celestial. Many beginning cruisers are weak in this area.

If you know the language spoken in the destination of a proposed cruise, you'll find a slot more easily. In much of the world traveled by yachts, Spanish and, to a lesser extent, French are the common languages. Spanish is the tongue of 200 million in Latin America alone, as well as the Spanish Mediterranean. French will stand you in good stead in many parts of the Mediterranean, Polynesia, and the Caribbean. You'll become the translator and as such have the closest contact with port clearance officials, markets, and mechanics.

When all other crewmembers must remain aboard, the translator often accompanies the captain.

Many cruising boats lack a licensed amateur radio operator. They all have heard how important amateur radio is for safety, communication with family, and weather information, but many skippers have problems passing the stringent Morse code requirement to get the license. If you already have a General Class amateur radio license or higher you might easily find a crew position on a boat equipped with ham radio. This is even more true if you are willing to supply your own portable rig. Most hams already own their own radios. This is an excellent way to get aboard, and is a great source of fun, too. Some hams are so devoted to their hobby and the thrill of talking to other hams from distant and exotic places that it's hard to tell if they go cruising to visit interesting locations or just to talk on the radio. (See Chapter 15.)

Anybody can cook, you say? The job of sea cook is a tough one. If you already enjoy cooking and don't mind becoming a "galley slave," you can find a crew position more easily with little seagoing practice. Pat took classes in microwave cooking and nutrition, and she developed vast computer files of seagoing recipes with accompanying shopping lists. Keep in mind that the job isn't easy in a tiny ship's galley, often without refrigeration, bouncing around in a seaway. It also takes experience in knowing how to set up food budgets and how to provision for offshore passages. (See Chapter 8.)

The cook's slot is a morale-keeping one as well. We once were asked to fly down to Cabo San Lucas with a crew to pick up a motor sailer and deliver it into the charter service in St. Thomas in the Virgin Islands. The owner had started this long voyage from San Francisco with a bunch of his buddies, thinking it would be a joy ride. Everybody, including the owner, was disillusioned with the adventure by the time they reached Cabo, so they jumped ship. That's when he decided that working in his law office was easier than delivering his own yacht, and that he needed the job done professionally.

When we got on board we found one big reason why. The boat had been completely provisioned with hot dogs. That's all! The freezer was still full of them. It doesn't take long to get disillusioned with any adventure that involves a steady diet of hot dogs.

Other skills can help you land a crew position, too. Scuba diving is important not just for recreation, but also for making repairs underwater or unfouling tangled anchors. Teaching and child care are valuable on larger yachts with children.

Being young, strong, eager, and willing to become a "deck ape" often is enough. Sometimes just having a current valid passport, being ready, willing, and able to leave on short notice, and standing in the right spot at the right time will do it.

How will you find these positions? Start tramping the docks and talking with people: yacht brokers, full-time boat captains, owners of boat-maintenance businesses, charter managers, etc. Don't waste your time on habitually underemployed dock loafers. Tell the right people that you're interested in crewing, and leave them a card with your name and phone number. If they don't have something for you themselves, they'll have you in mind when they hear of somebody assembling a crew. Or they may point you in the right direction. Meanwhile, leave ads or messages on marina bulletin boards.

The most effective approach is to run a classified ad in local yachting newspapers. If there's a "Crew Available" category, just list your skills. Otherwise, you must also say that you are interested in a crew position. Don't waste your ad by saying that you want to go only to Tahiti or want to sail only on a schooner.

A reliable telephone is vital. Return all calls immediately, or have someone knowledgeable return them for you, just to preserve the contact until you can follow up. If you have no phone, get a professional message service. Use a friend's phone only as a last resort. From a prospective employer's point of view, how "together" can you be if you can't manage to maintain a phone number in your own name?

Cruisers' "kick-off" parties are open to the public in some boating communities, expressly to link captains and boats with available crew. Aspiring crew often carry signs detailing their qualifications. Some even walk around inside sandwich boards. Similar to urban block parties, these social events are usually sponsored by ship chandlers or nautical publications. On the West Coast, they begin as small gatherings in early fall in the northern latitudes of Seattle and San Francisco and then follow the declining sun southward. By the time cruisers amass in San Diego, the Halloween party spills out into the streets.

Departing cruising boats begin crossing the U.S./Mexico border in late fall to spend winter and spring in Mexican and Central American waters. To locate a boat on which to make the beat northward, join the big spring blowout in La Paz.

Once you have landed a crew job, learn as much as you can by participating in as many facets of running the boat as you can, even those outside your previous area of expertise. Learn the boat's maintenance, mechanics, galley, navigation, ship's business, and provisioning.

Ask your captain to teach you how to maneuver the boat in close quarters. This is a very necessary prerequisite for skippering and a skill that you can never acquire by observation. You must actually take the controls yourself through the entire procedure. Many a captain is reluctant to relinquish the helm for the simple reason that if anybody is going to crash the boat, he wants to make sure it's him.

Ironically, it's to any captain's advantage to have another boat handler in his crew. What if the captain falls overboard and no one can maneuver the boat to retrieve him without running him over? Or what if the captain is stricken ill or becomes unconscious and you must find treatment quickly? You might point this out tactfully.

Once you're out there cruising, you will constantly be meeting other yachts. Keep one eye open for future paid crew positions on the larger yachts. In major cruising ports, crews tend to break up for a variety of reasons. The opportunity to sign on as replacement crew is great in places like Palma, Antigua, St. Thomas, Ft. Lauderdale, Acapulco, Cabo San Lucas or La Paz, Papeete, and Lahaina or Honolulu.

Crew changes may be in order, but never leave your first boat in the lurch. An unpleasant parting can haunt you for many years. You want to enjoy a good recommendation from every skipper you work for.

If you plan to get in the delivery profession, your objective is to gain one year of documented sea time toward the first level of your U.S. Coast Guard captain's license. Just the fact that you are aspiring toward a license will help you up the crew ladder, and meanwhile, it may lead to an unlicensed captain position.

CHAPTER 3
LEARNING FROM A DELIVERY CAPTAIN

One of the best ways to gain experience is to learn from a successful delivery captain. We continually need to hire temporary crew with varying levels of experience for different deliveries. Our thickest file in the cabinet is the one labeled "Crew."

If a crewmember is sufficiently experienced in his own right, and if we know him well and trust him, we frequently refer appropriate delivery clients to him. Most of the names on our list of skippers to whom we refer jobs are former crewmembers of ours.

Call all the skippers whose ads appear in marine periodicals under the yacht delivery category. Tell them you're interested in crewing for them and be prepared to answer questions about your experience. Have names and phone numbers of people who will vouch for your seagoing experience and your reliability. Be prepared to send a resume and to set up an appointment for an interview. This is much more effective than sending off a resume and cover letter.

On your initial contact, don't begin by telling the skipper that you want to break into the yacht delivery business, and that you want to gain experience from him. He may not care to train his own competition. By hiring you, he *is* going to train you, but once you've gained this experience, what you do with it is your business. (Never double-cross a former captain, but in this industry, working your way up the ladder is the honorable method; the fact that you're going to move on is completely expected, even if it's not expressly stated that way.)

We never hire anyone who has never been to deep sea before. You can never know how someone is going to react the first time they're out of sight of land for several days. Some people actually "nut out" at sea, and we can't afford to risk that possibility.

If you have a current passport before your call, your chances of getting a job immediately are much better. Passports can take anywhere from one to 30 days to attain. Expired passports are expired; you're dreaming if you hope you can squeak by or that no one will notice. Deliveries generally "congeal" in a flash, and we have to scramble to find people who are available on short notice. Many times we've had to turn down well qualified crew who didn't have current passports and hire others who just happened to call us at the right time, with passport in hand.

If you have to be extremely specific about the dates you're available for crewing on deliveries, you'll have slim chances. Because delivery work is fraught with unexpected occurrences, we can't hire people who have only, say, the first two weeks of December off from their regular job. We wouldn't want weather, or mechanical breakdown, or port delays to make someone late getting back to their regular job. But worse, we wouldn't want them to fly off before the job was completed, because we'd have to replace them en route, and that's very costly.

We get lots of calls from people wanting to crew, "preferably onboard a schooner going to New Zealand between June 30 and September 15," or something equally as specific. We tell them it would be nice if we could match each prospective crew member with the delivery of their dreams, but since we can't they'd better call a travel agency. But it never hurts to try.

If you're short on experience, offering to work for lower-than-normal wages might help you get hired, especially if the rest of the crew is highly qualified. On vessels that must be hand-steered, two crew should be on watch during each shift, one of whom serves as the "go-'fer."

We never hire inexperienced people and let them work without pay, even though we get such requests each week. We'd rather have someone with some experience and pay him or her something, perhaps not a great deal, but something. The theory is that when the chips are down, an unpaid crewmember may imagine he is just along for the ride and may not take his responsibilities seriously. That never works out well for anyone aboard.

John recounts how he got started in the yacht delivery business:

I owe my introduction to this profession to Captain Ish Fisher, an established yacht delivery skipper in San Diego. I had set myself up to go cruising on my own boat and had mentioned to a friend that I was interested in yacht delivery. My friend found out that Ish had contracted to bring two racing sailboats back from Mazatlan and needed another skipper. We were introduced, Ish hired me, and my delivery career was launched.

Ish had been delivering boats back and forth along the Mexican coast for eight years.

He would be the commodore of the two-boat fleet—he the captain of one boat and I the captain of the other, but under his direction. Ish contracted directly with the owner of my boat, paying me less than he was receiving in order to profit on the deal. By today's standards I wasn't making much, but it was something and it was a start.

I put together a crew of two others—Anne Brownfield, a good seagoing cook with lots of local cruising on her own boat, and Don Hess, a retired, 30-year Navy bosun who had already spent one season cruising in Mexico, and offered local knowledge.

Together with Ish's crew, we all set off from San Diego towards Mazatlan in the owner's car, a giant tank of a Chrysler Imperial. He was going to drive it back. Driving a thousand miles into Mexico is an adventure in itself.

We spent a couple days prepping the boat in Mazatlan. It was a learning experience for me to work under Ish's direction and to watch him handle the paperwork with the Mexican officials. *Vector,* my "first command," was a CF-37 one-ton ocean racer.

Raceboats usually are very spartan. Important to a delivery is the fact that they also have small engines and fuel capacities. The delivery from Mazatlan to San Diego was 1000 miles dead to windward, and that meant powering would be important. *Vector* had a larger than normal raceboat engine, capable of 7 knots, and had a range of 450 miles, more than adequate for the trip up Baja.

During the preparation, I had my first exposure to ham radio. *Vector's* owner, Herb Johnson, was then head of Atlas Radio, Inc. He also designed and built the Atlas radios that were very popular with cruising boats of the time. Using his radio, Johnson linked up with another ham operator and made a phone patch to his son in the States. I was impressed enough that within five years I got my own ham license.

Other than a brief *chubasco* (thunder-storm) when we first left Mazatlan, the weather for the trip back was unusually good, meaning that it was flat calm and we motored the whole way. We stopped in Cabo San Lucas and Turtle Bay. It was my first exposure to a vessel with autopilot and I was hooked. Other than coming in and out of port, we never touched the wheel.

After that trip I was infatuated with the idea of making a living in yacht delivery. I decided to use the savings I had accumulated for my cruising kitty to get started in the yacht delivery business.

I worked with Ish off and on for two years, going as captain on trips that Ish couldn't make and serving as his first mate on some of his trips. I am particularly indebted to Ish for introducing me to the world of powerboats. I was one of those purist sailors who said I would never be caught dead on a "stinkpot." After making several powerboat trips with Ish,

I became convinced that for a delivery skipper to be successful he must be willing to do both. It broadens the potential market. It also makes him a better-rounded seaman.

After a couple of years, Ish quit deliveries and went a common route for former delivery captains—into yacht sales. And I continued delivering boats as the result of the experience gained from him.

Since then, several people who have worked for me have gone on to become captains. It gives me pleasure to watch loyal crew-members who have proven their competence and ability succeed in the business.

Whether you want to be a yacht delivery captain or team, move your own boat with confidence, or prepare yourself for your cruise of a lifetime, working under an established delivery captain is a good way to get started.

PART II
PREPARING THE BOAT

CHAPTER 4
DO YOUR OWN SURVEY

A wise boater normally spends years of trial and error in the process of searching for just the right boat in which to go cruising. Then he might take months or years to get it ready for the sea. The delivery captain, on the other hand, must prepare an unfamiliar boat, usually not one he'd choose to own, for a long trip in a few days.

We'd like to share how we've learned to quickly prepare a boat for delivery, hoping that anyone making an offshore trip can benefit from this information.

On the professional side, one of the first questions asked by crew is, "Does the owner pay the captain and crew while they're prepping the boat?" The answer is a definite yes. Boat prepping is hard and serious work. It is an indispensible part of every delivery and ought to be done by the very people who are going to sea on the boat.

Prepping the boat is a constantly varying compromise between safety, time, and the owner's budget. The captain must be able to rank and organize each of the many projects involved in the prep stage, and each crewmember must know how to carry out his or her responsibilities for the prep stage. The captain must prepare the boat quickly, ensuring the vessel's ability to make a safe passage, without getting caught short of some vital item, and do it all on a budget.

More often than not, a professional delivery crew won't even see the boat until the end of a long plane ride to wherever the boat is waiting. Sometimes, that's a foreign country. For this reason our contract stipulates that if we determine upon initial inspection that the vessel is inherently unseaworthy for the proposed trip, or if vital deficiencies have not or cannot be remedied to render it seaworthy, the owner must pay a daily wage for our time spent, plus our expenses, which would then include return airfare.

To avoid wasting our time and the owner's money, we want to know as much about the boat as we possibly can to determine, *before* departure from our home base, if it merits inspection.

The primary consideration is what kind of boat it is. Is it a design that is inherently seaworthy for the proposed voyage at the specified time of year?

There are certain kinds of boats that shouldn't go certain places at certain times. It's the captain's responsibility to inform the owner if a proposed trip is not feasible. Owners often ask yacht deliverers to make trips that are marginal from a safety standpoint. No matter how badly you need the money or how much you'd like to make some exotic-sounding trip, don't let your good judgment become clouded. Your own safety and that of the crew and the vessel are at stake.

For instance, a 40-foot sportfisherman shouldn't make a trip from the West Coast to Hawaii. Small sportfishers generally aren't designed for the rigors of offshore voyaging, and they aren't large enough to carry sufficient fuel to cover 2,250 miles. We knew a delivery captain who took such a boat to Hawaii, specifically because everyone said it couldn't be done. He loaded the boat down nearly to its gunwales with fuel and had more than his share of trouble, including an onboard fire. He made it, but how much care was this captain taking for the lives of his crew? For the owner's property?

PREVIOUS SURVEY

Ask for a recent survey. Often the owner has just bought the boat, and as a condition of sale and financing, it has been hauled and surveyed. The written survey is a valuable list of equipment and an evaluation of the vessel's condition. Of particular interest is the section listing deficiencies and recommendations. Generally speaking you should follow these recommendations, but don't be misled by a survey; learn to read between the lines.

Trust seems to be a key factor in the marine surveyor world, and there are many fine surveyors whose livelihood depends on their trustworthiness. However, it is an unlicensed profession. Anyone can print business cards, advertise themselves as a marine surveyor, and then report whatever the person requesting the survey wants them to report. If a survey already exists, especially a recent one, find out who requested the survey and who paid for it. Sometimes a seller will request a survey before putting his boat on the market, ostensibly to save prospective buyers the expense. Beware of such surveys; they may well be hiding something.

John recalls one such survey:

Early in my career I was rather naive about surveys. I was contacted by a West Coast owner who had just purchased in Florida a schooner built in 1879. He needed a captain to take it around, through the Panama Canal. I am partial to old schooners for their aesthetic appeal, but have no great desire to deliver them. Since it was nearly a century-old wooden boat, I had my doubts, so I asked him for a survey. It was recent and done just before purchase. I never found out who requested it. The two-page document mostly listed the ship's equipment. On the last page under "Condition" were some flowery paragraphs stating in effect that this was a fine old vessel that should be preserved for posterity. That should have made me suspicious.

In my eagerness I flew to Florida. When I got out of the taxi, I could see the "fine old vessel" a hundred yards away, and my heart sank. Even at that distance I could tell she was a derelict. Closer inspection showed that she was even worse.

I told the owner, who planned to go on the trip, that I didn't think the vessel was seaworthy enough. However, he had assembled such a fine crew that I decided at least to give it a shakedown cruise 150 miles to Key West.

Just before we left, the previous owner took me aside and said, "You know she's old and has been sitting here a long time. When she gets outside she's going to start taking water, but she'll be all right." That didn't make me feel any better about the trip.

True enough, as soon as we cleared the Lauderdale breakwater she started taking water, and large quantities of it. The next 24 hours were some of the hairiest moments I ever spent at sea. Several times when the water level got high enough to pump, the generators or the main engine wouldn't start. The machinery room contained 100 years of jury rigging. Several times when I was right at the point of calling the Coast Guard, the engineer got things going and pumped out.

They were lonely hours for me. I couldn't

communicate to any of the rest of the eight crew how truly worried I was about whether we were going to make it. I had positively decided that this old tub was not fit for a 5,000-mile trip, and—short of a total rebuild—never would be. I did not want the responsibility of the crew's lives in my hands on this unsafe vessel.

Gratefully we made it to Key West and tied up at the pier at the end of Duvall Street. With all the machinery shut down, I could hear the water running into the hull from between her planks. I informed the owner of my decision. He was very angry, of course, and I had to pay my own way home to San Diego. It was not my fault that he bought a leaky antique. However I was so glad to have both feet on dry land that I nearly kissed the ground with joy.

Today, we learn as much about the boat as possible on the telephone before we even ask about a recent survey. But misleading surveys are the reason we've put an escape contingency in our contract. There is no rule that a captain must continue a trip on an unsafe vessel. To the contrary—his responsibility is *not* to proceed in such circumstances.

Here's our list of questions to ask an owner on the phone. We print them on a single sheet and leave them with our secretary when we are out on a delivery.

1 Name, address, and phone number of principals?

2 Kind of boat?

3 From where to where? When?

4 Age, condition, type of construction?

5 Last survey?

6 Photo and copy of listing?

7 Kind of engines and generators?

8 Fuel capacity, consumption, and range?

9 Autopilot?

10 List of navigation electronics?

11 Type of ground tackle?

12 Liferaft? EPIRB? Launch?

13 Is the boat actually purchased yet?

14 How did you hear about us?

An experienced delivery captain asking the right questions can usually estimate how much preparation will be needed for a vessel for the proposed trip. Occasionally, the captain can request specific but limited preparation work to be done before his arrival at the boat's location. He never is sure about all details until he gets there and makes his own inspection. Most owners have a tendency to grossly underestimate the amount of time necessary to do the preparation work, or think they can do it all for the delivery captain before he inspects the boat himself.

The manufacturer of a line of large power yachts once called us to deliver his biggest model from the East Coast to Los Angeles. The vice president told us to hurry out to the boat, to expect three days' preparation before we would be underway.

Great, we thought. That's the way we like to work: provision, sea trial, and go. Preparation time can sometimes be the most frustrating part of the trip. Upon our arrival, we found that the builder needed far more than three days for finish work before we could even begin our prep work; the building crew still needed to complete the interior cabinetry, lay carpeting, and install the electronics. We got as much done as possible, storing all the gear in a warehouse, but there was little we could do on board. They insisted we stay nearby, waiting for them to finish their jobs, while they paid us by the day plus food and hotel expenses. After two weeks, John voluntarily let the VP off the hook and we returned to the West Coast. Six weeks later, when the factory finished the boat, we traveled once again across the country to begin the delivery.

At the other end of the spectrum, we once flew to Honolulu, stepped aboard an unfamiliar 62-foot trawler, and within hours set out on a 2,600-mile passage to Cabo San Lucas. The former captain was a friend of ours, and over the phone he'd been able to answer all our questions, telling us everything we needed to know about the boat. His trusted first mate had remained on board in Hawaii to prep and even provision the boat for us. We arrived to find no surprises, and after a brief inspection and orientation, we cast off for a trouble-free Pacific crossing.

ONBOARD INSPECTION

Once you're finally aboard you can begin your inspection, becoming your own yacht surveyor. As such, you must go through the boat from stem to stern, truck to keelson. This inspection and your experience are all you'll have to determine if the boat can make the trip. Make your inspection thorough, and it does take lots of experience.

In his book *Surveying Small Craft*, Ian Nicholson writes:

> It is quite extraordinary how old, decrepit boats which are found to be in poor if not downright unsound condition make extraordinary passages across dangerous oceans, just to confound the surveyor's opinion. It all boils down to the fact that seaworthiness is a quality which is never found in a perfect form, and is in any case only attributable to the team of ship-plus-crew and never to the ship alone.

Don't interpret this to mean that a deliverer should make a habit of delivering old, decrepit boats. On the contrary—you and your crew may not live long using such bad business practices. We have found that owners of such vessels often are operating on a small budget; if something major goes wrong en route the owner may be financially incapable of correcting the problem, and the captain may become the scapegoat. However, Nicholson's comments do point out that an experienced captain might pull off a trip with a vessel in less-than-perfect condition where an inexperienced yachtsman might not.

While this is not intended to be a text on marine surveying, here are some of the important systems that need to be checked out.

Hull

Begin with the hull condition.

Wooden vessels are becoming more rare, but they present the most difficult survey because of the danger of rot and broken members. Go through the boat with a pick, poking in suspicious areas, looking for rot in major structural members and particularly around the stern gland, and looking for cracked ribs. On a wooden sailboat check the keelbolts.

On steel and aluminum boats, look for corrosion and electrolysis. Examine fiberglass hulls for cracks and buckling with particular attention to the hull-deck joint and bulkhead joints.

Check the bilges for signs of high-water marks. If you find them, you'll have to find the source of the leak. Inspect all through-hulls and seacocks, making sure they are not frozen. Are there wooden bungs to fit every through-hull? If not, buy them. Secure each one near its appropriate through-hull fitting. Replace connecting hoses and hose clamps if they're cracked, corroded, or broken. Memorize or diagram the location of all bilge pumps and check to see they work.

Steering System

Thoroughly check the steering system—hydraulic or cable—and see if the boat has an emergency steering system. If it's been altered over the years, was the job done cleanly? Little piles of powdered metal beneath the steering gear in the bilge or lazarette are an indication of wear. Check the fitted tops of rudder posts for weld fractures, indicated by hairline cracks or internal corrosion. If the system is cable, check the condition of the wire, the clamps on the ends, and the mounting of the sheaves. With hydraulic steering, check for leaks and check all mechanical joints to make sure they have keepers. Make sure the correct hydraulic fluid is being used.

We have lost steering at sea three times, and it's a frightening experience. In one case we were delivering a brand-new motor yacht, right from the factory, and as we were running down-swell in some rough seas, the boat started wandering off course. John thought perhaps the autopilot had gone out until, when we tried to steer by hand, we found we had absolutely no control. A crewmember had to keep us out of the trough by steering with the engines while we started tracing down the problem, starting with the steering gear. To do this, unfortunately, we had to move several 55-gallon drums of diesel fuel off the lazarette's

Check the cutlass bearing. Grab the propeller and shake vigorously. If there is movement, the bearing needs to be replaced.

Worn splines and a deteriorated outer wall will cause excessive vibration.

When inspecting a powerboat's hydraulic steering system, look first for any fluid leaks. Then tighten all nuts and check for sturdy cotter pins and keepers on the ends of all connectors.

access hatches, no easy feat while rolling around.

But that's where we found the problem—a hydraulic ram that connects to the steering quadrant had become disconnected and dropped into the bilge. Fortunately all the pieces were still lying right there, so it was just a matter of reassembling them before we

Deep splines and a thick outer wall signify a new cutlass bearing.

bor water is too dirty, wait until your sea trial to find some clean water.

On a sailboat, go over the rigging thoroughly, including standing and running rigging. Check the spars for cracks, dents, and corrosion. Pay particular attention to the tangs for wear and cracks. Check the sail track for straightness. Inspect all shackles, screws, clevis pins, turnbuckles, and cotter pins.

On a brand-new sailboat John was about to take to the South Pacific, he noticed that a stem deck fitting through which the forestay passed was suspiciously lifted a fraction of an inch off the deck. On further inspection he found that a long bolt, imbedded in the stem and connected to the forestay, was threaded the wrong way. As he tightened up on the forestay, the bolt unscrewed itself out of a large

could get underway again. The only part missing was the cotter pin required to keep the whole thing from vibrating loose. The scary part was that the factory had never put one in. With such lack of attention to a primary piece of gear, we began to wonder what other surprises this boat might have for us. As it turned out, there were many.

Out-of-Water Inspection

If the boat is out of the water when you arrive, you have a much better opportunity for inspection. Check the rudder, propeller, strut, cutlass bearing, and all through-hulls for electrolysis, dings, and general wear.

John once did his own inspection—only hours after a marine surveyor had completed his—of a twin-engine motor sailer we were about to deliver. When John grabbed one of the propellers and shook it, the whole thing rattled. The cutlass bearing was not just worn, but was completely out. This is one of the major items a surveyor should check.

If the boat is in the water, dive on her bottom to check out these same items. If the har-

On sailboats check all standing rigging, including the tangs, for signs of fatigue and wear. You will have to go aloft in a bosun's chair to do this.

nut that secured the whole thing in. The yard had to grind down the fiberglass in the stem, remove the bolt, and replace it with the right thread. This kind of problem isn't immediately apparent; it would have held together until the first good blow, perhaps a thousand miles from land, when it would have been damned inconvenient to have the mast fall down.

MACHINERY AND SYSTEMS INSPECTION

Because marine engines are used in a harsh environment, and because they're subject to periods of disuse in the same salty air, they require constant maintenance. Ignoring them is disastrous. Offshore cruisers and yacht delivery captains need to know as much as possible about them.

Ninety percent of this section on a boat's power plant is relevant to sailors with auxiliary power on board. For purposes of thoroughness, let's consider that we are inspecting the machinery for a long passage with offshore work involved. If it were a short coastal passage, requirements might be slightly less stringent. We will deal only with diesel power. Gasoline engines can be extremely dangerous, and we don't even deliver gas-powered boats.

Read thoroughly any engineering logs the boat may have, because they contain a wealth of information. First, if engine hours are excessive there could be trouble. If the vessel has been sitting unused and unattended for some time, evident by large voids in the log, there is likely to be trouble. Check when the oil was last changed. If it was not recent or if the date is unknown because there are no logs, you should start off with an oil and filter change. If time permits, consider sending off an oil sample for analysis.

Engine

Before starting the engine(s), conduct a thorough exterior inspection. Check the engine bed, shaft, and coupling for strength and any nearby signs of misalignment vibration. Look for loose or missing bolts, particularly in the shaft coupling.

Don't let a brightly painted engine deceive you. In fact, be suspicious of fresh paint. While an engine room should be neat and orderly, paint can cover a lot of ills. Look over the entire surface of the engine for evidence of oil, fuel, or water leaks. Inspect all lines and hoses for signs of decomposition, chafe, or collapsing. Tighten all hose clamps. If in doubt about hoses and clamps, replace them. Also measure the diameters of all major hoses, both inside and outside diameters, and make sure you have spares for all. Look at all the belts for wear. If you see cracks or excessive wear, replace them now; don't wait until they break underway.

As soon as you have done an initial inspection of the engine, check that it has oil and water and is clear of obstructions. Start it and run it at least until it comes up to temperature. Watch it under operation, looking for oil, fuel, and exhaust leaks. Make sure the docklines are secure, and put it in gear both fore and aft. Do this just long enough to check that the raw-water cooling flow is sufficient, that you have prop wash and that the boat is moving fore or aft. Listen, feel, and look again for abnormal vibration and signs of shaft misalignment.

Inspect the shaft packing gland. A tiny bit of water flow is necessary to cool the shaft and prevent excessive heat from scoring it. Tighten or loosen the packing nut as necessary. If you tighten the nut as much as possible and still have excessive leaking, you probably have to replace the packing material.

Run up the RPMs in neutral and look at the color of the exhaust. The best test of this is under a load during a sea trial. According to *Marine Diesel Engines,* by Nigel Calder, the color of the exhaust can tell you the following:

Black

1. Dirty air filter **2.** Defective turbo or supercharger **3.** Injector dribble **4.** Overload **5.** High exhaust back pressure.

Blue

1. Worn or stuck piston rings **2.** Worn valve guides **3.** Worn turbo or supercharger oil seals **4.** High crankcase oil level or back pressure.

White

1. Lack of compression **2.** Water in fuel **3.** Air in fuel **4.** Defective injector **5.** Cracked cylinder head or leaking head gasket.

Check all gauges that monitor the engine's behavior. Do they all work? Is there good oil pressure? Is voltage output correct? Are all temperatures within normal operating ranges, according to the manuals? Make a mark on or near the gauges to denote what their normal operating ranges should be. (See Sea Trials, page 42.)

The cooling system is notorious for causing problems. Take out the sea strainer and clean it. Notice what type of debris is in it. This might show that something has found its way into the engine. It's a good idea to pull the raw water impeller out, inspect it for wear and replace it if necessary. Make sure you have spare impellers and gaskets for the trip. Even if you replace the old impeller, be sure to replace the gasket on the inspection plate. On older boats consider taking apart the heat exchanger, cleaning it, flushing out the system and replacing the coolant.

Likewise, the wet exhaust system on old boats can rust out and allow seawater to enter the cylinders. If this happens, the next time you start the engine you'll bend a connecting rod, since water doesn't compress. Consider having the exhaust pressure-tested.

Fuel System

If there is any doubt about the injectors, pull them off and have them tested. If necessary, replace or rebuild them. Spare injectors are very expensive items, but so is a mechanical breakdown underway. If possible, carry a complete set of spare injectors. Even for coastal deliveries, you should always carry at least one.

Check the fuel lines, which often require a special tool for installation and removal. Look for kinks, stress cracks, unprotected hot spots, or leaky fittings. Do you have spare line and the tool?

The best insurance against future injector damage is proper maintenance of a good fuel filtration system. A good one is essential. The filter supplied by the engine manufacturer on a brand-new engine is not usually adequate for marine use. Install a heavier-duty one upstream, and be sure you have pumping power.

We've grown partial to Racor or Dahl filters, because they have a clear sediment bowl, allowing you to see sediment, water, or even air in the fuel when it's running. If the vessel is already equipped with these filters, shine a flashlight into the bowl. It could show fuel contamination problems.

If you can't determine from the logs whether the filters have been changed recently, go ahead and change them all. You can then analyze the material inside the filter. Rusty sediment, water, and algae are signs that the fuel is old and has been sitting for a long time, and you should probably clean the tanks and "polish" the fuel.

Snake a hose to the bottom of the fuel tanks and pump out a sample. If it contains water and sediment, have the fuel pumped out and the tanks cleaned. Large fuel docks have facilities to polish the fuel by pumping it through large filters and a centrifuge. If the fuel appears to be reasonably clean, put in a fuel conditioner such as Biobor.

By changing filters, you will also learn how to bleed the engine to get it started again. Better to learn now at the dock than some dark, stormy night at sea.

John tells how he got very familiar with bleeding a Perkins 4–108:

I was delivering a sailboat from San Diego to Zihuatenejo, Mexico. The owner was Jose Lopez Portillo, who was then President of Mexico. We called him simply *El Patron*. We were accompanied the entire way by a Mexican Navy vessel which was a WWII-vintage U.S. destroyer escort. We certainly didn't have to worry about pirates on that trip.

The initial leg to Cabo San Lucas was sailing at its best. We were well offshore, running dead downwind in a steady 25- to 30-knot northwesterly. During one 48-hour stretch we made 400 miles, surfing down huge breakers. Our escort ship wasn't having fun, though. She couldn't run that slowly and had to steam in circles around us, wallowing all the way to Cabo.

My crew, Mexican Navy officers who were appointment secretaries to *El Patron,* had fun sailing. But not Captain Rains. I had my head down and my posterior up, constantly working on the engine. The engine ran fine for the first few hours, then mysteriously began to die. Though we were sailing, I still had to run the engine often because we had a lot of navigational electronics. The batteries were weak and they ran down quickly. Every time the engine died I had to bleed it to get it going again. I could see air coming through the Racor filter and at first I thought perhaps there was an air leak in the bowl of the filter itself.

This was all manageable until we totally ran out of wind 100 miles from Cabo, a common occurrence. Now that I had to rely completely on the engine, it would only run for fifteen minutes and then die. I pumped fuel out of the ship's tanks and into a five-gallon bucket. I then ran fuel directly out of the bucket through the Racor and into the engine. It ran fine and we made port, though it was a messy operation.

Of course we could have been towed in by our escort, but professional pride made me want to depend on my own resources.

When I arrived I knew that the Racor was okay and that the problem had to be between the Racor and the tank. After backtracking all the way, I found that the fuel pick-up tube in the tank had a tiny screen filter. It was clogged with a black tarry substance. By cleaning it, I solved my problem.

Why didn't I look there to begin with? The boat had just come out of the yard, where they were supposed to have cleaned the tanks. Obviously, they didn't, even though *El Patron* paid for it.

If there is no filtration on the engine other than the filters, you will have to provide it. The ideal set up calls for two Racors plumbed in parallel, so if one clogs the other can be brought on line and the clogged one changed without shutting down the engines. With a single-screw power boat this is essential, because you don't ever want to shut down all main propulsion at sea unless it is an emergency. Perfectly running engines are notorious for not starting when shut down for something as simple as checking the oil. On twin-screw boats one additional filter per engine is sufficient if budget and time are a problem.

The clear bowl helps show what's going on inside the filter, but to be sure when filters need to be changed, you need vacuum

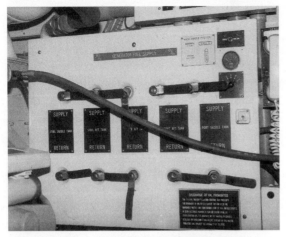

Make sure the fuel manifold works and you know
how to operate it. This one is conveniently located
and well labeled. Some boats have hidden valves
and lines that take a long time to trace.

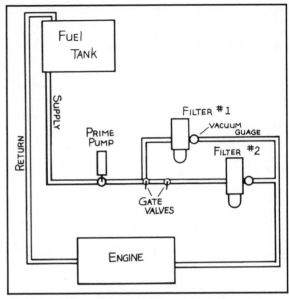

Figure 4-1. Proper fuel transfer and filtration system
for a diesel engine.

gauges. When vacuum builds into the red, it's
time to change filters. Again, this is ideal but
not essential.

Check out and prove the fuel transfer system (Fig. 4–1). If there are no diagrams on the
boat, you will have to locate the tanks and
valves, and trace out the lines. While you're
running the fuel transfer system to make sure
it works, consider what spares it requires: a

A first-rate fuel filtration system. These twin Dahls
(the small one is for the generator) are plumbed so
that one can be shut down and changed without
stopping the engine. There is a gauge on the panel
that shows fuel pressure and will indicate if the filter
is beginning to clog.

pump, impellers, solenoid switches. In an
emergency, how can you transfer fuel if the
main transfer system fails? Is there access to
the tank top? Could you get the fuel out with
a portable pump? What else would you need?

Plumbing

There are many kinds of fluids on board besides fuel: seawater, fresh water, hydraulic
steering fluid, stabilizer fluid, etc.

Look through all plumbing diagrams and
manuals. Even if there aren't any, you should
locate all tanks, pumps and valves, switches,
and their through-hulls. Trace their lines.

Run all the pumps and determine what
spares or replacements you might need. Open
and close all valves to ensure they are free and
that fluids flow at their required velocities.
Make sure all the heads work and that you
have rebuild kits for them.

Identify all bilge compartments and check
the limber holes and drainage into these compartments. Did you test the bilge pumps, manual and electrical? Make sure that the float

switches are working, that there's no debris to jam them on or off, that there are strainers on the ends of intake lines, and that you again have proper spares.

Electrical

Start your inspection of the ship's AC and DC systems with the electrical panel. Test each switch and the equipment that it operates. Older boats with lots of additions since the factory and with lots of incorrect labels on the panel can present a real mystery. You may not know what breaker works what, and you can only figure it out through a long process of trial and error. Once you figure it out, label it properly. If wiring is old, check around turns for deteriorated insulation.

Running lights, insignificant as they may seem, are one of the most important electrical items to check before leaving the dock. Even though they conform to Coast Guard regulations, are they large or bright enough and placed well enough to be of practical value? Could they be seen in heavy shipping lanes in bad weather? If not, consider enlarging or re-positioning them.

Running lights also are difficult to keep going at sea, especially in heavy weather when the boat takes more water than usual. Side lights and the stern light are often so low to the water that they eventually short out. Are

Poor running lights. They are so small and low that they will never be seen by shipping in a seaway. Their placement near the water may make them corrode and short out.

the bulbs well sealed inside the lenses? Do you have spares?

Run the AC generating plant (or plants) and bring it on line independent of shore power. These engine portions are subject to the same inspection guidelines as the main propulsion plant. Check to see that voltage output and cycles are correct. Determine how much of an electrical load the generator will carry by bringing different equipment on line until it bogs down. Often one generator is inadequate to handle everything on the boat at one time: battery charger, air conditioners or heaters, electric stove, boat launching crane, etc.

Locate and check the batteries. Are they adequately secured and ventilated? Add distilled water if necessary. Clean corrosion from the terminals and connections, and see if they're charged up. Is the charger working correctly? To check the battery discharge rate turn off the charger and run some DC items. It's not uncommon to have to replace batteries just before a delivery. If in doubt, do so.

Electronics

Turn on the navigation electronics and radios to see that they work. Radar usually takes a few minutes to warm up, so call for a radio check on the VHF and single-sideband while you're waiting. Can you transmit and receive

Good running lights. Large, bright, and high enough to be seen.

on the proper frequencies for ship to shore, ship to ship, and weather stations all along your route? Transmit the radar on both high and low power to see if you have a good picture on both. Program the Loran and Satnav to make sure they give fixes. Check the depth sounder. Leaving these electronics on for awhile is a good idea to ensure that they don't suffer from "sea buoy syndrome," a disease that makes them work fine at the dock but go haywire as soon as you pass the sea buoy. (Also see Chapter 6, Sea Trials.)

Ground Tackle

Give attention to the main anchor, windlass and rode. Everyone has their favorite type anchor for particular situations, so be sure what you have is right for where you're going. Is the anchor and chain heavy and long enough for the size of the vessel? Puny ground tackle is a common problem among occasional-use pleasure boats, but certain regions of the country seem to be worse in this department than others. Florida has lots of places for shallow-water anchoring and many marinas, so it is not uncommon to find 20 feet of chain on a fairly large boat's very small anchor. Fifty feet of chain is a bare minimum and we prefer 300 feet.

Operate the windlass to make sure it is not seized up. If the chain size doesn't fit the gypsy head, the links will "skip" and be very dangerous for anyone handling the windlass or standing near it. The improper match of chain to gypsy head also causes needlessly heavy stress on the windlass. We've delayed deliveries to install chain of the proper size.

Make sure that the swivel shackle's clevis pin is safety-wired and that the eye and thimble pass through the hawse without jamming. See that there is some means of solidly securing the anchor in place on the bow in a nasty seaway.

Lower and raise the anchor at dockside to make sure the chain runs out smoothly. Often after a long passage to weather in heavy seas, the chain is so balled up inside the chain locker that it won't run out. We once had to rent a crane in Honolulu to clear the chain after a rough passage against the winter tradewinds from the Marshalls.

Sometimes the windlass seems fine at the dock, but its true test is under load in an actual anchoring situation. You can do this later on sea trial.

You will need a backup anchor and rode. Even if you don't lose the main one, you may need it as a stern anchor or a second anchor in a storm. It need not be as large nor have as much chain as the main anchor; portability and stowage are desirable. Three anchors and three separate rodes are ideal.

Launches

Check out the launch and the davits, if that's how the launch is carried. Operating the davits to put the launch in the water is the only way to ensure that the davits work properly, that all clearances are adequate, and that the launch can be resecured in its cradle. Run the launch to make sure its engine works.

Every delivery requires a launch, even if it's intended to be a short delivery. What happens if you have to make an unscheduled emergency stop and must get ashore in a place with no docks?

For short deliveries, a small inflatable tender with oars will do. For a trip of any length, particularly foreign voyages, you need a substantial launch. An inflatable with a bottom stiffener and an outboard motor is the bottom line.

For deliveries, we prefer inflatables over large, rigid dinghies because they're light and easy to launch and retrieve. An inflatable dinghy used during a foreign or long-range deliv-

The only way to know if the crane or davits work is to launch the dinghy as part of the sea trial. Check for possible obstructions and learn how to keep the swing of the dinghy under control with the painter and lashings. Run the dinghy and then resecure it in its cradle.

This inflatable with bottom stiffener and hard transom is ideal for deliveries. It's easily launched, seaworthy, and speedy enough for long runs from the anchorage to shore.

Puntarenas, Costa Rica, is one of the main stops on the route between the East and West coasts of the U.S. To stop there you must anchor in the outer anchorage for inspection by officials before being granted permission to move into the sheltered "back anchorage." To do this you must put over your launch and summon the officials from the pier. The anchorage is little more than an open roadstead with swell, wind, and current—all opposing one another. On several occasions we have had great difficulty launching a hard dinghy from the boat deck of a motor yacht. Such vessels roll so badly in the swell that the launch begins to swing violently, threatening to bash in the side of the yacht. Inflatables are much safer in such circumstances.

Motor yachts with large launches on their upper decks are sometimes unstable. We've delivered a couple of such vessels, and in heavy seas wondered if we were going to roll over. Since then John has convinced some owners to sell their large launch, or to ship it ahead to the destination, and to replace it with

On some vessels the weight of a hard launch on the upper deck causes excessive rolling. Consider replacing it with a lighter inflatable.

ery needs an outboard engine. More often than not, you must anchor in not-very-well-protected waters a good distance from where you can land the dinghy. Dinghy docks are a wonderful Americanism, but you won't find them everywhere. Ask yourself if that dinghy and engine could get your crew and a load of provisions back through surf and swell. Sometimes sea conditions are rougher than small engines can handle.

an inflatable for the delivery. Instability of the whole vessel caused by too large a launch on an upper deck is sufficient reason to turn down a delivery.

You must have a means of carrying the launch on board. Towing a launch is only acceptable for short trips in protected waters. A launch towed for a long distance is a launch sure to be lost, so don't even consider it.

Safety Equipment

Ensure that you have all the safety equipment as required by the Coast Guard. Because of increased drug inspection, U.S. flag vessels should expect several boardings during a long delivery. You'll get a citation and fine if you don't have the proper equipment aboard. Beyond that, take along any safety gear that prudence would suggest for the proposed voyage.

A life raft is essential to any delivery, but see that it's adequate for the voyage you are undertaking. A coastal raft is not sufficient for an offshore passage. Life rafts should be repacked once a year; check the date. If it's past due, send it out to be repacked immediately. Since repacking can take two weeks, we ask the owner to check the raft's inspection date when we first speak with him on the phone. Rather than leaving with an out-of-date raft, see if you can trade with someone not going anywhere soon.

Horror stories abound about cheap-brand rafts being packed by amateurs inside top-brand cannisters, but it's only because such frauds were discovered during survey inspections that anyone lives to tell about it.

Familiarize yourself with the gear the professional life raft packers have stowed inside the raft. It's usually not much, but if you request it, they'll include as much as logistically possible. You probably will have to pack your own ditch kit, the bag of equipment you take into the raft with you should the boat sink. (See Chapter 17 for a list.)

Man overboard gear should include a throw ring with sea anchor and water light, a pole with flag, and a whistle. We buy each crew member his own whistle, and most of our regular crew have their own life harnesses.

Are the hand flares within date, and are there enough of them? Is the flare gun handy, and are there plenty of flares for it? Do you have a bell and horn? Don't laugh, if they don't work or aren't aboard, you're risking a costly Coast Guard citation. Banging pans together won't get you by anymore. Is there at least one serviceable life jacket immediately available for each person onboard?

Make sure that fire extinguishers are the proper type and have been serviced within the last year. Don't hesitate to install new ones.

An EPIRB (Emergency Position Indicating Radio Beacon) is essential. Test it and check the battery date. If the EPIRB is stuck away in a drawer, mount it now.

Inventory

Part of the surveying job is making a complete inventory of what's already aboard. Then you'll avoid purchasing duplicates.

Do this by compartments (such as berths, lockers, cabinets), labeling as you go. Keep the list of items compartmentalized this way, so you can find what you need later. Restow bulky items you won't need during delivery.

We each take our small, lap-top computers along. They are valuable timesavers for doing inventories. When we want to find anything, we enter the item name and the computer comes up with its location. We also use the computer for scheduling and accounting.

Work List

After this complete inspection of the boat, you'll probably have quite a work list. Some of it falls under Repair & Replacement, and some of it under Outfitting. How much of it gets done is a function of time and money, or what the owner is willing to pay versus what the captain feels is absolutely necessary. There may be some mutual concessions made, but the captain will have to ensure he does not compromise the safety of the crew and vessel in the process.

CHAPTER 5
SPARE PARTS AND OUTFITTING

For any voyage, you want to carry as many spare parts as your budget allows. But even if you towed a barge full of spares, you could still break down for want of some insignificant O-ring. Rank your spares list according to: (A) Would lack of one of these cause a major breakdown during the trip? Would we be stuck if we don't have it? (B) If we have this spare, are we capable of repairing the thing at sea?

An example of an (A) spare is an impeller for the engine's raw-water cooling pump. Yes, without this spare, you could possibly be stuck dead in the water, unable even to make port where spares could be purchased. For this reason, we always carry several impellers for each major pump.

If the spare in question is an internal engine part, it might get put into the (B) pile, because it's unlikely you could tear down an engine underway. On the other hand, oddball or hard-to-find parts come in handy in a port where you can find a mechanic but not the part.

The bulk of your spares are items often replaced on a regular maintenance schedule, like filters for fuel, oil, and water, and soft items that wear quickly, like gaskets, impellers, and belts.

The size of your spare parts inventory also depends on the nature of your trip. An ocean crossing requires a more extensive spare parts list than a coastal trip, because you must be totally self-sufficient in mid-ocean. And an ocean crossing on a single-screw boat requires more spares than would a twin-screw passage, because you can't cannibalize the second engine for parts to make port on the first engine.

If the intended route follows the U.S. coastline, the spares inventory need not to be quite so extensive, since most ports would have parts. Just ensure that you have the parts necessary to make port.

A coastal trip through Third World countries, Latin America, for example, requires an extensive inventory, because parts are often unavailable even in port.

It's not uncommon for an owner to complain about the cost of spares, so be prepared to give him an option. You can go without the more expensive spares, like starters and injector pumps, gambling that you will not need them. If you do break down underway and have to limp into a foreign port, you'll have to make every effort to get them locally. If your parts are unavailable, you may have to fly out a crew member to pick up the parts and bring them back. This sounds expensive, of course, but it may be cheaper than carrying a large spare parts inventory.

Flying someone from a boat in a foreign country to pick up the parts also sounds extravagant, but many times this has proved far

Twin watermakers on the cruising yacht *Las Americas* are a prime example of carrying back-up equipment. If all else fails, one machine can be cannibalized for parts to keep the other working.

cheaper in the long run. The crewmember must hand-carry the parts back as personal luggage, often as carry-on luggage, and walk the parts through customs. Because his passport verifies his first entrance into that country as legitimate crew of a boat in transit, the crewmember stands a good chance of getting the part cleared through the maze of hassles attendant to foreign customs inspections.

Bribery, extortion and the implacable *mañana* attitude have kept emergency repair parts tied up in quasi-official warehouses and back rooms for days and weeks. Some customs officials seem to thrive on others' misfortunes, and they have hungry mouths to feed. Meanwhile, the boat's expenses mount even as it sits idle, and the captain and crew are being paid by the day. A crewmember hand-carrying parts on planes and walking them through for-

eign customs is the only sure way of getting your part.

The following is a list of spares. It is general, so you can specify part numbers for particular repair or replacement parts for each individual delivery. Each boat will have a different engine and other machinery aboard. Certain boats with certain kinds of machinery will need other specific parts.

High on the list are fuel filters. Buy many more than you think you will ever need. Getting dirty fuel in foreign ports is one of the most frequent problems encountered in long-distance passagemaking. As the tanks get low and the weather gets rough, the fuel, dirt and water get so mixed you might have to change filters every hour to make port. It's rather reassuring to know you have cases of filters. This is one place not to skimp.

SPARE PARTS AND TOOLS

Main Engine

1 Complete rebuild kit for raw water and two impellers
1 Freshwater pump
1 Injector per engine (minimum)
1 Set of belts
1 Starter for each rotation, or at least solenoids and brushes
Engine manuals: shop, operator, parts
1 Spare fuel pump (optional)
1 Alternator, if it is the only way of making the electricity you need
Hoses and clamps of needed sizes for fresh and salt water
Filter cores (Racor), 1 case each engine
Engine fuel filters, 2 each
2 Lube oil filters
Spare fuel lines
1 Complete set of engine gaskets
Thermostat

Generators

1 Injector for each generator (minimum)
1 Set belts for each generator
1 Generator starter, or at least solenoid and brushes
1 Generator shut-down solenoid
1 Complete raw-water rebuild kit for each generator, 2 extra impellers
Hoses and clamps for fresh and salt water
1 Case Racor filters
2 Engine fuel filters for each generator
1 Case oil filters
1 Complete gasket set

Sailboats

2 Complete turnbuckles in each size found onboard
Cotter pins or circlips for standing rigging
Wire forestay and backstay, made up with fittings on one end
Nicopress swage tool, thimbles, and zincs to fit forestay and backstay
2 Winch handles
2 Halyards, made up with fittings
Many shackles
Assorted line, 3-strand and braided
Mast tangs, or flat stock to fabricate replacements
Sail cloth and repair kit
Hanks
Slides
Blocks

Tools

Craftsman socket sets in ¼-inch, ⅜-inch, and ½-inch drive
Box/end wrenches, ¼-inch to 1 ¼-inch
3 Crescent wrenches, 6, 10, and 16-inch
3 Pair Channel-lock pliers (water pump pliers) small, medium, large
2 Vise-Grip pliers, small narrow jaw, medium wide jaw
1 Side cutter (Dikes)
1 Good quality wire stripper/crimper

1 Set Allen wrenches, small to large
1 Set feeler gauges
1 Ball-peen hammer
1 Good-quality cold chisel
1 Center punch
Regular punch—2 sizes
2 Pipe wrenches, medium and large
Electric drill, ⅜-inch, and 2 sets of metal bits
1 Hacksaw and 2 coarse blades
1 Razor knife
1 12-volt test light
1 Multi-tester
1 Pair of pliers, wide jaw
1 Good-quality filter wrench
2 Sets of screwdrivers, Phillips and slot-head

General

Props, shafts, and puller
Distilled water
Hydrometer
Spare bilge pump and float switch
Freshwater pump, at least repair kit and backup motor in case of burnout.
Refrigeration belts, freon gas, drier, belts, solenoid valve
Assorted nuts, bolts, washers, and screws
Spark plugs for outboard
Adequate lube oil
Shaft packing material in proper width
Hydraulic fluid
Long jumper cables
Underwater epoxy
Wooden bungs for through-hulls
Gasket material, sheet and liquid
Electrical wire, black tape, and assorted lugs, connectors, switches, fuses, and breakers
Soldering gun and solder
Light bulbs for 110-volt, 12-volt, and 24-volt
Spare bulbs for running lights and navigation lights
Electronics: Check manuals for recom-

mended spares. Autopilot relays, replacement fuses for all electrical, fax paper and stylus, depth recording paper, PL-259 connectors, RG-58U cabling, SWR bridge.

OUTFITTING

After an extensive inventory of the boat, you may have many items to buy for the trip or none. It depends on the boat. We have delivered boats that were ready to go to sea as soon as we arrived. On the other side of the coin, we've delivered several brand-new boats that needed everything.

The following lists assume that the boat is already supplied with U.S. Coast Guard-required safety equipment and has necessary electronics (see electronics section), and has the minimal equipment the average builder supplies.

Miscellaneous Gear

Ensign and staff
Foreign courtesy flags
Q-flags
Ship's papers
Writing materials: pen, ink, ballpoint, paper envelopes, stamps.

Deck Gear

3 very large fenders
4 110-foot docklines (if transiting Panama Canal). Cheaper to buy spool
Dinghy and motor
Flashlights, spare batteries and bulbs
Backup anchor with minimum 35-foot ⅜-inch chain (if no second anchor)
Water hose for freshwater washdown, buckets, deck brush, chamois
Cleaning materials: paper towels, cotton rags, soaps, teak cleaner and oil, stainless steel polish, squeegee, ammonia, denatured alcohol, furniture polish, spot remover, head cleaner, varnish, sand paper,

Large fenders are mandatory equipment for docking delicate yachts in foreign ports with crude facilities.

brass wool, thinners, brushes, spray paints.
Hose for fuel transfer, with adapters.
Parachute sea anchor
Scuba tank, mask, regulator, fins, and snorkel for underwater repairs

Safety Gear

All necessary equipment to pass U.S. Coast Guard inspection
Inflatable liferaft
EPIRB
Medical kit
Strobe light, personal type
Flare gun and flares
Signalling mirror
Life jackets

Salon and Sleeping Gear

Bedding: sheets, blankets, pillows
Lee cloths
Towels

Navigation Gear

Hand-bearing compass
Sextant
Chronometer
WWV receiver
Binoculars
Hand-held VHF radio

Parallel rules or rolling plotter
Dividers (one with lead for radar plotting)
#2 Pencils, sharpener, eraser
Log book
Sailing Directions
Nautical Almanac
Sight Reduction Tables
Tidal Stream Atlas
Tide tables
Light Lists
Mariners Guide to Single Sideband, by
    Frederick Graves
WorldWide Weather Broadcasts
Charts

BUYING CHARTS

Purchasing charts for a long cruise or delivery can cost a great deal. Yacht delivery captains often supply their own charts, especially on a route in which they specialize. To ensure proper coverage without over-buying, you'll need to plan a bit.

The U.S. government formerly subsidized the information-gathering and printing processes needed to make charts. With its effort to recover those costs from users, it has hiked the price of charts to the point that proper coverage for a particular voyage is approaching the prohibitive mark.

A *small-scale chart* covers a large area, perhaps a continent, and thus has less definition. A *large-scale chart* covers a small area such as a harbor and has great definition.

So they don't have to buy so many, first-time cruisers and beginning yacht deliverers often try to get by using smaller scale charts than they should. It is said that all of life is a compromise, but this is a dangerous practice. You never know when you might just need good definitions of coastlines and their offshore dangers. Especially for places you never intended to be.

John illustrates the point:

Pat and I had just pulled into Cozumel from Key West when another captain came over to shake my hand. He told me that he had just arrived in Cozumel from Panama by using a hand-drawn planning chart in my book, *Cruising Ports: California to Florida via Panama.*

We were aghast. That 5 × 7-inch illustration covered everything from Panama to mid-Florida. It was a simple geographic reference to the second largest barrier reef in the world and the strong currents of the Gulf Stream, and never was it intended for navigation. Whole island groups and thousands of reefs and cays were omitted, and it contained not a single depth sounding.

If all his charts had somehow been swept overboard, that simple drawing might have helped to get him to port safely, but there was no reason for such reckless frugality. He was the worst example of a "chart skimper" we've ever heard of. And the luckiest.

On the other hand, it's easy to go overboard purchasing charts. Don't let yourself become confused by charts of varying scales that overlap one another, or by those that leave gaps between them.

Buy charts according to a definite plan. Get small-scale charts for overall route planning. Your selection of coastal charts then depends on how close your routes come to shore. If you are coast-hopping you will need more charts. If you stay offshore, you will need fewer charts. Research which harbors have repair facilities or airports should you need to put in for some emergency. Some of these harbors may be off your initial itinerary route, but you may wish you had large-scale charts for them anyway.

Be sure to have *Sailing Directions* (for foreign waters) or *Coast Pilots* (for U.S. waters) aboard in addition to the charts. These are written descriptions of coastal waters. When

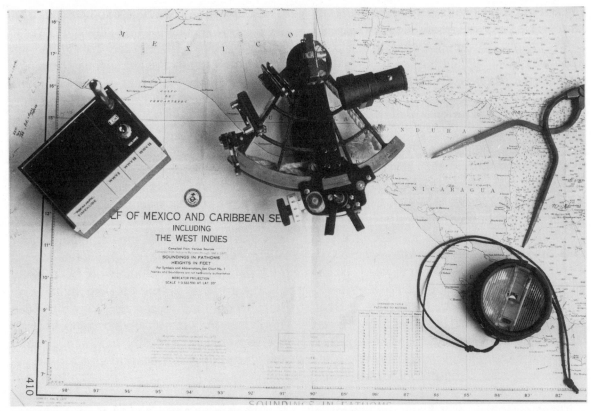

Part of our delivery kit. Portability is important here. The sextant is half size, yet accurate. In the lower right is a hand bearing compass, tiny yet superior to most larger ones. To the left is a compact back-up radio receiver for picking up the WWV time tick and weather reports.

we made an unscheduled stop in Port Royal, Jamaica, we only had a chart that showed the entire eastern half of Jamaica and lacked detail of the harbor. We couldn't obtain the harbor chart in Panama, where we came aboard the boat. The *Sailing Directions* talked us in and we timed our entrance for ideal conditions for pilotage through coral: high sun at our backs so we could see the many coral heads.

Since the price increase in government charts, private companies have published books or charts that thoroughly cover specific areas, using a variety of large- and small-scale charts and harbor charts. These are real bargains compared with buying all the government charts needed to gain the same coverage.

DELIVERER'S KIT

The fact that we supply many of these items ourselves can be a selling point for a delivery, especially if the owner doesn't have them and doesn't need them after the delivery. However, on big-ticket items like radios, you could help defray your own costs by adding a rental fee for these items to your delivery fee.

The most expensive items we offer to supply are a radio and Satnav. If the boat doesn't have ham radio gear aboard we supply it, along with tuner and antenna. The set we have also contains marine SSB frequencies, which can be used to transmit in an emergency, and all the necessary frequencies for picking up weather forecasts. Supplying this radio has gotten us several long-range deliveries, because it saved the owner several thousand dollars. We also provide a hand-held VHF radio.

We supply all the non-electronic navigational gear listed, including charts, which represent quite an investment. If deck fuel is needed, we can bring along our own fuel bladder and fuel transfer pump.

We've accumulated these costly items over the years not to make money, but because they were essential to safety and expedience.

We pack all our delicate equipment in a large, hard suitcase, cushioned inside with styrofoam and bubble plastic. Traveling with all this extra baggage is inconvenient and rings up extra baggage and insurance charges. We get some strange looks in airports and hotel lobbies because of our mass of luggage, all loaded with boat gear. People's humorous looks seem to say, "Those people certainly must not travel much to carry all that luggage.

They'll learn to travel light someday like we do."

Years ago, having just finished a delivery in Mallorca, Spain, with paid tickets back to San Diego, we planned to spend several weeks touring Europe. Reservations were impossible to make, since we couldn't promise exactly what day we'd finish the transatlantic passage. We had a ton of luggage, too.

Because it was the height of summer tourist season, every village was packed full, and we couldn't find storage for our collection of boat gear or get hotel reservations. We had to change hotels every few days with all this luggage. We were so exhausted from our rough Atlantic crossing and from dragging around all the extra bags of radios and boat gear that we flew home to get some rest, after spending only two weeks in Palma, Barcelona, and Madrid.

CHAPTER 6
SEA TRIALS

Your sea trial should tell you whether the vessel can make the trip, what work must be done to the vessel before departure, and what kind of voyage lies ahead. While surveying at the dock is important, the sea trial is the bottom line.

How soon into the project should you take the boat out for a sea trial? Prudence dictates that it be done as soon as possible. But because of the constraints of time and money that often are placed on a yacht delivery, the sea trial is often done at the last moment or even underway to your destination.

If your initial survey leaves you with serious doubts about the vessel's state of health or its inherent seaworthiness for the proposed voyage, you should plan a sea trial as soon as you can get the boat to move. If the boat fails the test, i.e., exhibits insurmountable problems, you have wasted the least amount of time.

Coastal trips require less extensive sea trials than do offshore passages. If the boat surveys well for a coastal trip, we dive right into the normal preparation work. Once that's done, we go for a sea trial, which may constitute just moving the boat to the fuel dock, running around in a few circles and, on a sailboat, hoisting the sails on the way there. If it passes that small test, we will conduct the rest of the sea trial enroute to the next port. This abbreviated type of sea trial is fine for coastal trips within U.S. waters, in benign localities with fair weather.

Typical of our work, a vessel departing Ft. Lauderdale for the long voyage to the West Coast starts with a 150-mile run to Key West as the first leg. This is an ideal run for a sea trial. If we find trouble with the boat, this first hop offers plenty of marinas to duck into to cure the problem. We're still in the U.S. (though in Key West you sometimes wonder) and have access to parts and service if we should need them. If all goes well, and if the boat has enough fuel, we may not need to stop in Key West at all.

If your first leg lands you outside the U.S., or in areas without yacht facilities, you'd better conduct a more thorough sea trial before you jump off on a long trip. The frustrating lack of facilities and parts is a delivery captain's nemesis.

Offshore trips require more critical sea trials; your life is on the line during an ocean crossing, so you want to make sure you no longer need those handy marinas and ship chandleries.

Several years ago, we had the opportunity to deliver a large sailboat from the West Coast to an exotic port in the Far East. After his initial inspection of the boat, John had some doubts about its design and inherent seaworthiness for offshore trips, but he reserved final judgement until we could do a sea trial, which we planned as a 24-hour trip offshore from Point Conception.

Southern California wind is often too light

for a good sea trial, but 100 miles offshore and out of the lee of Point Conception you may find a gale blowing. A gale was exactly what we wanted for this particular sea trial. Typhoons and lofty tradewind seas are nothing to take lightly, but John was concerned about getting into the violent storms that brew suddenly between Guam and Southeast Asia in all seasons.

As we motor-sailed off the coast, conditions were indeed calm, but the offshore weather forecast called for 20 to 30 knot northwesterlies and 10-foot seas.

Just as we passed Santa Barbara Island, conditions stiffened and began to build quickly, and we were able to drive the boat hard into a headwind and head seas. Of course, this was harder than we'd choose to push a boat, but we wanted to see her seagoing characteristics under conditions similar to what we were very likely to encounter on the way to the Far East.

Within minutes, waves were crashing over the length of the boat. As we sailed along, the mast began to pump, growing into a more and more violent motion. Suddenly, a large cleat securing the running backstay sheared off, and we slowed her down. As we examined the severed gear, it was obvious that the metal cleat was of cheap quality, not at all what it was said to be. We suspected every piece of rigging on the boat was the same poor quality. In a very short time, John had determined that nothing short of a major redesign would make her fit for such weather, and he refused the trip. Even though the money was good and a downwind trip to the Far East was a tantalizing adventure to contemplate, our lives and the lives of the crew would have been excessively endangered.

Later, another captain phoned us to say that he was going to deliver that boat, but he was very concerned about its ability to hold up. He admitted he'd never do it if he weren't completely broke. This is one of the worst positions from which to make a life-or-death decision. He said he knew that, so all we could do was wish him well.

Fortunately, they made it, but the key to their safe trip was that they had abnormal weather the whole way, in the form of gentle, favorable wind and flat seas.

Taking off on a boat that you know or suspect is not fit for the trip is exactly like playing Russian roulette. The gun didn't go off for our friends on the way to the Far East, but that means they have one less empty chamber. Rough weather and equipment failure are natural parts of moving boats; we all get our share. But nobody stays out of trouble long by courting disaster.

Since that incident, we've faced the same sort of decision several times: an enticing destination or point of origin, a lucrative contract, but an unfit boat. Each time we've turned it down. And we're still in business and going strong.

HOW TO CONDUCT A SEA TRIAL

Before getting underway the first time, check all fluid levels. Then test the running gear at the dock. With all lines still secured to the dock, try each engine slow ahead for a few seconds and then slow astern. This could save quite a bit of embarrassment once you have cast off the lines. Make sure you have raw water pumping through the engine and discharging overboard.

Once underway, bring the vessel slowly up to speed, keeping an eye on the instruments to make sure you have proper oil pressure and are not overheating. Note the "normal" readings on the gauges and mark the gauges with tape or crayon. This allows everyone standing watch to tell at a glance if any readings are abnormal.

If on this first run the engine water temperature is within normal range but close to marginal, you should investigate, especially if you are going into tropical waters. Sea and air temperatures are higher in the tropics, so engine temperature rises with them and may cause overheating. If engine temperature is excessively high in cooler latitudes, you may have a simple thermostat or impeller problem. Otherwise, boiling out the heat exchanger is a more expensive solution.

Gradually climb to full cruising speed and check for excessive vibration, which could be caused by a dinged prop, collapsed strut, bad cutlass bearing, or misaligned shaft. Put your hand on the shaft packing gland to feel if it is hot. If so, you will have to loosen it to allow a trickle of water to cool it, or it will score the shaft. If too much water is dripping in, tighten down on it.

Test all the electronics again on the sea trial to make sure they don't have a case of "sea buoy syndrome," that malady in which equipment works fine at the dock, but quits as soon as you clear the sea buoy. Warm up the radar and, if you haven't already done so, try out each radio's transmission and reception by calling for a radio check.

The autopilot can only be proved underway, and in a location where you have plenty of sea room. Sometimes autopilots take a few minutes to get oriented. The autopilot's best test is with a strong following sea. If you have a watermaker it should only be run in clean water, so test it at the same time.

If it's a sailboat, sail it. Run up all the sails and set them in every position imaginable. Lay out any spare running rigging and reef anything that's reefable. Even a straight-looking sail track has been known to jam due to corrosion or crimped rails.

Find a place to anchor and drop the hook. You can check ground tackle at the dock to see if the windlass works and the chain runs out, but the only true test is under the strain

Test the anchoring gear under load during the sea trial. Make sure the chain fits the gypsy head and doesn't skip.

of actually anchoring, backing down on the anchor to set the hook, and then retrieving the full amount of chain. Make sure that the wildcat locking wheel engages and disengages, and that the chain runs out freely and can be controlled by the hand brake. It's common to find that the chain skips or pops out of the teeth of the wildcat once it's under strain of anchoring, even though it looks like they're a perfect fit. This is how sailors lose fingers.

If chain needs to be guided while it's coming onboard or going out, *never* use your hands. Pat uses a small length of 2 × 2 to manipulate chain in motion. She uses it to flake wet chain into the chain locker, pushing it into alternating corners as it comes in. This prevents chain from piling up and then tumbling into a snarled ball.

Is the windlass motor strong and fast enough to lift the chain and get you out of harm's way in a hurry? If you need to moor Mediterranean style (stern to a quay), you need a windlass that's reliable the first time.

Sea Trial On The Open Ocean

Protected-water sea trials are helpful, but only in the open ocean can you see how the vessel truly behaves. Make sure that everything is secure above and below decks. Don't assume everything is secure or even take somebody else's word for it.

At sea, we have had chandeliers, books, built-in furniture, bridge electronics, microwaves, trash compactors, and even refrigerators break loose from their supposedly secure locations.

We once were asked to deliver a 54-foot motor sailer from San Diego to San Francisco. The owner had been living aboard in a quiet marina slip for several years and had converted one forward cabin into an office, complete with an IBM computer sitting on a counter. After mutually extolling the virtues of computerdom, we asked the owner if he was going to UPS it to his new home in San Francisco or carry it with him in his car as he drove up. He couldn't understand why it couldn't just stay on the counter during the delivery. Pat finally convinced him by comparing his peaceful home-on-the-water to a 1-inch toy boat that was about to get tossed into a washing machine on heavy duty cycle. Even if we wrapped the computer in plastic and shipping blankets and packed it away in a closet, its internal circuit boards and wiring would get shaken badly on the normally bounding sea, especially bashing uphill around Point Conception and Point Sur.

During sea trials, drive the vessel hard into a head sea to discover how she handles while beating. Does her bottom pound? Does she slice through seas or resist them? Then put her beam-on the seas to learn how she rolls.

Is there a snap at the end of a long roll? Severe roll can be a problem. We've delivered several powerboats that were designed and built so top-heavy that in heavy weather we had to maneuver carefully to prevent them from rolling right over on their ears.

You can get a quick fuel consumption check by topping off with fuel before you leave and then again after the sea trial. It's better to conduct a sea trial with a full load of fuel anyway, just to see how the vessel trims out and how it behaves full laden in a seaway. If you're going to be carrying deck fuel on the actual delivery, now's the time to make sure you won't be putting her decks under in a seaway.

During the fueling operation, you'll learn how well the tanks are vented and subsequently how quickly you can take fuel. Inadequate fill venting can be a problem, as the tanks take fuel very slowly, the fill lines get air locks, and then fuel burps up through the fill holes. Always have rags ready.

In foreign ports that don't cater to yachts, you may find only the high-speed fuel pumps designed for commercial vessels. Unsympathetic fuel dock operators quickly lose patience with us "yachties" when they have to stop and start their pumps, allowing short bursts of diesel to dribble down the teensy fill lines of our expensive toy boats.

If you have a serious venting problem, see what can be done now to improve it. Sometimes opening other fill caps or altering the fuel transfer valves will help. Never take water while you have fuel caps open, and don't forget to return the fuel transfer valves to their normal operating positions.

CHAPTER 7
FUEL MANAGEMENT

Whether sail or power, the lifeblood of a yacht delivery is diesel.

Yacht deliverers more often than not are hired to take sailboats straight upwind. Whether they're getting paid by the mile or by the trip, they must get the trip completed as quickly as possible to get paid the most for their time. Tacking upwind is a painfully slow process, so that means motoring.

Sailboat fuel tankage is generally smaller than that of powerboats of approximately the same size, but even those who specialize in delivering large power boats often need to carry more fuel than will fit into the built-in tanks below decks.

Our bread-and-butter route through Central America requires a range of at least 650 miles in order to bypass refueling ports in unfriendly or dangerous countries such as Nicaragua, Cuba, and El Salvador.

Staying at sea as long as possible between fueling stops is highly cost effective. Every port stop is expensive, especially in foreign countries where port clearance procedures are time consuming. It often takes 48 hours just getting in and out, to say nothing about port clearance fees and dockage charges. In addition, every port call offers a potential grounding or collision.

You can carry extra fuel by converting tanks, bladders, and barrels.

Converting existing tanks from other uses may be the simplest solution, provided the owner doesn't object. Tank conversion is safer than other methods discussed below, because the tanks are already secured below decks and are capable of being plumbed. Your first thought should be of the waste holding tank, because it's already "contaminated," or unsuitable for potable water. On some voyages, a waste reservoir may be superfluous. After the trip, it can easily be converted back to holding wastes.

If the boat has two 250-gallon water tanks, for example, you might convert one to diesel. You'd still carry a decent quantity of water, depending on the length of the offshore portions of the trip. But you could never again use that tank for drinking water.

Even a bait tank might be used for a temporary fuel tank. Whatever type of existing tank you consider converting, it must first be "cleanable," so you don't contaminate the fuel you put into it with fish scales, water or other foreign matter.

If the ship's extra water tank is not well baffled, you might consider what one of our customers did. He ordered a heavy-duty waterbed mattress custom made to the dimensions of the inside of one of his monel water tanks. A small portion of the top of the tank contained baffles and therefore was too intricately divided to bother with trying to line. Otherwise, most of the tank space could be lined with the pliable, heavy-mil bubble, which was then filled with diesel. It was relatively inexpensive and worked like a charm.

To do this, the tank's access plate must be large enough to admit the scrunched-up mattress. Make sure diesel won't eat the vinyl or whatever material the mattress is made of. Ask for a one-foot sample of the material and soak it in a bucket of diesel for a week before ordering the whole liner made up. Then you need to be able to pump fuel from this temporary tank into one of the ship's regular fuel tanks when needed.

If you can't convert a tank, you will have to carry deck fuel. The primary danger with carrying deck fuel is that it's hard to secure. This brings up an old argument of whether to use barrels or bladders. We use both, but our preference is for bladders, because they are more portable.

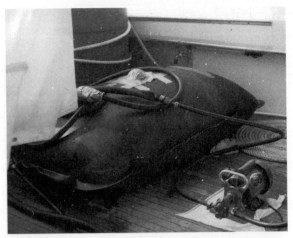

Deck fuel increases your range, but carry the right equipment to make fuel transfer underway a smooth operation. The portable fuel pump must be a powerful, high-volume model, preferably gear-driven like this Oberdorfer. The 100-gallon bladder made by Goodyear is built of thick, rubberized fabric. Notice that the larger-diameter fuel hose, which is cheaper, has collapsed and is barely allowing as much fuel to pass as the smaller-diameter hose, which cost more per foot. Chafe pads were taped for the first part of this delivery, when the bladder travelled inside a dinghy on the foredeck. Note the plastic barrel lashed into the cockpit corner. Never leave a fuel transfer operation unattended.

BLADDERS

A fuel bladder is a big, soft bag designed to be filled with diesel, stashed somewhere onboard until it's needed, and then drained. They come in various sizes, but usually can be rolled up and stowed when not holding fuel.

Bladders are expensive, but as with so many other things in life, you get what you pay for. The cheapest and least desirable models on the market are made of plastic. We've heard many horror stories about these breaking when a vessel pounds in a seaway. Imagine the mess of 200 gallons of diesel spilling all over a yacht, and then the worry about running out of fuel before the next port. We don't recommend this type bladder.

The best bladders are made of a nearly indestructible rubberized fabric. John has a 100-gallon bladder made of this tough black fabric that is 20 years old, and it's still as serviceable as the day it was made by Goodyear to haul

helicopter fuel in Vietnam. You can still buy them now.

We don't recommend any bladder over 100 gallons for two reasons. First, it places too much weight in one place, especially on a pleasure boat's deck. Second, if it did get punctured, that's just too much loose fuel to have in your bilges or to put into the ocean.

Let's look at the bad news about fuel bladders. They're difficult to secure when full. They get rather round and bloated, and they tend to creep or walk around with every roll of the boat. The fishing cockpit of a sportfisher or yacht fisherman is a reasonable place to carry a bladder. We have been known to fill them and leave them unsecured in the midships section of a sportfisher cockpit that's clear of any puncture dangers. Even in a heavy sea, all they will do is walk themselves slowly over to the low side against the gunwales, after which there is no where else to go.

If you have a good pump that will lift the fuel well, you could find a place for a bladder below the main cabin sole. Use hefty line to secure it where you want it and check often for chafe.

Bladders aren't compatible with yacht interiors because they may emit diesel fumes and invariably dribble from the fittings. If you don't want the boat's interior fabrics (curtains, bedding, wall coverings) smelling of diesel by the end of the delivery, you'd better find some other home for the bladders.

Once when delivering a new 53-foot Hatteras sportfisher, we were able to fit John's Goodyear bladder below decks, beneath the fishing cockpit, where it fit right between the stringers. We didn't even have to tie it, because the tall, hefty stringers gave it nowhere to move. This kept the fuel low, out of sight, and any drips went into the bilge. The key was a good gear-driven pump, because we had to lift the fuel several feet to get it into the deck fill of the ship's tanks.

Carrying bladders on foredecks can be difficult. Make sure you have more than one strong, through-bolted fitting to tie them to. Are you absolutely sure the deck underneath the bladder is strong enough to support the additional weight as the bow lifts and pounds down in heavy seas? The farther forward you place the bladder, the more accentuated its motion will become, the more it can and will move, and the more likely it will come loose.

Ordinarily, you want to get rid of deck fuel as soon as you have burned enough from the ship's regular tanks to make room for more. But if your bladder is well secured on the bow, you might want to wait until you have made enough room in the ship's regular tanks to allow you to dump in the entire contents of the bladder. Why? Any less than the full amount of

POTCH·N·TOOKUS
— PHILADELPHIA. PA. —

Nine plastic drums in the stern of this 60-foot sportfisher carried us an extra 350 miles, and the 100-gallon fuel bladder on the bow balanced the trim and took us another 75 miles. We were able to eliminate an intermediate fuel stop in an unpleasant port where fuel would have been expensive. Instead, we pressed on while the weather was good and made Acapulco, where fuel is relatively cheap. Each drum holds about 60 gallons. They must be lashed securely, yet not cover deck hatches, clog scuppers, or block cleats.

the bladder, and you will have to tighten up the lines securing the bladder. That's not practical when the bladder is partially full and its remaining contents are pitching in a sea. It's like wrestling a giant amoeba. On the brighter side, fuel on the foredeck is generally higher than the boat's deck fills and easily drains by gravity without pumps.

BARRELS

For enclosed cockpits on large boats, barrels are a decent means of transporting extra fuel. Fifty-five- or 60-gallon barrels are common sizes. Smaller sailboats can get by with plastic jugs lashed to the shrouds.

Don't use steel drums on yachts unless you have no alternative. They are heavy, difficult to move, difficult to secure, and are usually rusty and dirty. Use carpet scraps for chafe gear all around them.

The advent of plastic or PVC drums or barrels has made the use of deck fuel much more practical for yachts. Plastic drums are much lighter, easier to handle, don't rust, and are generally cleaner.

When we're in the South Florida area getting a boat ready to take around to the West Coast, we often find all the blue plastic, 60-gallon barrels we need at a tiny junkyard called Symons Surplus, which is on the west end of the runway at Miami Airport.

We'd just flown into Miami airport to begin prepping a brand new, 60-foot sportfisher in Dania, Florida, for the long route. As usual, we had reserved a station wagon rental car just so we would be able to haul the huge load of provisions in one trip, and the 60-gallon fuel drums in another trip. But after we arrived at the airport we found that they had given our station wagon reservation away.

It seems that in Miami, vans and station wagons are always difficult to rent. Transients appear to need them for hauling a load of something or other here and there, and if they can't find one, they just flash somebody a hundred dollar bill and presto—they have a car somebody else reserved.

The only car available with a trunk large enough to hold the barrels was a "full-size" model, and to make up for their error, the rental agency wanted to give it to us at the same rate as our station wagon that had mysteriously disappeared. It turned out to be a brand new, four-door, metallic gold Cadillac.

Pat arrived at the junk yard in grand style, and the senior Mr. Symons remained implacable and congenial as she helped him lash four barrels on the roof, two in the trunk, and three more in the back seat, thanks to the fold-down back of the passenger seat. What a sight. Pat called it her nine-barrel Caddy.

The barrels still contained small amounts of Argentinian apple juice that had grown ripe in the South Florida heat, so they smelled rather strongly of alcohol. Make sure you get a sealing cap for each barrel, that you keep the air conditioning running, and that you don't speed. That aroma attracted half the highway patrol in Dade County.

We had to flush the barrels with water and set them upside down in the sun to dry, but 24 hours later they were ready to fill with diesel.

Always clean used barrels, because you never know what residues remain in corners to contaminate the fuel. Apple juice is water soluble and easy to clean, but beware of toxic or noxious chemicals that are impossible to remove or to dump.

Securing barrels is another creative challenge. Fishing cockpits are the easiest, depending on the number of barrels needed. If you need only 100 gallons of deck fuel, secure one barrel in each corner to the good, strong points such as the stern cleats and a hawse.

If you need more, see if you can't line several barrels across the taffrail. Use as many as you need so they fit tightly without moving and then secure them to each other and to the stern cleats and hawse holes. We've also put a 2 × 4 across the front of the drums and laced all the drums to it. Carpet scraps secured underneath and around the drums will prevent chafe.

Even with the best job of lashing, barrels try to move in heavy weather. Never let them break loose.

When lashing barrels across the stern, make sure you leave access to the deck hatches and the lazarette below.

Murphy's Law says, "If anything can go wrong, it will, and at the worst possible moment." We once lost our steering underway and needed to get into the lazarette to fix it. Another time a hose broke off a through-hull and was flooding the aft bilge. Both times we had barrels on the hatches, and we had some anxious moments while trying to keep the unlashed barrels from moving while we rolled in a heavy sea.

Deck fuel invariably affects the boat's trim. Don't overload the boat so freeboard is dangerously diminished, or so the boat loses maneuverability in heavy seas.

We once loaded nine barrels in the cockpit of a 60-foot sportfisher, and they put her so low in the stern that the swim step was under water while sitting still. To counter-balance this we carried a 100-gallon bladder on the bow, stored nicely inside an Avon inflatable we were carrying flat on the foredeck.

Never carry drums on the foredeck of a pleasure boat. There is no place sturdy enough to secure them properly, certainly not a rail stanchion, and when they break loose, they'll carry away whatever is secured to them. This could mean tearing holes in the foredeck.

PUMPS

To pump the extra fuel into the ship's tanks, you'll need high-volume and reliable pumps. Sometimes you can place bladders and barrels so they will flow by gravity, but it's still a slow and messy job.

Both AC and DC pumps are available. If you don't have an AC generator you'll have to get a DC pump operating off the batteries, which is much slower.

Impellers are crucial to fuel transfer, so take plenty of spares, the kind intended for fuel, not water. The best class of fuel pump is gear-driven, so you don't have to mess with impellers at all.

Make sure you have plenty of hose for transferring the longest distance from the spare fuel to the tanks. Get good-grade fuel hose and carry extra lengths for any shore refueling operations you may get into. Also take extra plumbing pipes, adapters and reducers. Since fueling operations in foreign ports may

Small, 110-volt impeller pumps are barely adequate for the job of moving deck fuel. They pump too slowly and the expensive impellers bind up and have to be replaced frequently. Use them only as backups to larger pumps.

be set up for commercial vessels, you may have to reduce down to the size of the fuel fill.

FUEL CONSUMPTION

Next to safety, the aim of a delivery captain is cost efficiency. Though many powerboats are designed to run at high speeds, they are not fuel efficient at those speeds, and must be run at lower speeds for optimum fuel consumption.

For example: An owner is taking bids from several captains for a 5,000-mile trip. You bid $15,000 for fuel based on an 18-knot cruising speed. Another captain bids $8,000 for fuel at 10 knots. Who do you think is going to get the trip?

The most limiting factor to a boat's speed is

A constant crosscurrent and beam wind make for a precarious fueling operation at the old cannery pier in Cabo San Lucas, Baja California, Mexico.

its range between fuel ports. High-speed boats rarely carry enough fuel to make the 650-mile minimum range that is necessary for the trip from Florida to California via Panama. Running slower greatly extends the range. This allows you to avoid additional ports that cost extra time and money. Slower running isn't nearly as hard on the machinery or on the rest of the boat and crew for that matter. This is a hard idea for full-time yacht captains to accept when faced with doing a delivery. They are so used to running at full bore that they don't even think of slowing down.

Once as we were tying up at the Henry Morgan Yacht Club in Port Royal, Jamaica, we watched the Jamaican Coast Guard tow in a 54-foot sportfisher that had run out of fuel 10 miles offshore. Her captain had last topped off his 1,000-gallon tanks in Great Inagua, about 350 miles away. He ran down toward Jamaica well in excess of 20 knots and didn't quite make it.

That means he was burning three gallons per mile. With the 8V92TI GMC engines he had, he could easily have gotten 1.5 gallons per mile at a speed of 10 knots, which would have given him a range of 666 miles. He wasn't trying to outrun any weather problem in the

area, he just thought he was always supposed to go fast—until it meant he didn't make it.

Here's the formula for figuring cruising range:

T ÷ GPM = Range
Total Tank Capacity ÷ Gallons Per Mile
    = Range
1000 ÷ 1.5 = 666.66 = Range

Generally with fast boats we back off to 10 knots. However, high-performance turbo-charged engines (TI and TA) don't like to run at low RPMs for long periods. Unburned fuel coats the turbo blades, eventually getting them off-balance, which can cause the bearings to go out—or worse.

To counter this, we run at about 1000 RPMs, but no slower than 800 RPMs. Every two hours we run the engines up to 1,800 RPMs for about 15 minutes. When we know we have sufficient fuel, we run the last several hours at full cruising speed into port. We have never had trouble with any turbo engine using this method. However, if you neglect to run the engines up on a regular schedule, you will ruin them.

With GMC engines of the 8V71TI, 12V71TI, and 8V92TI series, we've enjoyed remarkable consumption at low RPMs—1.5 gallons per mile or better. This is just a ballpark figure for powerboats averaging about 60 feet. Of course, weight makes a lot of difference.

Talking about slowing down the engine may sound ludicrous to the auxiliary sailboat skipper, but it still applies to him.

We delivered a 44-foot Peterson sailboat non-stop 3,700 miles from San Diego to Bora Bora. We had a range under power of 700 miles at seven knots, and during most of the passage we had light winds.

If we had motored at full speed we would have run out of fuel and been at the fickle mercy of the wind god. However John cut our speed back to four knots and arrived in Bora Bora with a thimble full of diesel. Four knots is slow, but 100 miles a day is better than drifting aimlessly, day after day, in the doldrums near the equator.

The late Eric Hiscock wrote in his classic work, *Voyaging Under Sail*:

I am glad to have had the opportunity of making a passage through the doldrums under sail, for I feel that is an experience which every sailorman ought to have once in his lifetime, so that he may learn to be patient and to appreciate some of the difficulties with which his forefathers had to contend. But once is enough, and if I ever have to pass through that area of calms, squalls, rain, and heat again, I hope to have an engine of greater power and a *plentiful supply of fuel* for it. There is also this point to consider: a powerful engine running slowly is longer-lasting, quieter, and cooler than a less-powerful unit giving its maximum output.

The emphasis is ours, but Hiscock might have added that a powerful engine running slowly is much more fuel efficient than a small engine burning itself up.

FUEL RESERVE

How much reserve fuel should you carry? Robert Beebe, in his book *Voyaging Under Power,* recommends 10 percent. He qualifies this depending on the design characteristics of the vessel, with certain types needing more than 10 percent. Overall we don't think that 10 percent allows for the additional fuel you might consume making your course in bad weather, nor for some loss of fuel due to in-

accessible corners of the fuel tanks. To be safe, we use 20 percent across the board.

Most vessels have a certain amount of fuel that, because of the design of the tanks, you can't transfer to the engines. We don't think that the amount of unusable fuel should be calculated in the reserve figure. If you can't get at it, don't even think about having it.

A crossing from Los Angeles to Hawaii is about 2,200 miles. If you get 1.0 gallons per mile, you'll need 2,200 plus 20 percent, or 2,640 gallons.

To calculate the amount of fuel needed for a given distance:

$$(D \times GPM) + .2(D \times GPM) = GWR$$
$$\text{or}$$
(Distance × Gallons Per Mile + 20%) =
Gallons needed with Reserve
$(2,200 \times 1.0) + .2(2,200)$
$(2,200) + (440)$
$2,640 =$ Gallons needed with Reserve

Apply this to the declining balance. For instance, if you get halfway (1,100 miles) and you only have 1,200 gallons left or about 9.1 percent reserve, you should slow down, because you are eating up your reserve too fast.

To calculate percentage of fuel reserve:

$$[G - (M \times GPM)] \div M = \text{fuel reserve}$$

[Gallons remaining − (Miles remaining × Gallons Per Mile)] ÷ Miles remaining = Percentage of fuel reserve

$[1,200 - (1,100 \times 1.0)] \div 1,100$
$(1,200 - 1,100) \div 1,100 = .0909 = 9.1\%$

John delivered a 62-foot trawler-type motor yacht from Honolulu to Cabo San Lucas, a most unusual route, 2,600 miles dead against the winter trades. This little ship had been cruised from San Diego to the Caribbean, back around to Alaska, and then across to Hawaii. It had extensive logs about its fuel consumption that told him that it had adequate range and reserve at full cruising speed.

The ship also had a very good method of monitoring fuel consumption on a daily basis. The engines ran off a large day tank and every day he would pump fuel from the other tanks into the day tank. He made a mark near the top of the day tank's sight gauge, and every 24 hours he'd pump fuel exactly to this mark. The pump was the same as you find in automobile filling stations and had a very exact counter for measuring the gallons pumped.

The first 48 hours of the trip the ship punched against Force 6 tradewinds and the fuel figures showed that the fuel consumption was higher than the logs ever reflected, leaving zero reserve under those conditions. Never had this vessel made a trip against headwinds this strong for so long a time. John backed off the speed from eight knots to seven. The following 24-hour check showed much better consumption and sufficient reserve under those conditions.

Though this was the tropics, for 10 days they drove on under these uncomfortable conditions and the sun never broke through the cloud cover. The last six days the trades died gradually to flat calm as they closed with the Baja California Peninsula. The change in weather showed up immediately in better per-mile consumption. When he ran back up to full cruise, it became apparent that they had more than adequate reserve under these new conditions. However, he couldn't push the engines any harder.

They arrived with 800 gallons of fuel left. That's a conservative approach, but it's better to have too much fuel than not enough. The psychological anguish of pushing speed to the maximum is not worth the mental wear and tear of wondering if you really are going to make it. Going slow and knowing beyond the shadow of a doubt that you will arrive is well worth it.

CONSUMPTION PER HOUR AND PER MILE

Yacht deliverers often use *gallons per mile* (GPM) as opposed to *gallons per hour* (GPH), because it is easier to estimate overall fuel costs on long-range voyages. At the same given RPM, current and windage are what affect fuel consumption per mile. Gallons per hour at the same RPM remains the same no matter what the current, but speed varies as does time to the destination and therefore your total consumption. You should have a thorough knowledge of how both GPM and GPH work.

Be skeptical of fuel consumption figures given you by the boat manufacturer, yacht broker, or owner. Bet your life on them only after your own verification.

We were asked to deliver a 50-foot motor sailer from Mystic, Connecticut, to Mallorca, Spain. Time was crucial to the owners; they had a charter party waiting for the boat and therefore wanted us to go the 3,200 miles non-stop. The selling broker had told them the boat had a 5,000-mile range at full cruise.

John had serious doubts about that range. Even though her six-cylinder Gardner diesel was fuel efficient, his previous experience did not allow him to believe that 1,000 gallons of fuel would go 5,000 miles at eight knots.

We did have the option of fueling in the Azores, which we were sure we had the range for. And fuel there we did, 800 gallons worth. The salesman's range figure was inflated by 100 percent. This kind of marketing hype is very typical.

To complete the picture, we will talk about the effects of current and windage. Here's an example of how to figure consumption. The crossing from Key West to Cozumel is 380 miles. Having started with full tanks, we top off in Cozumel with 500 gallons.

Here's how to calculate GPM:

G ÷ D = GPM
Gallons used ÷ Distance = Gallons Per Mile
500 ÷ 380 = 1.32 Gallons Per Mile

The leg from Key West to Cozumel took 38 hours, so we averaged 10 knots.

This is the formula for GPH:

G ÷ H = GPH
Gallons ÷ Hours = Gallons Per Hour
500 ÷ 38 = 13.2 Gallons Per Hour

Let's look at what happens when we return to Key West at the same RPM. We top off with 418 gallons. 418 ÷ 380 = 1.1 gallons per mile. The trip took 31.7 hours for an average of 12 knots. 418 ÷ 31.7 = 13.2 gallons per hour.

What happened on the return trip? Speed went up, consumption went down and gallons per hour remained the same. Why? The Gulf Stream current. Roughly speaking, this current accounted for about half the difference between 10 knots and 12 knots, which is one knot. Actually, a 1-knot effect was quite light for this stretch. Gulf Stream current is generally 1.5 knots or more.

Once, on a 30-mile stretch between Isla Mujeres and Cozumel, we made 10 knots through the water and four knots over the bottom. That's a six-knot adverse current. Imagine what that does to your gallons per mile figure. Or what it does to a five-knot sailboat.

To find the gallons per mile average for the Key West–Cozumel example, use the formula G ÷ D = GPM.

918 total gallons used ÷ 760 total miles = 1.21 Gallons Per Mile

So, 1.21 gallons per mile is your fuel figure for currentless passages, assuming that current is running at the same speed and direction on both trips. That's something you rarely find.

We've shared these examples to illustrate that there is a direct relationship between gallons per mile and gallons per hour. Though yacht deliverers commonly use gallons per mile, double check your figures using gallons per hour. Always double check.

Engine manufacturers are a reliable source of hourly fuel consumption figures. At a given RPM the engine or engines will burn the same amount of fuel per hour no matter what the weight or design of the boat, the kind of propellers, current, or windage. Often the manufacturer will give a graph of fuel consumption at various RPMs. However, they often will not give hourly fuel figures for the low RPMs you may have to use to extend the boat's range. Then you will have to make your own graph. This is the only true test anyway.

CHAPTER 8
MEAL PLANNING*

Nothing quickens the spirit of a hard-working crew faster than a good meal. In the one or two days that the captain and engineer are busy preparing the boat's mechanical systems, the cook and deckhand should be provisioning the boat's larder and setting up onboard shipkeeping for the voyage.

Meanwhile, you and your crew will be working very hard and need to eat. Sometimes the galley doesn't contain one pot or pan, and the larder isn't stocked yet.

If you're prepping the boat in an urban area, you might bring aboard some donuts, coffee, deli sandwiches or pizza and sodas just to ignite the first spark of warmth in the boat's hearth. Then, as the cook and/or deckhand begin making runs for provisions and gear, time your comings and goings from the boat so you can bring the ready-made food on time for regular meals. If you're prepping the boat in an isolated area, make one of your first priorities the purchase of a multi-purpose non-stick pan, a dozen eggs and an assortment of canned soup.

Provisioning is as important to the delivery's success as getting the engine running. And for the sake of harmony right from the start, the cook needs to keep people fed.

*By Patricia Miller

PROVISIONING

Before you so much as buy a can of beans for the trip, you should calculate your food budget. The "bottom line" of the food budget is a major consideration in establishing the original cost of the delivery, so you'd better be sure it's accurate. If you're too high, you may either miss out on the account altogether, or just create expensive waste. If you're too low, peanut butter gets real boring!

Here's my simple budget formula, tried and true, to determine how much money I'll need to buy food for the entire voyage, based on a figure of $15 per person per day:

Persons × days × $15 = food budget
3 × 30 days × $15 = $1,350

This example is for a 30-day voyage from San Diego to Ft. Lauderdale with three people on board, buying as much as possible from membership wholesale discount houses in San Diego. The remainder was purchased from retail groceries, using bulk-buying techniques (which can save money and space) explained in detail on page 59.

This figure, $15, is the average cost of feeding one person three balanced meals and one night-watch snack (called "mid-rats") per day, based on food prices as of August 1989, in Southern California. Besides a few meals ashore during the voyage, this bottom-line figure includes some essential non-food items like paper plates, bath soap, and Ziploc bags, but no alcoholic beverages. You'll need to adjust your budget for inflation and regional price differences.

You probably won't spend the whole $1,350 during the initial provisioning—not that a good galley engineer has any trouble spending money. Produce and perishables just don't last long enough to give you crisp salads or fresh veggies 30 days later, no matter how well stored. You'll need a reprovisioning reserve of between 8 and 10 percent of the total food budget to restock perishables during one or more brief port calls along your route.

If you're unfamiliar with the ports you'll be putting into, count on the high end of this reserve. Don't expect to leisurely ferret out all those great buys you've heard so much about from other cruisers. If you're being paid to deliver a boat, your time is money. Reprovisioning normally means you'll shop at whichever market you can reach in 10 minutes, spend 30 minutes buying, 10 minutes returning, 10 minutes stashing it away, and immediately cast off the lines for sea again.

After you're familiar with what's available in your reprovisioning ports and have gleaned your own local knowledge, you may have two or three percent left over (and will have found how to shop for your own trinkets on the fly). Until then, count on using up the whole 10 percent reprovisioning reserve.

The United States is truly the land of plenty. Compared with a Safeway or Winn-Dixie, much of the rest of the world is the land of Next to Nothing. Quality and availability are always better here, and sometimes price is better here, too. I can't overstress that you should buy as much of what you need here. Unlike cruising or even chartering, there's never going to be anyone to bring you something from home.

Provisioning in exotic ports can bring joy or frustration to cruisers and yacht deliverers alike. Willemsted, on the Dutch island of Curaçao, lies just north of the Venezuelan coast. Local captains sell directly from their produce-laden vessels lined up along Willemsted's canal system, which threads through an area of 18th-century colonial architecture.

To custom-fit this food budget formula to your needs, keep receipts for every nickel you spend during initial provisioning in the port of origin and in the ports you visit while restocking. At every check-out counter, be sure to separate items like paper plates and dish detergent, which are part of your food budget, from bilge detergent, engine room garbage bags, and muslin to cover furniture, which are housekeeping and engineering items. Get separate receipts and label them in ink. This may seem like a pain in the kazoo at first, but it will rescue you from an ocean of accounting snarls later.

Inflation over a 10-year period pushed the $15 figure up from $9.50, so calculate this change, too, to extrapolate your own base cost per person per day. If you must do your initial provisioning in ports such as Tahiti or Hawaii, count on $17 per day per person.

A 30-day master meal planner is a thorough list of specific meals, containing each entree and side dish to be served for breakfast, lunch, dinner and mid-rats (easy snacks for the nighttime watches) for each of 30 days. If you do this precisely enough, you can draw your gigantic shopping list (the ingredients and quantities for each entree or side dish) directly from this master meal planner list.

The list of entrees I've drawn up (see Appendix II) includes a close approximation of the quantity of each ingredient I'd need for each meal to feed a crew of three for 30 days. In the five-day master meal planner, I've calculated ingredient quantities for breakfasts, lunches, and dinners. Your own intuition comes into play in the end, of course, but here's how to start with mathematical precision.

Gather up all the recipes you're familiar with and throw out all those that contain ingredients your crewmembers are allergic to. Then toss out all those that can't be made underway aboard the particular boat you're about to deliver. Souffles are out, and jello sets only on calm days.

Meals should be tailored to the particular equipment onboard, such as the number of square feet of freezer space, type of stove, oven, microwave, and dining facilities. Is there a toaster or blender that can be used underway? Is there a broiler pan that fits in the oven? A Sea Swing back-up stove? A drawer full of utensils? A fillet knife? A lidded-bowl for jello? The answers bear directly on how you decide to provision. If you don't know, find out before you plan for something that isn't onboard.

This may not seem immediately important, especially to other crewmembers, but it will become very important to everyone onboard once you're far at sea with a lot of food that you can't prepare. I often have to ask a broker or owner on the other coast to walk down to the boat and look to see if there's a microwave, a freezer, any cookware or silverware at all.

I have one set of recipes for powerboats and one designed solely for sailboats. Sailors usually eat more simply than do power-boaters, because there's more likely to be freezer space and a larger galley on a power-boat.

However, powerboat galleys are notoriously awkward to work in during heavy weather, even to the point of being dangerous, so plan several "storm meals" that you can prepare and eat with one hand, even on a luxurious power cruiser. One 96-footer leaving Panama for a Caribbean crossing was so badly tossed by the trades that no one ate anything but mugs of oatmeal and saltines for two days.

Even if you have a large freezer and two generators, plan for emergencies. On one Atlantic crossing, I had provisioned not only for our passage from Connecticut to Mallorca, but also had to lay in several hundred dollars worth of top-quality meats in the freezer for the owners' charter guests for a month of Mediterranean cruising. When the freezer died halfway across and couldn't be repaired underway, I had to spend two days in storm conditions cooking all the meat on a gimballed alcohol stove as it thawed. Then when the refrigerator also failed, it broke my heart to toss all the food overboard as it began to spoil. We sailed in eating our emergency canned food. It's amazing how fast you can go from abundance to nothing onboard the closed system of a boat making passage.

If the cook does nothing other than cook, the meals can be more complex than if the cook also stands regular watches, including night watches. I've enjoyed planning the next few days' meals during long night watches. Never leave the helm unattended, but before or after you go on watch, you'll be able to start a pot of beans soaking for the next day, set out a frozen pot roast to thaw in the sink, or marinate a pound of tofu in tamari in a closed Tupperware container.

It's nice to prepare one meal a week that's

an elegant knockout, just to keep up spirits. On the other hand, no one's trying to impress anyone else during a delivery, so the best general plan for selecting recipes is to keep it simple.

Allergy or Craving?

Be considerate of each crewmember's food preferences. Special diets, however, can be impossible to maintain on passages. When cruising on your own boat you can enjoy more consistency than when you're working in the delivery business with a different boat each trip, with different routes and changing faces.

Before you start planning meals, sit down with crewmembers and discuss what foods they love, what foods they think are absolutely revolting, and what they are honestly allergic to. One crewmember might normally drink a gallon of milk a day, while the other gets hives from soup made with milk. One of our engineers requests peanut butter and jelly sandwiches three times a day, everyday.

Mild allergies to common foods such as wheat, dairy products, onion, sugar or cured foods may not crimp your meal planning drastically; there are tasty, convenient substitutes that the rest of your crew may not mind at all.

Diabetics, strict vegetarians, or picky eaters may simply prove to be incompatible with the "expedient" nature of yacht delivery. No delivery cook should be asked to routinely prepare separate meals for individual crewmembers. Even if they select their own foods and prepare their own meals, it still means more elbows in the galley or scheduling separate times for meal preparation. To be fair to everyone onboard, it's wise to screen out prospective crewmembers who require too much special attention during hard deliveries.

Don't let someone's ephemeral cravings send you into a tailspin, as I once did. An engineer we'd hired many times before decided

that on this particular delivery he was going to go on a diet and he wanted nothing but Le Menu and Lean Cuisine microwave dinners. Since on this boat we had plenty of freezer space for the extravagance of frozen dinners, I just rearranged the food budget and devoted one entire freezer just for them.

Unfortunately, the engineer tired of his new diet only a few days out and decided he'd rather have what we were eating. (We were eating many tuna and noodle casseroles, since that's all the remaining budget allowed.) I gently reminded him of his agreement to eat them, no matter what.

Well, guess what. That same day, the Le Menu freezer mysteriously quit working, causing him to have to throw overboard the thawed top half of its contents. He'd have thrown them all over if I hadn't intervened and decided to eat them myself!

Food allergies are a different matter. I once threw away a perfectly good bottle of peanut oil because a woman I knew was very allergic to peanuts. A month later I learned she'd been rushed to the hospital in an ambulance, unable to breathe, with eyes, mouth and throat swollen to freakish proportions.

At a party she'd eaten some grocery-store coffee cake made with peanut oil. The hostess had said it was her own recipe and contained no peanut oil, not believing anyone could tell the difference. Susan recovered after 48 hours on radical antihistamines, but I wonder what the outcome would have been had the peanut attack occurred at sea.

The moral is, pay attention to crewmembers' allergies when you choose recipes for your master meal planner.

SHOPPING

At least 24 hours before you go shopping, order all your frozen meats from a good butcher, so they can be cut, packaged and frozen solid while you do the rest of your provisioning and stowing. Make it your last pickup before you shove off.

Finding a good butcher is essential. If you're in a marina area, see who regularly provisions for week-long charters or who supplies commercial fishing expeditions. They'll be experienced in packaging and freezing just the way you order it, based on your meal planner.

I once had to defrost 15 pounds of ground beef all at once because an inexperienced butcher changed my packaging order. I'd written 5 packages of 3 pounds each, but he froze one package weighing 15 pounds.

If you're in Eastern Mongolia and all the butchers you can find seem staggered by your quantities or by your request for such specific packaging, find a good restaurant chef who will introduce you to his provisioner.

If all else fails, just find someone who's in the vicinity of the boat, so your meat won't defrost on the way back. And don't mention the word *yacht,* or it will cost you triple.

Plan to pay a deposit of 30 to 50 percent when you place your order with the butcher. This is customary. Depending on the area, or your businesslike appearance, or the butcher's method of doing business, you may be asked to pay an estimated total. That's not uncommon, either. There's no way the butcher can know the exact total until it's all cut and weighed. When you pick up your order, take a peek inside the freezer box before it goes into the hot trunk of your car.

In Ft. Lauderdale, my favorite butcher is Smitty's, near the Southport Raw Bar—exceptionally delicious meats, perfect packaging every time. I normally give him my non-frozen meat order, too, because it's handier to pick it all up together. If my budget isn't blown by then, Smitty's superb condiment counter is where it vanishes.

Bulk Buying and Apportioning

If you are cruising on your own boat, the quantity of food you buy is not too crucial. Non-perishables all will be eaten eventually, so there is little harm in overbuying, particularly if you find a bargain. If you are delivering a boat, on the other hand, plan your meals carefully and try to follow your shopping list to avoid waste at the end of the trip.

Start your shopping in volume-discount houses, where all those giant-size cans and case quantities might save you money. If you don't already have a membership in such a wholesale/retail group, go with a friend who has and pay cash for your purchases. If you're legitimately in the yacht delivery business, such membership fees are tax-deductible, so you may as well invest in one.

Take your meal planner along and be prepared to adjust your menus when you find that six cans of corn are cheaper than two. This is the place to buy sodas by the case, cheeses by the block, boxes of 1-cup packets of instant coffee, and barrels of paper plates. Beware of getting such good deals that you go broke or that you unbalance your menu.

Bulk buying can save you money, and portioning of bulk quantities will be a tremendous convenience once you're underway, but not every item lends itself to this trick. For example, giant bags of spiral noodles are easy to split three ways for three meals. You can cut a 10-pound brick of cheddar into three blocks, re-seal two blocks and slice up only the first one you want to use. But a giant can of tuna means that once it's open, you must store half or two-thirds for a day or two, before mixing it into tuna salad or whatever. This can be done, but make sure you have the storage containers and refrigerator space to carry out this plan.

Resealable bags, an indelible felt pen, a small scale, and a few hours are required to portion down most of your King Kong-size

For a crew of four or more, Pat provisions with large-size cans whenever practical, to keep us within the food budget. Tuna disappears quickly, but three people may not be able to consume such large quantities of other foods, before the foods spoil.

purchases. Here's how to handle a 10-pound box of pancake mix:

Read the directions on the box, then measure out the amount of mix needed for one morning's worth of pancakes for all crewmembers. Three pancakes each for five people equals 15 pancakes, which requires 2 cups mix. Easy. Seal it in a small Ziploc bag and write on the outside *2 C. mix, ½ C. milk, 1 egg, yield 15 pancakes*. Portion out small bags until you empty the box. Cut the instruc-

Resealable bags, an indelible felt pen, a small scale, and a few hours are all you'll need to portion down your bulk purchases.

tions off the box and toss them into the last runt bag.

Retail Grocery and Specialty Shops

Anything you didn't order from the butcher or couldn't find in the Amazon Aisles will have to come from a regular grocery store, and this will be the majority of your initial provisioning.

Go late at night or early in the morning, when you pretty much have aisles to yourself. This way your caravan of five or six shopping carts accumulating in the corner of the store won't cause undue congestion.

Take a helper with you if possible, and start him or her off at the other end of the store with half your shopping list. Save produce or chilled foods for last. Cross things off as you go. Ask the floor manager where you can park your filled carts in one place while you fill your next.

Once, in a small town, a most hospitable manager happily walked the aisles with me, making sure I didn't miss anything and have to double back for it. It was summer and he rolled my filled carts into the refrigerated produce storage area until I was all finished. Here's where the magic word *yacht* made someone's day.

One major grocer may not have all the items on your list, so leave yourself time to take this load back to the boat, maybe stow the perishables, and to make a second trip to another major grocer.

Specialty items like flaked rye berries, brewer's yeast, and powdered sour cream might have to come from a health food store or the marine chandlery's cruising foods corner. These specialty items might be as costly as Smitty's gourmet bargains. If you keep even vague track of your budget as you load the grocery carts, you'll know if you can afford to stop for the treats or not.

Now that we've purchased all the food, let's get it aboard and start stowing it.

STOWING PROVISIONS

The cook's toughest job in prepping the boat is stowing all the food. It's often done in a chaotic rush, punctuated by frowns from the captain and crew, who are eager to cast off the dock lines.

Stowing hundreds of pounds of cans, glass bottles, boxes, and frozen packages is physically exerting. As much as you might like to recruit help, it's a one-person job. The cook's the one who won't mash 12 loaves of sandwich bread into a small ball in the corner of the freezer, or who won't fill the only cupboard over the stove with engine room cleaner. When the sun's down, the sea's rolling, and the frying pan's empty, the cook can't afford to wonder where that bottle of safflower oil was put.

For this massive stowage job, your best helper is the stowage diagram (see Figure 8-

Long-range deliveries require lots of groceries, and there'll be no 7-Elevens along the route. This was one of three provisioning hauls for a crew of four for 30 days.

1), which you should make before stowing the food. Here's how:

Map out the boat with a sketch of the salon, galley, state rooms, bridge, engine room, or what have you. Draw each area on a separate sheet of paper. Within each area, identify each food storage place, such as "Bridge, port settee seat, aft bin," or "Guest head, hanging locker," or "Salon floorboard, amidships forward, lower bilge."

On lined paper, make one outline for each major area, breaking it down into each bin, locker or bilge compartment where you plan to stow food. Below the bin location, list the exact contents and quantities.

To make your stowage diagram into an inventory keeper as well, cover the outline paper with clear plastic and write on this overleaf in wax pencil or crayon only the quantities. This way you can wipe off and correct the numbers as you use up your supplies. Look in K-Mart's stationery counter for the clear plastic sleeves, which come folded over black construction paper with holes punched for a ringed notebook.

Nowadays, I keep my master meal planner

Getting food on board for a major provisioning can be a logistical problem, compounded if you're at anchor. Even when berthed stern-to in the marina on Raiatea, French Polynesia, Captain Marc Paris receives a basket of provisions with difficulty.

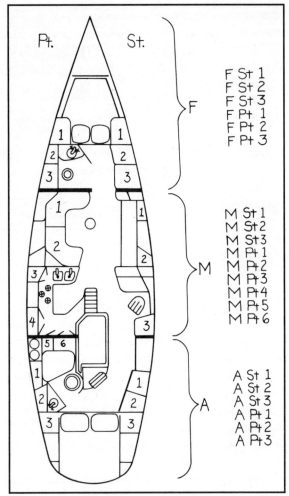

Figure 8-1. A stowage diagram can be a cook's best helper.

		Pt.	St.
		F St 1	
		F St 2	
		F St 3	F
		F Pt 1	
		F Pt 2	
		F Pt 3	
		M St 1	
		M St 2	
		M St 3	
		M Pt 1	
		M Pt 2	M
		M Pt 3	
		M Pt 4	
		M Pt 5	
		M Pt 6	
		A St 1	
		A St 2	
		A St 3	A
		A Pt 1	
		A Pt 2	
		A Pt 3	

"Metomi kai" inventory (pg 2 of 3)

item	size	original qty	location	qty left
asparagus spears, tall		3	mPt2	2
artichoke hearts, marinated, sm jars		3	mPt1	2
beans, green, French cut		3	mPt1	
beans, green, whole		3	mPt1	
4-bean salad, marinated		3	mPt1	2
beets, whole		2	mPt1	
beets, sliced		2	mPt1	~~0~~
corn, creamed		5	mPt1	3
corn, niblets, sm		4	mPt1	2
okra, cut		2	mPt2	
olives, black, pitted		4	mSt3	3
olives, green, jars		2	mSt3	
pimento pieces, sm jars		2	mPt3	
peas		6	mPt2	5
sauerkraut		2	mPt2	
spaghetti sauce, w/shrooms		1	mPt2	
spaghetti sauce w/ sausage		1	mPt2	
spinach		2	mPt2	
turnip greens		2	mPt2	
tomato juice, sm boxes		24	mSt1	19
tomato juice, med cans		8	mPt2	
tomato paste, sm cans		4	mSt1	3
tomatoes, stewed w/ herbs		6	mPt2	
apricot halves, unsweetened		2	mPt6	~~0~~
cherry puree, lg		1	mPt6	1
blueberries, whole		2	mPt6	~~4~~
grapefruit juice, lg		5	mPt2	3
lemon juice, sm bottles		4	mPt3	3
orange sections, sm		6	mPt6	5
peach halves		3	mPt5	
pears		3	mPt5	1
raspberries, whole		2	mPt5	

An inventory list showing original quantity, location, and amount remaining.

and multi-page stowage diagram/inventory keeper, in plastic sleeves that I staple together and store in a handy drawer for quick reference.

Most veteran cruisers know a zillion clever tricks for keeping canned goods and perishables: varnish the cans, salt and cheese-cloth the cheeses, wax the eggs, smoke any extra fish, wrap each apple in tissue, vacuum-seal the wheat germ, etc. However, if you are about to begin a delivery you have a few hours—not days—to stow everything perfectly. When you reach for that can underway, it's likely to be in a night gale with a flashlight stuck in your mouth and a pot boiling over on the stove. Think expedience. Just write "cr corn" on one end of the creamed corn can with an indelible marker and put it in the bin.

Remove all paper labels from cans that may end up in the bilge. You could take on serious water, which could soak off the labels, which would likely clog the bilge pumps. A lot of drama could result from not removing all those paper labels.

Unless you're leaving civilization for a year at sea, you don't need to buy so many cans that you overflow all other storage places. Cans don't normally rust through during a six-week passage, unless you've stored them in a very wet bilge. Anything likely to deteriorate

For small sailboats, the many cans needed for a long delivery may not fit anywhere but in the bilge. If so, make sure you remove the paper labels and write the contents on one end with an indelible marker. Paper labels clog bilge pumps. Spray oil or varnish help prevent rusting if bilges are damp.

that would otherwise tumble around in a seaway. Scotch tape will hold small boxes together in rows, so you can slit them apart and discard them as they're emptied.

Keep small portions of things you often use handy to the galley and stow their larger quantities elsewhere. I learned this the hard way on a trip to Hawaii. I stowed all the cans under two handy bunks in the main salon. As the trade winds rose and the voyage fell into its natural rhythm, we were forced to devote both these bunks to "hot bunks" for watch rotations. That meant that two-thirds of the time when I needed to retrieve a can, people were sleeping on both bunks. The solution was to move the cans elsewhere.

Temporary Stowage Methods

If you'll be taking more food than the boat is equipped to carry in lockers in bins, you'll need to improvise some stowage space.

Consider buying an inexpensive ice chest just for sodas. Put it where crewmembers can help themselves to a cold one without opening the main refrigerator or getting under foot in the galley. This puts less strain on the main refrigerator and helps keep food cold.

It's normally impractical to ice down the bulk of your sodas or bottled water all at one time. Just chill a day's supply at a time. The task of keeping the soda chest replenished with ice and warm sodas becomes a favorite duty for any of the crewmembers.

If you have more frozen meats than the boat's freezer can handle, pack another ice chest with dry ice and your pre-frozen meats. Seal it with duct tape. This will last only a few days, especially when you must open it, so use it up first.

I find that flimsy styrofoam ice chests work fine for storing sodas and excess frozen meats, *if* you reinforce them with duct tape before you put anything inside. Wrap it all around the

should not be stowed in an inaccessible spot. Don't let crewmembers change your storage locations without your knowledge.

It's unlikely your longest passage will outlast a dozen eggs, refrigerated or not, so you can probably forget the wax job. Just store them where they won't get sat upon. Fresh eggs are available wherever you'd stop for diesel, water, or repairs.

The main glitch with hanging mesh hammocks for fruits and vegetables is that they swing, mashing their contents, and then drip juices that stain carpet and fabric wall coverings.

Stow glass jars and bottles amidships with wadded newspaper between and underneath, to cushion them and absorb liquids if they should break. Don't pack newspaper where it can be sloshed into the bilge. Stow cans low, and keep fruit juices from heat. Bags of noodles double as cushions between boxes outside of the rim and make a duct-tape hinge to keep the lid from wandering away. Secure ice chests where they won't become loose cannons in beam seas. Duct tape them into a corner or to the floorboards under the salon table if necessary.

On about half the boats we deliver, the galley cupboards already are crammed with the owner's food, which we don't use. Rather than move it all elsewhere, or simply to expand my galley stowage space, I make a temporary pantry for non-refrigerated produce and dry staples. You can make a temporary pantry out of lightweight plastic baskets, the oblong variety that dime stores sell in many colors and sizes. Duct tape two or three together and secure them in a dark, ventilated corner (for produce) where they won't trip anyone, yet where you can reach them. Line the bottoms with newspaper or brown paper bags to absorb moisture and act as a slight cushion.

In hot, dry climates, you may need to cover vegetables loosely with damp muslin, the same fabric recommended for covering upholstered cushions at sea. (See Chapter 9.) In the tropics, keep the muslin dry. Why? You can always cook shriveled pippins. But once they're moldy, all you can make with them is a sacrificial offering to Neptune.

A pantry for staple goods (cereal, mixes, chips) fits easily into most sportfisher designs on the ledge above the amidship bulkhead, under the forward windows. If you have inside steering, don't obscure navigational visibility. Secure one basket or a string of them to the bulkhead with duct tape. About half the boats we deliver have windows or ports that leak, so keep a close eye on this pantry area once underway.

Heavier plastic milk crates work well in the engine room for stowing spares, but they cost considerably more.

The drawback to any temporary stowage is that it can get to looking sloppy underway. A tidy ship contributes to a cheerful attitude among the crew. The muslin cover may help.

SETTING UP THE GALLEY

Now that the food is aboard and well stowed, carve out an hour or so to set up the galley.

If you've ever been a short-order cook, you already know how to make certain things highly accessible: dish soap, paper plates, spices, mugs, instant coffee, ground coffee and filters, paper towels, juice jugs, and sodas.

Now imagine being a blind-folded short-order cook on a pogo stick.

If you have an alcohol, kerosene, or propane stove, you may need to fill the main tanks and clean priming pans and burners. If there's a sticky valve or dead burner, get it fixed before you depart, or plan around it. It's better to get it fixed. One of my worst cooking ordeals occured when two electric burners went dead underway, leaving me one corner burner on which to cook for a crew of five. It also was a stove that offered top burners or oven, but not at the same time.

A sea cook's best friend is a cook's sling. (See Figure 8-2.) Imagine you're lifting a pot of steaming food from the stove to the sink with your left hand, and are holding a lid on a secured spider on a stove burner with your right. Even if you're accustomed to the boat's

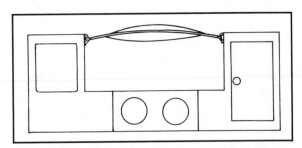

Figure 8-2. A cook's sling can prevent serious injury in rough weather.

motion, all it takes is one lost cross-wave to cause a serious scald, burn or cut.

The main purpose of a cook's sling is safety. It gives you something additional to lean against, normally in the galley's main work area, so you won't get flung across the salon. In heavy weather, a good sling can actually keep you strapped in place, while an assistant (at arm's length) passes full plates to the crew.

Cook's slings are used mostly during passagemaking where you are likely to encounter heavy weather, but coastal trips can present plenty of crossed seas. When the going gets really rough, there is a point when no sling will help, and you should pass out granola bars.

If the boat you're about to deliver has no provision for a cook's sling, here's what's involved in the installation. Screw or bolt two sturdy "pad eyes" into two hidden places in the cabinetry, so you can clip each end of the sling. If you choose pad eyes or eye bolts, the holes you drill will have to be mentioned to the owner, who may never leave his slip and never need a cook's sling. Be sure to use rubber washers. If you choose screw eyes, make sure the threads can hold your weight two or three times over, as if you were being thrown into the strap, because you may well be.

In especially heavy weather, you might need to rely on just one eye, either by clipping both ends into that eye, or by clipping one end into the D-ring of the other end, which is clipped into the "weather eye." If you cannot use a hefty eye bolt for this task, you probably shouldn't risk your safety by cooking in especially heavy weather, when a small screw eye is likely to pull out during a lurch.

To position the sling, have one crewmember on each end of your sling holding the clips in various places on the cabinetry, probably right under the counter overhang, with the strap going across your bottom at hip level as you stand at your station. Too low on your

bottom, and the strap could trip you backward. Too high on your back, and it could yank your shoulders forward. There is a height just right for your weight and size. It's best if you can do this with full knowledge of how the boat rolls.

A cook's sling is made of seat belt webbing or strap, similar to safety harness used on deck. Its usable length should be about four feet, enough to span most galleys. If you have a sailmaker sew it up, ask that it be adjustable in length with a sure-grip-type tension ring. Install a D-ring and carabiner on each end and you're set for safety.

Frequently-used items must be secured against rolling or flying around, and put where you can grab them in the pitch dark, or while you're strapped into your work station. Again, plastic baskets come to your rescue, this time the smallest size. Again, use duct tape or fibrous strapping tape to secure them to the countertop.

By being thoughtful about where you tape these small baskets, you might also create a wedge to constrict the missile properties of toasters, blenders, coffee makers, and other appliances that some boats carry and sooner or later must be used underway in bad weather. I've created containment wedges with cardboard and duct tape, too, by folding

Rubber-coated mesh keeps galley objects from sliding. It's flexible, washable, and is sold in varying widths from commercial fishing-boat suppliers. Although intended to cover entire counter surfaces, rubber mesh is practical in small pieces, too.

Most powerboats have ungimballed, household-type stoves. Improvised sea rails for such stove tops are always a challenge to the yacht deliverer's sense of creativity. Without some means of securing hot pots in place over burners, there could be no cooked food while underway. This version, designed by one of our engineers, is made of flat, stainless steel stock and gives the adjustable, screw-on pan holders a firm hold from all sides. When the rail unit is removed, the four screw holes are filled with chrome-headed brads.

A properly gimballed stove.

a rectangle of cardboard lengthwise and taping its two longer sides to the counter.

Tinfoil makes a great constraining material in the oven and refrigerator. Wedge tinfoil pie pans around the baking pan you intend to use most often. You can't allow hot, juicy dishes to move around inside the oven underway. Slip the edge of the pie pan between the rods of the wire oven rack if necessary. You can always straighten out the tin foil.

The same trick works in the refrigerator, but if you had trouble finding storage space for some of your paper towels, use some of the individually wrapped rolls as wedges in the roomy top shelf.

As soon as the voyage settles into its own rhythm, you'll see how to rearrange things, and eliminate squeaks and bumps.

As soon as the galley is secured, it's time to secure the rest of the boat's interior, either before the sea trial, or before you cast off for the first leg of your journey.

CHAPTER 9
SECURING FOR SEA*

SECURING THE EXTERIOR

Step back for a moment and imagine a two-story wall of green water washing over the deck at about 20 knots.

If forward-facing ports on the cabin or house are particularly large, and if they are made of glass, seriously consider adding storm windows. In an emergency, plywood sheets cut roughly to fit can be "glued" in place with large, messy quantities of seagoing epoxy or a hot batch of resin, but the prudent mariner will have lucite storm windows cut to fit, and install through-bolts or mounting slots to secure them properly.

Test the seals around the hatches and ports by squirting them with a high-pressure hose. Compared to replacing a stained interior, it's far cheaper to draw a few beads of silicone and replace a few yards of gasket material now.

Stuff the hawse hole for the anchor chain with a wad of kid's modelling clay. Unlike potter's clay, it's just waxy enough not to wash away, yet it's plastic enough to mold right around the chain. This is another neat trick we learned from Larry Briggs, owner of the schooner *Invader*, when we brought *Neptune's Chariot*, his liveaboard motor yacht, from Hawaii. We found modelling clay at K-Mart.

*By Patricia Miller

Clear the decks. Only those items that absolutely must remain on deck should be lashed in positions where they will be used. Avoid shock cord, which relaxes in the sun and salt. Lash with braided line or anything non-stretchy. If you must carry deck fuel, secure containers separately to the rails and don't block your scuppers or primary cleats. Make sure all scoop ventilators have flush, screw-in plates that fit. If this is a passage, can you stow the windsurfer inside an on-deck dinghy rather than against the lifelines?

See that the liferaft is ready to launch, not screwed or bolted into its cradle. Lean hard on the lifelines, noting any wobbly stanchions that need to be firmed up from below. Replace their backing plates if necessary.

If you're using clip-on life harnesses with a jack line, try out the system to see that the jack line permits access to the forestay and boomkin, and that it doesn't trip you or roll under your feet. We keep it stowed until weather calls for it.

A dinghy in davits should be secured better than if you were merely running between anchorages. We've had sturdy-looking davits begin to collapse in rough weather, due to the extra inertia of the wildly swinging dinghy. Even though the upright inflatable is covered, remove the drain plug.

Inspect all standing and running rigging. Check that shrouds and stays are tuned, turnbuckles are in working shape and secured, and clevis pins are sturdy and free of stress fractures.

Look for potential chafe problems in the rigging and on deck. If chafing gear is missing, cut up sections of old rubber hose and lash them in places to reduce friction.

Securing through-hulls below the waterline requires testing seacocks to make sure they can be shut off. Tape an appropriate-size wooden bung near each through-hull fitting.

SECURING THE INTERIOR

Potential missiles lurk silently everywhere on boats that seldom pass the breakwater. Comb the interior of the boat and try to spot them before they start flying.

Imagine a worst-case scenario. If that picture frame could slide around and scar the bulkhead behind it, take it down for the trip. Nicknacks, catchall baskets, lamps, pictures, TVs, blenders, books on shelves overhead all must be secured. Look around.

If you are delivering a boat for someone else, you might offer suggestions such as, "Since we're responsible for your lovely, etched-glass, 300-pound dining room table top, can we lift it off its legs and secure it flat on the carpet in the corner with pads all around? That way, we can stow the carved ebony legs in your stateroom closet where they couldn't possibly get scratched."

Maybe you don't even need to mention that the table top would slice a man in half faster than a buzz saw if it ever got to moving around, or if it broke by having someone fall onto it. If the owner balks at moving potential missiles, I wouldn't hesitate to point out the dangers.

My nemesis is the chunky wooden cutlery holder that sits out on the counter presenting half a dozen knife handles to the galley gourmand. Great at the dock; not at sea.

Designate one knife drawer for all sharp knives. Never leave a knife loose on the counter, but slip it down into the sink basin instead. Wipe knives and put them in their drawer rather than leave them drying in a dish rack.

In heavy weather, large appliances that aren't through-bolted tend to bounce or even "walk," which can be lethal.

We once had a wrestling match with a refrigerator. We were heading south through the Yucatan Channel against a stiff current that was bristling in a stiff adverse wind. At 0300, a favorite time for disaster to strike, we heard a terrible crash in the galley. The boat's motion had sheared off the factory bolts securing the huge household-type refrigerator into its cubicle in the cabinetry, and not only was it walking around the galley, but the door's latch was smashed off and the entire contents of the fridge, including a broken glass bottle of Mazola oil, were disgorged onto the floor under it's metal "feet." The monster was skating around quite freely on the greasy mess, flapping its door and threatening to walk right through the side of the boat.

John put the boat on a more comfortable course and the engineer, who weighed 250 pounds and stood 6 feet, 6 inches, wrestled the slippery beast back into its corner, but it took the rest of that stormy night. Isla Mujeres was only a few miles away, so we ducked into its lee to clean up the mess and secure the fridge.

On another boat, another ocean, we were delivering a liveaboard motor sailer. I asked the boat's owner, "Is that microwave through-bolted to that shelf up there?" and he said, "Oh yes, it's even screwed down. A friend of mine installed it for me."

I was skeptical but he reassured me that he knew the difference between screwed down and through-bolted. Because the counters were full of food that had to be stowed in a hurry, I didn't take time to check for myself. Off we sailed, beating to San Francisco.

We were reefed in anticipation of an approaching squall, but when it hit, complete with hail, it laid us over on our beam end. From the cockpit we heard the proverbial crash from the galley. As the microwave fell, it tore a huge gouge in the teak drawer facings, landing in a heap of worthless parts on the galley floor. If I hadn't been on deck at that moment, I'd have been making dinner.

It's a shame to have to delay departure for small details like bolting down a microwave, so look around for potential missiles and secure them now. Get out the drill. Install hook-and-eyes.

If you are delivering a boat, particularly a powerboat with lavish furnishings, you may need to convince the owner to let you pack up certain belongings and ship them ahead. The first time I did this, I felt terrible. It was a set of white silk, barrel-type salon chairs that the builder's decorator had just brought onboard for the Miami boat show. During a sea trial, they tumbled across the salon like a pair of 50-pound beach balls—even with their castors removed.

The owner grumbled about the extra expense, but agreed to let me ship the chairs to his West Coast address. It turned out to be a very rough trip with lots of beam seas. The windows leaked and required constant sponging. Even if I'd wrapped the chairs in plastic and secured them with line to the couch, they hardly could have escaped damage. They fared just fine by UPS, and in the end the owner thanked me for convincing him.

Mirrored closet doors made of real glass also are missiles waiting to launch themselves. Make a big "X" over each large glass panel with masking tape, but don't pull it tight. Glass flexes naturally, and you want it to flex all it can, rather than to break. The "X" will help contain large sections of glass, should it break.

Taping glass allows flex while preventing larger pieces from becoming airborne missiles.

Then, tape newspaper over the whole mirror surface, to contain fine splinters.

Beware of sliding doors with flimsy, pegged stoppers at intervals, because the pegs could sheer off once the door starts slamming around. Instead, make a wooden dowel to drop into each floor track. Cut it to the exact length so the sliding door cannot open or close more than half an inch. Before securing the door with the dowel, wedge a short piece of rubber hose between the glass edge and the door frame to cushion it from jerking.

SHIPKEEPING

Shipkeeping begins before you leave the dock, so you may want to buy several important items during your provisioning rounds.

In addition to the indelible marker, styrofoam ice chests, duct tape, plastic baskets, and plastic sheets for your inventory diagram, you may want to buy muslin fabric by the yard and a set of mugs and flashlights, one for each crewmember.

Muslin dusters, those white furniture coverings you've seen in Gothic romances, have a real function at sea. In fact, with yacht decorators sending smaller and smaller boats to sea with more and more luxurious interiors,

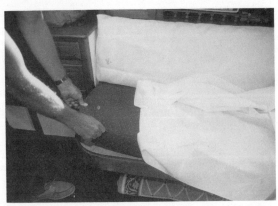
Muslin dusters are a practical solution for protecting expensive fabrics.

those traditional dusters are the only practical solution for protecting expensive fabrics.

No matter how you try, sweaty bodies will invariably land on any furniture coverings not stowed away, especially in bad weather. Airborne salt crystals filter into the interior as a fine mist, even if you keep all hatches to the outside closed as much as possible. The salt can even sneak in through air conditioning.

My solution when delivering boats that have no tailored furniture covers is to buy unbleached muslin by the yard, as cheaply as possible. Measure the seats and backs of all couches, chairs, settees, or anything upholstered that you can't stash away in a closet. Figure total yardage based on the width of the muslin. Narrow widths may work fine for the backrest part of the entire curved conversation pit in the main salon, while only the wider muslin will cover the seats in one run. If you must use two runs of the narrower width for seats, you may have to "make the bed" often during the trip. One large sportfisher required almost 200 yards of muslin. Instead of going to a retail fabric store, I bought it from a fabric wholesaler in two bolts.

For couches, simply tuck in one end, roll out the bolt, cut off what you need, and tuck in the other end. The most practical solution

for smaller chairs is to tear tassels in both ends of the muslin and tie them together. Don't trust stainless steel pins, which can rust and bleed through before you know it.

Buy a crew mug for each person on board. Let each one be responsible for returning his own mug to the galley or even for washing it and returning it to its place. This way the cook never runs out of mugs or has to make a mug retrieval mission. This keeps colds from spreading, too.

I buy a plastic, two-wall insulated mug in a different color for each crew member, or I buy a set and write their names on the bottoms with an indelible marker. Porcelain mugs, though they come in a million great designs, tend to crack or lose their handles under duress.

Most boats have one good flashlight on board, but I buy one small flashlight for each crewmember, write his name on it in indelible ink and make him responsible for it. Buy lights powered by two or four AA batteries that are small enough—don't laugh—to be held by mouth. Now nobody has an excuse for thrashing around in the dark, or for having to turn on shipboard lamps that destroy the night vision of whomever is at the helm or navigating.

Buy one extra flashlight with a red lens and reserve it for navigation. When I can't find a red lens, I just make the ordinary lens red with nail polish, red tissue paper, or red indelible marker.

If you are delivering a new boat, it may be completely bare of cookware, and linens, yet the broker or new owner may not be ready to put on the monogrammed sheets and towels, the Revereware, or the family silver service. Buy inexpensive starter sets of each just to get through the delivery, and leave them onboard to become spares once the good stuff arrives. If you expect the owner or broker to reimburse you for the cost, make sure that's understood, and don't get carried away.

In one quick sweep through a K-Mart store you can outfit the boat with cotton sheets and starter sets of stainless steel flatware, light-duty non-stick cookware, Melmac-type plastic plates and bowls, or paper plates with wicker holders, plus a spatula and cooking spoon.

I often arrive at a delivery job carrying my own galley kit, a plastic milk crate jammed with what I consider the minimal shipkeeping necessities for the galley. If the boat already has everything, I usually only take the first two items.

Galley Kit

Good fillet knife
One-burner propane backpack stove
Large frying pan with lid
Large soup pot with lid
Large saucepan with lid
Large baking dish or casserole with lid
Roll of heavy-duty tinfoil
Tinfoil pie pans and loaf tins
Tinfoil stove burner liners
Full-length apron and potholder mitts

Many are the times I've cooked on the tiny backpack stove aboard luxurious yachts, when, for a number of reasons, their electric stoves weren't operational.

PART III
UNDERWAY

CHAPTER 10
WATCH STANDING

After you finish the hectic preparations and the dock slips away behind you, the rhythm and routine of life at sea are quite pleasant. While occupied in these seemingly mundane shipboard tasks, you can feel yourself engaging in a time-honored life that has been shared since ancient times by thousands of sailors, famous, infamous, and unknown. However, in today's world of 20-knot shipping and heavily trafficked sea lanes, your round-the-clock watch standing and a vigilant lookout are more than routines to pass the time. They are fundamental to your safety at sea.

COLLISION AVOIDANCE

The captain should have an intimate knowledge of the Rules of the Road. Without it, he is exposing his vessel and crew to excessive danger. Whether the trip is a professional delivery or a pleasure cruise, the captain must be able to react instantly and correctly to confusing right-of-way situations, to course changes in tight quarters, to light and sound signals from other boats and navigation aids, and he must be able to take correct action when visibility is restricted.

Imagine the chaos on city streets if stop lights and turn arrows didn't exist, if there were no traffic lanes and cars didn't have blinkers. What would happen if we had no traffic rules, or if only a few drivers knew what they were?

The U.S. Coast Guard requires every skipper to pass a very thorough examination on Rules of the Road before obtaining a captain's license. The Rules-of-the Road portion of the test is exactly the same for a supertanker captain as it is for the captain of a small charter boat, and a score of 90 percent is the minimum passing grade. Even licensed captains working at sea full time tend to forget some of the less-frequently used Rules of the Road. Every skipper who goes to sea should keep a copy of the Navigation Rules on board and brush up periodically. The Coast Guard requires the rules to be kept on board anyway.

There are no federal laws requiring a noncommercial small-craft skipper to have a license or show any proficiency in the use of the Rules of the Road. However, ignorance of collision regulations can lead to dangerous situations.

John recalls a particularly trying year as captain of *Invader,* a 150-foot steel schooner displacing 265 tons, which operated as an excursion boat in San Diego Bay:

Often, drivers of small boats would pass dangerously close under my bows, forcing me to sound the danger signal, back down hard, or change course, even when I unequivocally had the right of way. Their ignorance of the Rules of the Road was much more dangerous to them than to *Invader.* She might have lost some paint if I hadn't avoided a collision, but they'd have suffered major damage, possibly even been sunk.

The Coast Guard Auxiliary and U.S. Power Squadron teach classes on Rules of the Road aimed primarily at pleasure boaters. This is a great help. Further, if you are a cruising skipper, we suggest that you take a course designed to prepare you for the U.S.C.G. license exam, even if you don't intend to get a license. By getting an in-depth understanding of the rules, you can better assure the safety of your vessel, your crew, and the other vessels you encounter.

"Might is right" is the unwritten, common-sense rule skippers should observe. If the other vessel is bigger than yours, do whatever you can to stay out of its way, because if you collide, you have the most to lose.

Operators of small craft (which includes 99.9 percent of all yachts) need to be aware of their own near-invisibility, when viewed from the bridge of a large ship, even in daylight. Add to that a moderate sea running, or haze, or darkness, or background lights, and you can always assume that the big ship doesn't see your boat.

It's a sad fact that many large merchant ships stand poor watches. Also, they rely primarily on radar for collision avoidance. If your boat doesn't show up on a big ship's radar, it doesn't exist. Yachts make very poor radar targets at any distance. At close range they get swallowed up in the larger ship's sea clutter (the return signal from wave tops on a radar scope). We can attest to this from years of staring into radar scopes.

A good radar reflector helps your boat to be seen on radar, but only to a minor degree. *Practical Sailor* once compared the effectiveness of many models of radar reflectors available for pleasure boats. The results indicated that small craft seldom show up on radar. Thus, skippers should assume their boats are radar-invisible.

Even if a ship sees your vessel on the high seas and you undoubtedly have the right-of-way, she may not alter course or yield right-of-way to you. Ships operate on tight schedules and don't like delays. The watch officer may be very reluctant to change course, because often his standing orders require him to wake the chief engineer in order to reset the auto-pilot after even a slight course change.

Assume that the other vessel's captain does not see you and will not alter course to avoid you. This requires that you take very early and appropriate action to stay out of the way. Modern ships travel at speeds of 20 knots or faster, so close-quarter situations develop quickly.

Try calling the other vessel on the VHF. In U.S. coastal waters the law requires all large vessels to stand radio watch on VHF Channels 13 and 16. Thirteen is for bridge-to-bridge communication. If you see a tug and tow bearing down on you in Chesapeake Bay, you can rely on him to hear you on Channel 13.

Outside U.S. waters, ships monitor and respond to calls on 16, the international hailing frequency, and seldom monitor 13.

Identify your vessel and the other by relative and absolute positions, courses and speeds, so you don't unwittingly get the wrong boat to respond. The silliest thing heard on 16 in crowded coastal waters is a frantic voice pleading, "To the boat off my bow, this is the *Wild One*. Do you read me? Over."

Instead, try, "To the northwest-bound fishing vessel two miles abeam of Boca Mitla and one mile off my port bow, (repeat this twice more, then ...), "this is the south-bound sailboat *Ragtime*, one mile dead on your bow," (repeat twice more). Do you copy? *Ragtime*: Whisky, Victor, three, three, seven, three on Channel 16. Over."

If he responds, but doesn't suggest switching to another channel, and if there's not a lot of traffic on 16, you can say something like this: "This is *Ragtime*. I wish to know your intentions, so we can avoid close maneuvering, (or, because we may be on a collision course). Can you please switch to Channel six? Over." This gives him time to figure out what's going on, since he still may not see you.

Then you should suggest what course of action you each should take. Normally, if there's time, you should each turn to starboard as hard as necessary to bring your closest point of approach to a safe and comfortable distance.

On the high seas, you may get no response from larger fishing boats and freighters because their watch officers don't speak English. Most of the world's merchant mariners are Japanese, Filipino, Norwegian, or Greek and do not speak English. Don't let this inhibit you from trying to contact them.

A woman usually has better luck getting a response to her radio calls on the high seas than does a man. To hear a female voice calling in the middle of nowhere is a novelty to any watch stander. The difference was evident during an Atlantic crossing we made. Halfway to Europe, our weatherfax machine went out. (Unless you can copy international Morse code at 20 words per minute, you'll find no broadcasts of high seas weather for the eastern North Atlantic, in any language.)

We resorted to calling passing ships on the VHF for weather reports, but they seldom replied to John. Whenever Pat called, even to ships at great distances, she invariably got a response and they agreeably gave her their latest weather reports.

The radio officer on one cruise ship traveling in our direction kept calling us back as he got weather updates, until the ship speeded beyond us, out of VHF range. He even offered to set up a radio schedule with Pat on SSB, but when other crewmembers came on watch, no

contact was made. In another part of that ocean, a lonely Korean officer kept trying to make contact with Pat. She tried English and Spanish, and he tried Korean and something that sounded Arabic, their efforts bringing some much-needed humor to the crews of both vessels.

We believe that all vessels should have a proper, *visual* deck watch at all times. All vessels are legally required to do so by Rule #5 of the Navigation Rules, Part B, Section 1:

> Every vessel shall at all times maintain a proper lookout by sight and hearing as well as by all available means appropriate in the prevailing circumstances and conditions so as to make a full appraisal of the situation and of the risk of collision.

The *degree of alertness* depends on the conditions. In heavy traffic close to shore, the watch stander must be extremely alert and pay constant attention. An ocean crossing in a remote part of the world is the other end of the spectrum. There, watch standing can be more relaxed.

On a non-stop passage from San Diego to Bora Bora, we sailed two weeks without seeing a ship, but there was at least one person on deck on watch the entire way.

We don't advise cruisers or delivery crews to simply leave the vessel on autopilot so everyone can go to sleep for the night or day. Even in mid-ocean we've seen vessels appear out of nowhere, far from any shipping lanes. In addition, many unmanned objects drift aimlessly in mid-ocean: whole trees, large cargo containers, and life rafts. Pat once encountered a huge, stainless steel, salad bar refrigerator that had fallen off a U.S. Navy carrier. It was bobbing inches below the surface, invisible to radar, directly on her bow, and it could easily have holed the vessel below the waterline if she hadn't spotted it in time to take evasive action.

In spite of numerous stories of close encounters, here's what Jimmy Cornell discovered and revealed in his *Ocean Cruising Survey:*

> (According to) the findings of my Suva (Fiji) survey, when the system of watches on long distance boats had also been investigated: Among the 62 boats in the survey, on only 45 was a full system of watches in operation, with all adult members of the crew taking their turn at watch keeping. The remaining 17 boats, and not necessarily those with smaller crews, kept very loose watches, the crew going to sleep at night when on passage and keeping a minimum of watches at other times.

Hmm ... This means that those of us who stand watches have to watch out for those who don't. A boat without a proper watch is nothing more than a very dangerous piece of flotsam that the rest of us must avoid running into.

WATCH-STANDING SKILLS

Make sure that at least one other person on board is able to make port if something happens to the captain, regardless of whether the trip is a day's outing or an ocean voyage. Here's a tragic example of why this is necessary:

A few years ago, we delivered a brand new, high-performance sportfisher from Florida to its owner in Los Angeles. A few weeks later he took some friends for a spin to show off his new boat. They were just a few miles off the coast and cruising at about 20 knots in a five-foot sea. Everyone was on the bridge as the owner started down the bridge ladder. The boat lurched and he fell over the side. The horrified guests watched him go over, but no one knew how to turn off the autopilot, change course, or stop engines. Eventually they figured it out, but because the boat was traveling at 20 knots in five-foot seas, the owner was already out of sight. A Coast Guard search ensued but was abandoned after 24 hours. They found his shoe and his pants, but the body never was found. He probably was overcome by hypothermia and drowned.

Even on a short trip, all crew and passengers should be briefed on the basics of stopping the boat and throwing the man-overboard gear.

The example of Tami Oldham underscores the importance of having a backup skipper.

In 1984, Tami and her fiance, Richard Sharp, were delivering a 46-foot ketch from Tahiti direct to California. Several hundred miles east of Hawaii they met a hurricane. The vessel was rolled and dismasted, throwing Richard overboard and knocking Tami unconscious. She came to 27 hours later with a bad gash on her head, her fiance gone forever, and the vessel full of water but still afloat.

She had the skills and presence of mind to jury-rig a sail, navigate by the heavens, and head downwind for Hawaii, where she arrived safely 42 days later.

Tami Oldham is a true nautical heroine whose survival serves as an example to cruising couples everywhere: If there are only two of you, make sure that both of you have the seamanship and navigation skills to make port.

The captain should train all watch standers in the following skills:

1 *Engines*—How to bring the boat to an emergency stop without killing the engine(s), how to put the transmission in neutral, and how to kill the engine(s) in case of fire.

2 *Autopilot*—How to disengage it, dodge traffic or lobster pots, reset it to the original course, or to change to a new course.

3 *Steering*—How to hand-steer a compass course or hold a course by the set of the sails.

4 *Sails*—How to douse any sail immediately and how to fine-tune the set of the sails to maintain the desired compass course.

5 *Log Entries*—How and when to enter vital information in the ship's logbook. We make entries in our navigation logbook every hour on the hour, and make entries in our engineroom logbook every hour on the half hour. The logbooks list specific data that change hourly, allowing one to compare and note trends. Logbooks are legal documents, not personal journals.

6 *Chart Work*—How to plot on various-scale charts using all the electronics and navigational gear you have, how to work up positions as opposed to dead reckoning, and very importantly, how to recognize when current or wind are setting you off course. Celestial confirmation is helpful, but we don't assign this to crewmembers.

7 *Engine Room Check*—See the section on Engine Room Logs (page 87).

8 *Radar Watch*—How to recognize an approaching radar target that appears from either side of the screen. How to plot multiple approaching targets (vessels and points of land alike) on the screen. Stress the importance of checking the radar and scanning between high and low ranges.

9 *Visual Watch*—Point out that this is the most important aspect of watch standing. Scan the horizon often with binoculars, particularly just before diverting your attention to making log entries, doing chart work, or making an engineroom check.

10 *Calling the Captain*—Give specific instructions about when to call the captain (for example, whenever any radar target comes within six miles). Also stress the importance of calling the captain whenever they have any doubt about anything.

All captains should support this last instruction by not arriving on the bridge in a grouchy mood, or at least by feigning amiability. Otherwise, someday a timid crewmember will hesitate calling until it's too late. A good captain should sense a crewmember's hesitation to call for advice and should dispel such fears.

Change of Watch

The change of watch is a critical time. The offgoing watch may be very tired and anxious to go below as quickly as possible. The offgoing watch should rouse the ongoing watch as early as necessary for them to get prepared, without unduly cutting into their rest period. Ten or fifteen minutes is about right. Crewmembers who habitually arrive late can be a source of irritation. If a crewmember continually arrives late, then the offgoing watch might well call him earlier and earlier until he gets the message. It's a thoughtful gesture and a boost to morale if the offgoing watch prepares a fresh pot of coffee for the next watch, so sparing them the effort of groggily preparing their caffeine fix.

The offgoing watch should instruct the on-coming watch on the following:

1 *Traffic*—Note both visual traffic and that picked up on radar and the relative motion of an approaching vessel and whether it poses an immediate threat.

2 *Navigation*—Notify them of any special considerations, such as course changes, sightings, or dangers ahead.

3 *Engine Room*—Note anything special that might be happening in the engine room, such as a slow oil leak, or a drop in fuel pressure.

4 *The Moment the Watch Changes*—Ensure that the ongoing watch knows at what point they are in charge. The relieved watch should not simply wander off the bridge, but should say something to the effect of, "You've got it?," and get an affirmative answer.

LOG KEEPING

Keeping logs is an integral part of the watch routine. Even though the data being recorded seem boring, those log entries contribute directly to important decisions about the delivery. Logs are legal documents. They are routinely demanded by the U.S. Coast Guard and insurance companies for the investigation of a collision, accident, loss of life or loss of property. Besides, updating the log keeps the crew on their toes, paying attention to what's going on.

We keep three kinds of logs: navigation, engineering, and a daily log. Because each vessel is different and requires its own array of entry headings, we don't use preprinted logbook forms found in nautical bookstores. Instead, we prefer using two hardbound, stitch-backed composition books sold by office suppliers or stationers. Ring notebooks and spiral-bound logs can be altered too easily and may not hold up in court if they must be used as evidence.

It's more practical to use one notebook for both the navigation log and the daily log, dividing the book in about half. The other book will be the engine room log. Somewhere on the cover of each book, inside or out, write the vessel's legal name, her rig (sailing vessel, motor sailer, motor yacht), the official number from the document or registration, her port of registry, gross registered tonnage, the extent of the trip (from where to where), and the owner's name, address and phone numbers. This information is useful when documenting your sea time for the Coast Guard when you wish to renew or upgrade your license.

We normally keep the daily navigation log on the chart table where it is used. The engine log can get greasy, and it should live in or near the engine room where it is used.

We recommend that you stagger the time designated for making both entries, and that you keep both books in their respective places. Whoever is standing watch should makes his own navigation entries every hour on the hour, and his engine room log entries every hour on the half hour. If both tasks were done at once, the watch-stander's attention would be too long diverted from keeping a proper watch for traffic. Alternating the entries breaks up the hour pleasantly and keeps the watch stander more alert, knowing that he has a specific task to do each half hour.

One hour is the longest period an engine room should go unchecked. Undiscovered fires and leaks sink ships in minutes. If the autopilot makes an unnoticed hiccup, you could drive straight into trouble very quickly. That's why a good engineer never sleeps with both eyes closed, and a good captain never closes both eyes at once.

We lay out the *navigation log* by making column rules and writing headings across the

date	hour	PSC°	SOG	RPM	conditions	Lat°	Long°	Remarks
5.20	1500	298°	18.7	1800	N5 flat	19° 05.8	105° 01.9	Rad Fx - Pta Chamela
	1600	298	17.2	1800	N5 flat	19° 20.2	105° 15.1	Rad Fx - Pta Chamela
	1700	305	14.8	1600	N12/3ft	19° 30.0	105° 30.0	Rad Fx - Roca Negra
	1724	305	10.7	1400	N15/5ft	19° 33.6	105° 40.3	Sat Fx/Rad confirmed
	1800	305	6.7	1000	N20/8ft	19° 35.2	105° 43.1	Sat DR (36 min)
	1839	305	6.4	1000	N20/8ft	19° 42.4	105° 45.5	Sat Fx.
	1900	300	6.5	1000	N20/8ft	19° 45.5	105° 50.7	Sat DR (21 min)
	2000	300	6.7	1000	N18/8ft	19° 48.3	105° 55.2	Sat DR (1:21 min)
	2100	300	6.5	1000	N20/8ft	19° 55.1	105° 59.8	Sat DR (2:21 min)
	2124	300	6.4	1000	N20/ugly!	19° 59.7	106° 04.2	Sat Fx.

Figure 10-1. The navigation log should be updated hourly.

top of a two-page spread, as shown in Figure 10-1. In the left margin we enumerate the times that hourly entries will be made.

There are many ways to record information. The captain should decide which data are pertinent for that particular boat when setting up the logbook. Our normal categories include the following:

1 DATE

2 TIME—Will you use GMT or local time? If local, then note how many hours it is different from GMT. Unless we're navigating primarily by celestial, we use local time on the 24-hour clock. For instance, 2355 is five minutes before midnight, and 0005 is five minutes into the new local day.

3 COURSE—Specify which compass you are reading. PSC is "per steering compass." Also designate T (True), M (Magnetic), or C (Compass).

4 SPEED—Enter in knots, not miles per

hour. Specify whether speed was determined by actual plotted speed for the past hour, or by a knotmeter reading. We enter "SOG" for actual speed over the ground.

5 ENGINE RPMs.

6 WEATHER—Wind in knots or Beaufort Force, wind direction, rain or sun, squally or calm.

7 SEA STATE—Direction and size of waves.

8 BAROMETRIC PRESSURE—In millibars or inches of mercury.

9 LATITUDE AND LONGITUDE—Degrees and minutes, of course, but are those seconds or tenths of minutes? Be careful when you change charts.

10 FIX—If the above latitude and longitude were determined by two or more LOPs from radar, enter "Radar Fix." If they are a good fix from the Satnav or Loran, enter "Sat Fix" or "Lor Fix." If they were obtained by electronic dead reckoning, write "Sat

DR" and be sure to enter the number of minutes since the last true fix. If they're only an estimated position, enter "E P." If they're determined by celestial navigation, enter "Venus, Sirius and Deneb," or whatever heavenly bodies you used.

11 REMARKS—This catchall column may include one or two of the following: Distance off Point Whatsit, change of a time zone, ETA at the next port of call, notations of set and drift, "crossed into Tropics on Joe's watch," or "caught 2 dorado," or a terse evaluation of the sea state.

Make navigation log entries in dark pencil (perhaps your plotting pencil) or in ballpoint pen. Neither will bleed away if the book gets wet, which can happen for the strangest reasons. If you have to abandon ship, take this book with you in a Ziploc bag.

Additional, supportive navigation entries can always be made. When you're creeping along some zig-zaggy channel in the fog, or picking your way among reefs, you may want to make critical notations as often as every 30 seconds, in which case you'd ignore some of the columns. At any time, the captain may want to work up his own fix, just to confirm the crew's navigation. Crew should be briefed in advance not to take this as an insult.

The *daily log* (Figure 10-2) is written by the captain, not by the crew. We keep our daily log in the same book as the navigation log. It should always be kept in ballpoint pen or indelible ink. It is a written summation of important events that occurred during the day. Personal entries should be kept in a separate diary or personal journal.

Cruisers have a penchant for recording what they ate each day, and indeed many won-

Nov 2 '87
Wind dropped in night. Storm warnings still up. Departed 0600, ran 1900 RPMs at 16 kts. Fixed trim tabs, rudder still flakey. Storm watch dropped at 1100, but may have to reissue it. Arrived 1575 at fuel dock. 9½ hrs, 125 miles, 13.2-Knot avg. Took 594 gallons at .85/gal. Wind came back up with heavy rain 3 hrs after arrival, stayed at A&B Marina.

Nov. 3
Wind gusting to 40 kts w/heavy rain & lightening all night & early Am. Trop Dep #14 passed w/i 60 miles. Worked on boat: ① Freed up garbage disposal, ② Compensated barometer, ③ Watermaker-interior pump keeps clicking off-fixed. ④ Salon-STBD A/C unit fan burned out-bought small fan to move air, installed in seating unit. ⑤ Bought + cut plexiglass for top of chart console on fly bridge. ⑥ Whipped ends on manilla line. ⑦ de-mildewed bimini ⑧ Radar-had tech out because image shrinks on screen intermittantly. He said he'd have to take front frame of cabinet, but after he did, he learned he didn't need to. Couldn't find problem, charged $150. Still have problem intermittant.

Nov 4
Departed Key West 0545. Wind calm, Ran 1100 RPMs in Gulfstream current. After 12 hrs pumped fuel from barrels: 1.35 gal/mi @ 7.66 Knots. Wind came SW.

Nov 5:
Rough night in beam sea. Turned corner Cabo San Antonio, west end of Cuba, Wind now aft of beam.

Nov 6:
1045 Switched to FRWD tank-reading just under 7/8. (509 gal.) AFT tank reads just over 3/4 (1048 gal.) High water bilge alarm went off-FRWD compartmt flooded-Pump burned out. Water came in through frwd shower sump thru-hull. Replaced pump and shut off thru-hull. Also, discovered fresh H_2O leak in line, down to 1/4 tank. Water cloudy-giving all p.o.b the shits. Short water rules.

Nov. 7
0345-FRWD tank down to 1/4, pumped 100 gallons fuel now reading just over 1/2. Ran 15 hrs on 4, 1/8.
1550-Switched to AFT tank reading 3/4 +. FRWD Tank now reads 1/16. 342 miles to go at 1.5 = 513 gal needed. Possible 786 gal - 10% = 707 usable.

Nov. 8 '87
1550: AFT tank reads 15/32, used 9/32 in 24 hrs, (295 gal) Only 128 miles to go 387 gal usable remaining- 177 gal needed.

Nov. 9
0530 = arrived Cristobal, Panama (9.1 Knot avg).
0900 = moved to Pan Can Y.C, changed oil, contacted agent, washed down, (1.66 gal @ 9. Knots)

Nov. 10 Tuesday - Admeasurer arrived. Agent aboard to arrange transit. Installed check valve. FRWD bilge

Figure 10-2. The daily log is written by the captain.

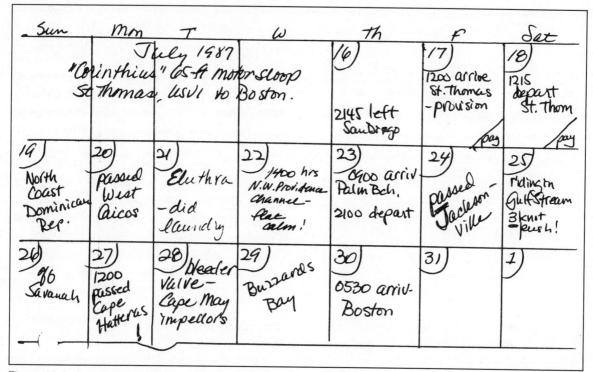

Sun	Mon	T	W	Th	F	Sat
	July 1987 "Corinthius" 65-ft motor sloop St. Thomas, USVI to Boston.			16) 2145 left San Diego	17) 1200 arrive St. Thomas -provision ~pay	18) 1215 depart St. Thom ~pay
19) North Coast Dominican Rep.	20) passed West Caicos	21) Eleuthra -did laundry	22) 1400 hrs N.W. Providence channel - flat calm!	23) 0900 arriv. Palm Bch. 2100 depart	24) passed Jackeson Ville	25) riding in Gulfstream 3 knot push!
26) 9/6 Savanah	27) 1200 passed Cape Hatteras	28) Heater Valve— Cape May Impellors	29) Buzzards Bay	30) 0530 arriv. Boston	31)	1

Figure 10-3. A grid-type calendar shows at a glance what transpired on each day of the trip.

derful memoirs and histories have been written from such diaries. Instead, we keep a provision inventory list in the galley to cross off what's been used up (See Chapter 8—Meal Planning).

On yacht deliveries, the daily log documents for an owner how the captain and crew spent their time, which translates to "his money." Besides noting port calls and positions along the route, the daily log should note what work or repairs were done to the boat, if any, how much money was spent, the reason for unusual expenditures, a detailed explanation of significant engineering happenings and an out-of-commission list.

Data from a daily log can be very useful in preparing a *recommendations list,* which we present to the owner when turning over the keys at the end of the delivery.

We always construct a grid-type *calendar* (Figure 10–3) at the front of the daily log, so we can tell at a glance where we were on a given day, what was the single most important event of any day, and on longer trips, how many days or weeks we've been at sea. For the final bill to the owner, this calendar also notes which were laydays and which were regular days under way.

The *engineering log* (Figure 10-4) is in a notebook of its own and should be kept in or near the engine room. After designating the far left margin or column for the hourly time entries (on the half hour), rule and enter column headings on the left page for the various gauges (oil pressure, water temperature, gear oil pressure, fuel pressure, fuel level, vacuum pressure, hour meters, etc.). Put the readings in logical order according to how you move through the engine room while making your inspection. On twin-engine boats, it may be

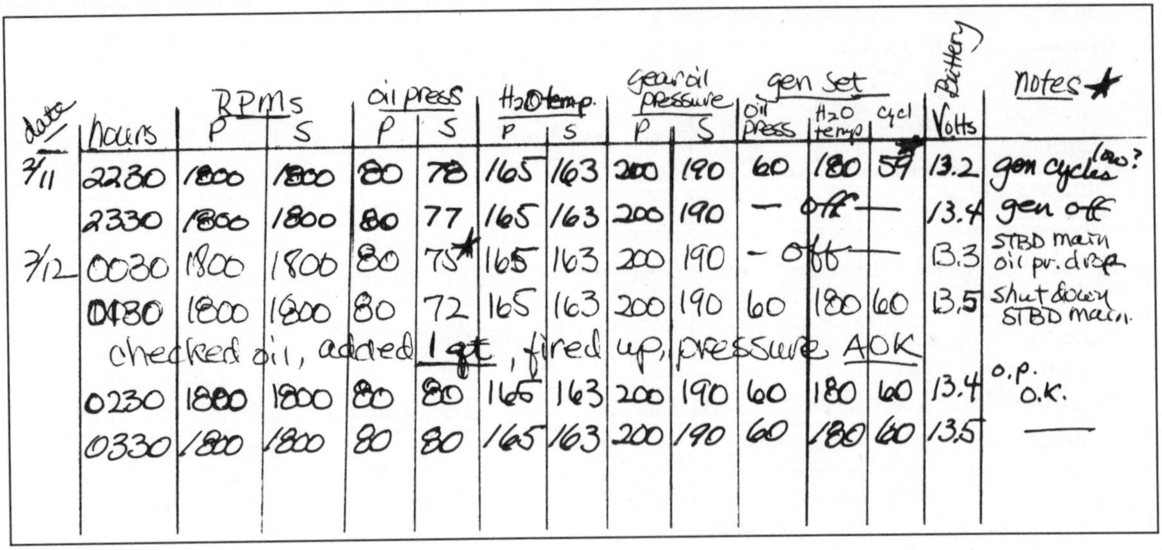

| date | hours | RPMs | | oil press | | H2O temp. | | Gear oil pressure | | gen set | | | Battery Volts | notes ★ |
		P	S	P	S	P	S	P	S	Oil press	H2O temp	cycl		
7/11	2230	1800	1800	80	78	165	163	200	190	60	180	59	13.2	gen cycles 120?
	2330	1800	1800	80	77	165	163	200	190	—	off —		13.4	gen off
7/12	0030	1800	1800	80	75★	165	163	200	190	— off —			13.3	STBD main oil pr. drop
	0130	1800	1800	80	72	165	163	200	190	60	180	60	13.5	shut down STBD main.
	checked oil, added 1 qt, fired up, pressure AOK													
	0230	1800	1800	80	80	165	163	200	190	60	180	60	13.4	o.p. O.K.
	0330	1800	1800	80	80	165	163	200	190	60	180	60	13.5	—

Figure 10-4. The engine log should be kept in or near the engine room and be updated hourly.

easier to record all the *port engine* data together, then move on to the *starboard engine,* or vice versa.

Keep the opposing page for significant comments about abnormal readings, about questionable findings from the checklist below, and for notes about when maintenance procedures were done such as oil and filter changes, cleaning of sea water strainers, replacement of belts, etc. These should be done in ink.

The engineer (or captain) should establish what abnormal readings or questionable findings would constitute a need to awaken him. Most engineers would rather forsake a few minutes of sleep than to have to repair serious problems underway.

Some crewmembers grumble that these hourly entries are unnecessary. Boring as they may be, they are absolutely necessary. If nothing else, they force everyone to know what normal readings are, so they will recognize abnormalities long before they become problems. If you spot a slow drop in oil or fuel pressure or increase in water temperature, you'll have time to find out the cause and do

something about it before you totally lose the engine.

On a commercial vessel we delivered, we found some humorous entries in the engineering log from a previous engineer. It contained very little engineering data but rather was a day-by-day description of how he wasn't getting along with the cook!

The engine logbook should also contain a simple checklist of items you want the crew to inspect during the hourly *engine room check.* Important items in the engine room log (Figure 10-4) are:

1 SMOKE OR FIRE—Give instructions about what crew should do if they see or smell smoke or fire.

2 BILGES—Show crew where to check bilge levels and how to pump them whenever necessary. Note this in the log if pumping is done manually, so you can monitor the frequency. If it is increasing, you'd better find out where the water is coming from, why, and do something about it. Automatic bilge pumps should have red lights on the bridge that indicate that they are pump-

ing and from which compartment. If a light is winking too often, investigate the cause. If it comes on and stays on, you have an emergency situation to be resolved immediately.

3 BELTS—Check for wobble while in motion and signs of wear when stopped.

4 ENGINE OIL, WATER, OR FUEL LEAKS—Look for evidence of these and monitor and note them. Some engines like GMCs are notorious for spitting oil from every orifice. Monitor the leaks, wipe them up, and if they get excessive find out why. Look at hoses for signs of chafe, leaks or clamp failure. Check engine drip pans for evidence of oil, water, and fuel.

5 FLUID LEVELS—Check all reservoirs for correct fluid levels, especially the tank you are burning fuel from so you don't run it dry. Likewise look at fresh water tanks and hydraulic reservoir levels and check them for leaks.

6 RAW-WATER PUMP—If it's safely accessible, touch the facing to feel if it's cool. If it isn't, the impeller may be deteriorating or water flow may be restricted. This can uncover an overheating problem before it occurs.

7 PACKING GLAND—If it's safely accessible, touch to see if it's hot. If it is, notify someone that the nut needs to be loosened or it will score the shaft. If excessive water is coming in, the nut needs to be tightened. There should be a slight dribble of saltwater coming in to cool the shaft.

8 SEA STRAINER—See that a proper flow of water is coming in and doesn't contain excessive foreign matter.

9 FUEL FILTERS—Shine a flashlight into the bowl of the primary fuel filter to see if there is water or other contamination.

10 VIBRATION AND NOISE—Listen for excessive vibrations or unusual noises, not just during engine room checks, but at all times everywhere onboard.

Hourly engine room checks are very important. Don't go any longer than that. We have many times caught problems such as a breaking hydraulic hose and a sudden drop in gear oil pressure in the very act of happening and been able to avoid serious problems and prevent damage.

On the other hand, a too thorough engine room inspection may take the watch stander away from the bridge for too long. Five minutes should do the job. On larger boats that require a lengthier, more complex engine room inspection, we carry additional crewmembers and stand two crewmembers to a watch. This way one can remain on the helm while the other is checking the engine room. If the boat has no autopilot, two to a watch is almost essential.

We stress that traffic and navigation considerations take precedence over the engine room. Never leave the bridge with a freighter bearing down on you, just because it is the appointed time for the engine room check. Keep an eye on traffic flow and on your watch, and leave for the engine room only when traffic is free and clear or when you have determined that it's not near enough to be a threat. If you have only a small amount of time to be away from the helm, at least stick your head in the engine room for a cursory check, looking for fire or smoke or spewing liquids.

Several times during each 24-hour day, the appointed engineer should make a more thorough inspection and investigate any comments written in the engine room log by watch standers since the engineer's last thorough inspection.

WATCH SYSTEMS

The captain, who is constantly on call, must learn to sleep when possible or he will become exhausted and begin to make bad judgments. Even catnapping is better than not sleeping at all. The captain must learn to pace himself.

We have been to sea with some captains whose sense of responsibility kept them awake on the bridge constantly, even when there was no reason for them to be there. They would get very run down during a long trip, and that was overdoing it. The other side of this coin is the captain who sleeps until disaster is unavoidable.

The whole crew must have proper sleep and rest, and the only way to assure this is to pick qualified crewmembers, train them to stand a proper watch, and then establish a workable watch schedule. Regular watches are crucial to maintaining a vigilant lookout. The choice of watch schedule depends on the vessel's rig, the size of the crew, and the nature of the voyage (coastal or offshore).

We believe in standing regular watches in which every crewmember is well aware of when his watch begins and ends, who he relieves and who relieves him. We know of other crews who operate on an irregular schedule: "I'll take it for awhile until I get tired, and then you take it." This can lead to sloppy watch standing and results in irregular sleep patterns. What happens when everybody is too tired to stand watch?

The human body and mind are used to regular sleep during a 24-hour period. Most of us sleep at night, but this pattern can be broken if done on a regular daily schedule, as people who work night shifts have discovered. They work while others sleep, and sleep during the day while others work. After the first few work periods, they settle into their new sleep pattern and get as much rest as they did at night.

The same is true of running a boat 24 hours a day, day after day.

Most of us suffer from jet lag when our regular sleep habits get interrupted as we change several time zones very quickly; our biological clock gets out of sync with the position of the sun. We recently took a 12-hour nonstop flight from Madrid to Los Angeles and it took us nearly a week to get back into our normal sleep pattern.

Though not as drastic, this is what happens the first few days you go to sea. That is, unless you happen to be the lucky one who gets a watch that allows you the same hours of sleep you are used to on land. Usually after three days, everyone adjusts, even the unfortunate ones with the mid-watch—0000–0400.

ROTATING WATCH SYSTEMS

Don't introduce a *dog watch,* which breaks the watch cycle so that crewmembers stand watch at a different time each day. Dog watches will lead to a permanent jet lag on board. Witness what happens with the following rotating watch system when a crew of three people stand three hours on watch and six hours off:

Day 1

Watch		
	A	0000 – 0300
	B	0300 – 0600
	C	0600 – 0900
	A	0900 – 1200
	B	1200 – 1500
	C	1500 – 1800
	A	1800 – 2100
	B	2100 – 2400

Day 2

Watch		
	C	0000 – 0300
	A	0300 – 0600
	B	0600 – 0900
	C	0900 – 1200

A	1200 – 1500
B	1500 – 1800
C	1800 – 2100
A	2100 – 2400

Day 3

Watch	B	0000 – 0300
	C	0300 – 0600
	A	0600 – 0900
	B	0900 – 1200
	C	1200 – 1500
	A	1500 – 1800
	B	1800 – 2100
	C	2100 – 2400

Look at the plight of the crewmember on Watch "A", the person standing the 0000–0300 the first day out. Every subsequent night he has to adjust to sleeping at a different time. This type of rotating watch schedule has a built-in fatigue factor, because it never allows anyone to fall into a sleep pattern.

Such a rotating watch schedule is very egalitarian, however, since no one can complain about always having "the crummy watch." It's also easier to stay alert for a three-hour watch than for four hours.

The rotating watch system has limited use. It's best suited for two-day coastal hops. During periods of rough weather, or when a four-hour watch is simply too draining, we will temporarily shift to this rotating watch schedule. However, if rough weather continues for more than two or three days, we shift to a watch that permits regular sleep patterns. Going without regular sleep is more draining than standing the longer watch.

The minimum number of crew required for an offshore passage or lengthy delivery is two, because singlehanded voyages of more than 12 hours are dangerous. The Coast Guard feels so strongly about this that it requires vessels carrying passengers for hire to

have two licensed operators on trips longer than 12 hours. Voyaging with only two watch standers can be very fatiguing, unless both have the same high level of skill and experience and the boat has some form of self-steering. Couples who cruise together should keep this in mind.

Before we teamed up, John once made a 1,100 mile, short-handed delivery from Manzanillo non-stop to San Diego aboard a 58 foot motor yacht. The only other person on board was another experienced, licensed captain. It was no strain on either of them and they both got plenty of rest because they trusted one another's ability to handle traffic or engineering situations during their watch. That trust made it unnecessary to wake the other person who was offwatch unless it was an emergency. They stood three hours on and three off, which gave them the same hours of sleep each day. However, things would have been more difficult had the autopilot acted up, or had they been delivering a sailboat, which requires calling the offwatch to help with a sail change.

Three crewmembers. The most common number of crew for a yacht delivery is three. For any type of passagemaking, three is safer than two. Having a crew of three allows the standard four-on, eight-off watch system that is used on both yachts and merchant ships. Here's how it works:

Watch	A	0000 – 0400
	B	0400 – 0800
	C	0800 – 1200
	A	1200 – 1600
	B	1600 – 2000
	C	2000 – 2400

This is the watch we use most often. It repeats itself each day, with each watch-stander having the same rest periods each day so he can fall into a regular routine of sleep. If all goes well—and it seldom does—this allows both off-watch crewmembers nearly eight uninterrupted hours in the rack.

John likes to stand the "B"-watch, 0400–0800 and 1600–2000, which is traditionally the *navigator's watch*. It allows him to be on watch during nautical twilight both morning and night, which is the best time to take star sights. Stars usually are visible and there's still enough light to illuminate the horizon for a good sextant measurement. It also allows the captain to be on watch at sundown to ensure that running lights are on and that the bridge is sufficiently darkened for good exterior visibility.

Watch "C" is the most popular, because the crewmember gets off at midnight and has until 0800 in the rack. This closely conforms to most people's schedule on land and it requires little or no adjustment when going to sea. We normally reserve this watch for the cook. Even when everything on board is going smoothly, the experienced, sea-going cook on "C" watch has the most amount of work to do, squeezing all meal preparation between the two regular watch periods. The "good watch" is compensation for that extra work.

It's important to balance work loads among a crew. With a standard delivery crew of three (captain, cook, and engineer), we find that this watch system works well and everyone has roughly the same amount of work over the long haul.

Watch "A" is the notorious "midwatch." Staying awake from 0000–0400 and sleeping during daylight hours are the toughest adjustments to make when going to sea, even though crewmember "A" gets the same number of hours of sleep as both other watches. "A's" sleep/work period is diametrically opposed to most people's land schedule. Some people adjust well to the midwatch, finding it easy to lie down after their watch and just drift off to the land of nod. These make the best crewmembers. Others who find it difficult to sleep at odd hours unfortunately also find it difficult to stay awake and alert during their watch. This is not a good crew trait.

The captain should be considerate of the needs of those on this watch. Most people adapt easily after three days of a long offshore passage. Normally our midwatch crewmembers will sleep from about 0415–1000 and again after the evening meal from about 0900–1130.

However, on long deliveries composed of many short coastal hops, the crew on midwatch can have great difficulty adapting. Just as he's beginning to adapt, port is reached and then he has to readjust to the normal daytime routine of getting the boat prepared to leave on the next leg. If possible, while in port be sure to allow him to sleep in late, at least on the first day. This doesn't normally take much arm-twisting.

If we have a midwatch stander who has great difficulty adjusting, we'll rotate the midwatch between ports. In other words, "B" will swap watches with "A" until the next port, perhaps three or four days away, and then they can switch back.

The other option for short coastal hops is the egalitarian three-on, six-off schedule.

Four crewmembers. As the size of the crew increases, the possible watch combinations increase. A common watch with four is this:

Watch	A	0000 – 0400
	B	0400 – 0800
	C	0800 – 1200
	A	1200 – 1600
	B	1600 – 2000
	C	2000 – 2400
	D = Cook, who does not stand watch.	

This works out to be quite fair, because as the size of the crew increases, the cook's job becomes that much more time-consuming and difficult. The fourth crewmember then slides into the "B" or "C" watch. The "D" person may find he or she has an inordinate amount of free time. Because our cook is also a licensed captain, we keep her constantly "on call" and she fills in as a back-up watch stander. She is particularly useful for keeping an eye on less experienced crew who are standing watch, and in heavy traffic, to allow the captain to sleep.

A case in point: when making an Atlantic crossing one summer from Mystic, Connecticut to Mallorca, Spain, we had freak bad weather most of the way. Hurricane Charlie, which according to the pilot chart had 0 percent possibility of spawning, dealt us very rough weather for six days. It became too rough for the crew of four to stand the watch mentioned above, so we quickly added the cook to the watchbill as follows:

Watch	A	0000 – 0300
	B	0300 – 0600
	C	0600 – 0900
	D	0900 – 1200
	A	1200 – 1500
	B	1500 – 1800
	C	1800 – 2100
	D (Cook)	2100 – 0000

This is a well-balanced watch system that gave the crew long, regular sleep patterns with shorter hours at the helm, which was very draining while hand steering in Force 9 sea conditions. Due to the extreme heel, rough motion, leaking portlights and a constantly wet cabin sole, it was impossible to remain standing in the galley, let alone to attempt to cook in it, and in such motion, no one had a *bon apetit* anyway. One-handed guzzling of instant soup and oatmeal were all anyone could manage at the wheel.

After maneuvering out from under Hurricane Charlie's influence and reaching the Azores, we returned to the three-on, nine-off routine, which is not a bad watch to use on a regular basis anyway.

On coastal passages in heavy traffic lanes, the captain might go for several days without proper rest, if he must be called onto the bridge several times during his night off-watch hours. In such cases John will ask Pat to fill in for him to help catch up on a few winks. This is one advantage to having a cook who can handle traffic situations and navigation as well as the captain can. Likewise, if another crewmember, such as the engineer, is giving up or losing sleep from some difficult engineering problem, Pat often will stand part of his watch.

Five crewmembers. Here's a workable watch system for a crew of five:

Watch	A and B	0000 – 0600
	C and D	0600 – 1200
	A and B	1200 – 1800
	C and D	1800 – 2400
	E = Cook, who does not stand watch	

With five in the crew you can use two on a watch team, freeing the cook from watches. As the size of crew increases, the cook must spend more time preparing meals, cleaning up, and other shipkeeping duties. If the cook is an experienced watch stander, he or she can remain on standby, to be called to the bridge for navigation or traffic emergencies instead of calling the captain, and can fill in for sick or overworked crewmembers.

Larger crews. As boat size increases, or as the complexity of the boat or rig increases, so too should the number of crewmembers increase. Two crewmembers may be required on each watch as follows:

Watch	A and B	0000 – 0600
	C and D	0600 – 1200
	A and B	1200 – 1800
	C and D	1800 – 2400

We used this system when we sailed nonstop, 3,650 miles from San Diego to Bora Bora, French Polynesia, on a 44-foot sailboat with no autopilot. We all got plenty of rest. Six hours seems like a lot of hours for one watch, but one person was steering while the other was on immediate standby. One person would hand-steer for an hour and a half, while the standby person either rested or slept, remaining in the cockpit, dressed and immediately available for a sail change or to help the helmsman in any way. Most nights the standby person could get quite a bit of rest. But when the trades were blowing strongly with frequent rain squalls, the standby watch was harnessed up and standing by, mostly at the base of the mast in order to reef several times a night.

This watch system works well on larger vessels, allowing "B," the standby, to remain on the bridge while "A," the primary watch stander, does the engine room check. Halfway through their six-hour watch, they can trade jobs. The only time both watch standers need to be awake is during engine room checks and sail changes. Cockpit cushions on a sailboat or a pilot berth on the bridge of a powerboat make this very easy.

Larger engine rooms and more complicated mechanical/electrical systems mean that engine room checks should be more extensive, and on larger vessels it simply takes longer to get from the pilot house to the engine room and back. Big-boat engine checks

should include a "walk-through" of the entire vessel, checking for anything amiss. A fire or leak in some remote area could go unnoticed by crew on the bridge until smoke, lights and alarm sirens tell them there's a big problem.

Assigning watch partners also is safer, because "B" is aware that "A" is in the engine room. If "A" is gone too long, "B" can investigate or call for help. Maybe he got his arm caught in some machinery or is in some other dire predicament.

The possible combinations of watches grow with increasing crew. We had a crew of 12 on a very traditional 112-foot Baltic ketch. With large crews, the captain can eliminate himself from the watch bill and put himself on perpetual standby. On the Baltic ketch, the captain and mate were on rotating standby, acting as watch captains. But the basic combinations are the same as outlined, the only difference being the addition of more crewmembers to the watch.

On long ocean passages, particularly going east to west, we like to adjust the watches by changing local time as we cross into different time zones. You can set up watches based on GMT and never have to do this, but that throws people's schedules off the natural periods of light and dark.

When sailing through time zones, the navigator traditionally stands the 0400–0800 and 1600–2000 (local time) watch, so he can use nautical twilight for celestial observations. This is fine when first starting out on a voyage, but after a few days of westing or easting, his schedule is thrown off so much that nautical twilight falls outside of his watch schedule. The human body and mind are accustomed to a "sun time" schedule, which is the same as local time. Without it, sleeping and eating patterns are disrupted. How would you like breakfast at 2300?

While traveling west, we set all clocks back

as we enter each new time zone. We generally do this at some change of the watch during the daylight hours, because it's easier then to absorb the extra hour.

Suppose the new watch comes on at 1200 hours. We then set the clocks back to 1100 hours. It adds an extra hour to this midday watch, which is normally relieved at 1600. This one day only, it becomes a five-hour watch (1100–1600) instead of the normal four hours (1200–1600). Most off-duty crew are roaming around at this hour, and it's probably the most social of all watches. You can spread out this extra time by having the 1600 watch relieve the previous watch at 1530, thus sharing the extra hour.

Going west to east is seldom a problem. At 0000 you set the ship's clocks ahead to 0100. The oncoming watch's time period has just been reduced by an hour, and nobody will grumble about that. As you enter other time zones, try to move the clock ahead at 1900 to 2000, or at 1500 to 1600, so that other watch-standers get to take advantage of the time gain, and so on.

The most important points of good watch-keeping are:

1 The crew should be able to stand an alert, visual watch 24 hours a day.

2 They should get enough rest and sleep during the same regular sleeping hours in a 24-hour period to avoid perpetual "jet lag."

3 Establish and post the hours and crew names so there are no misunderstandings about who's supposed to be on watch when, and so that everyone is clear about when others need quiet for their sleep periods.

4 Be flexible enough to adjust for emergency weather conditions, mechanical breakdowns, and serious accidents or illness.

Night Watch

Standing watch during the night can be boring, but it is one of the most critical responsibilities delegated to a crewmember. While everyone else aboard is sleeping, that person standing night watch is the only human safeguard against collision, shipwreck, fire, and the whole host of disasters that befall boats at sea. Dull? Sure, sometimes it gets very boring. Ideally, it would always be boring, free from adrenaline-pulsing calamities. Don't worry, excitement comes when you least expect it. Meanwhile, never should the night watch be taken lightly.

Before nautical twilight, the captain should do two things: *darken ship* and establish the *night orders.*

The term "darken ship" ironically means that you turn some lights on and turn off others. You turn on the boat's exterior running lights (the red and green side lights and white stern light), plus any other legally required lights, such as steaming lights (powerboats and sailboats making way with the engine engaged).

Officially, all required exterior lighting must be turned on not only at sunset, but also whenever atmospheric conditions (fog, rain, snow, smoke, smog) restrict visibility; that is, whenever other boats might have a hard time seeing you, regardless of the time of day.

If for any reason these exterior lights don't function, it is the captain who is held accountable. The Coast Guard will be unsympathetic toward any claim that the lights always worked. Wise skippers climb the rigging, if need be, each time the lights are switched on to see with their own eyes that they're working.

Take along plenty of spare bulbs, lenses, gaskets, and fuses. It's surprising how many exterior running-light assemblies short out the first time they get good and soaked.

To darken ship also means to turn off all other lighting that interferes with visibility, yours or that of another vessel. Brilliant quartz lights on a sportsfisher may help another boat notice you at the last minute, but generally, such extraneous lighting just makes it hard for other boats to distinguish your red and green, bow and stern lights, which tell them in which direction you are moving.

More importantly, to darken ship means to darken the bridge. Night vision—the ability to see into the darkness—is imperative to the person standing night watch. The longer your eyes adjust to the dark, the better your night vision becomes and the less strain you feel. White light destroys your night vision, so turn off all normal lights within the helm area and keep them off until daybreak.

Beyond this, you must keep ambient light from infiltrating the helm area. On a power boat, close interior doors onto the bridge; you can't always demand that the rest of the crew not use any lights below deck. Even when most lights below are off, one accidental flash from a sleepy crewmember foraging in the galley or gathering his gear to come on watch will ruin your accumulated night vision for a few moments. Better to just keep the door closed. Pin up blankets if you must.

Instrument lights are often too bright at night. Some don't have dimmer switches or opaque plastic caps. This extra light reflects off pilothouse windows and makes it impossible to see through them. This means you can't see your own bow, let alone any traffic.

You can't turn off or ignore crucial instrumentation. Find something that allows you to peek easily. Incredible as it sounds, we often have to jury-rig elaborate blindness preventers—"peek flaps" if you will—for high-tech, megabuck instrumentation, out of cardboard scraps and duct tape. Color video depthsounders that don't dim are the worst offenders.

The bow (steaming) light often will shine down on the foredeck and the reflection will diminish your night vision. You should check this out before departure, since you may not notice it in port where there are other surrounding lights. At sea you may have to move the light, or put a shade underneath it so it shines only forward and not down onto the deck. This is the way it should have been designed in the first place.

The darkened bridge or nav station also requires a *chart light,* a red-colored light that doesn't destroy your night vision, preferably fixed over the chart table, because you must continue plotting throughout the night. The best chart light is a goose-neck lamp with a narrow shade that creates a defined beam. This allows you to aim the beam just where it's needed and it doesn't diffuse light off to the sides. A chart light is important enough to install solely for a delivery.

Beware of trinket lights that don't do the job. We see a lot of old airplane navigation lamps with the lever that slides a red lens over the normal clear lens. Nifty as they seem, many of them are too small to illuminate even a folded-up quarter of a chart, while you need two adjacent edges of any chart lying flat and well-lit enough to measure degrees of latitude and longitude.

We've struggled through by painting red fingernail polish on a clear lens of an overhead light (never on the bulb itself, since nail polish is highly flammable), by painting the lens of a flashlight and cramming it in the navigator's mouth (you need two hands to plot), and by wrapping the assistant navigator's fingers loosely over the flashlight beam while the navigator directs, "Lower, lower, lower."

You can jury-rig small things, but nothing is a good substitute for a proper chart light.

We assign individual flashlights to every crewmember, and even write their names on them with an indelible marker. Each person is then responsible for keeping it working with fresh batteries and bulbs, and for bringing it on watch with him. Several spare flashlights are kept in handy locations. Even during daylight, the hourly engine room inspections require a flashlight for peeking into dark corners of an otherwise brightly lit engine room.

The engine room is the other source of temporary blindness at night. You can't darken it as you do the bridge, yet once an hour you must peek in, inspect, walk around, fill out the engine logbook, and in the process destroy your night vision. This is an unavoidable problem. All you can do is make sure before you leave the darkened bridge that nothing is looming off your bow, then get the engine room check completed swiftly, and return to the darkened bridge as soon as possible so your eyes are readjusted before trouble has time to pop up.

Now that the captain has darkened ship, he establishes the night orders.

Standing night orders. Night orders are specific instructions (often written) to each crewmember who will stand watch during that night. They may refer to traffic on the *visual and radar watch,* to course changes on the *navigation watch,* and to maintenance tasks on the *engineering watch.* They include anything the watch standers should do while the captain is away from the bridge during the night, including specific circumstances when the captain should be called to the bridge.

Night orders depend on the experience and competence of the watch stander.

We often work with a whole crew of licensed captains. This is ideal, because we know that these people have at least undergone training in the Rules of the Road, and we can give them more latitude in handling traffic and navigation situations. However in the beginning of a trip, we closely observe how they handle traffic during the day and night. If

we're comfortable with the way they go about it, John's night orders will merely establish a *closest point of approach* (CPA) of perhaps two miles or half a mile, depending on many other circumstances. This means they are qualified to read and plot the motion of all other vessels and to maneuver our vessel to maintain a distance of two miles, or half a mile, between us and another vessel. Or the CPA might refer to our closest point of approach to land or off-lying reefs.

Qualified watch standers are also issued night orders to make critical course changes at predetermined waypoints, and to alter course whenever they see we are being set off our course.

We tell all crewmembers not to hesitate to call either of us if they have any doubts or questions.

We don't expect or permit unqualified crewmembers to make waypoint course changes or to maneuver at their discretion in regular traffic. We instruct all watch-standers how to turn off the autopilot, how to turn the boat manually, and how to stop the boat, in case of emergencies, such as a submarine surfacing 100 yards off our bow.

Night orders for unlicensed or less-experienced crew are much simpler when the boat is equipped with radar and autopilot. "Wake me if any blip appears on the radar screen anywhere within five miles of us." The captain should familiarize crew with how to switch ranges, what to look for, and then should fine-tune the radar gain and any other settings. This way, crewmembers need only touch the dials that change ranges. The captain should set his desired range on the screen with a variable range marker (VRM) if there is one. Many radar units have an alarm, but overreliance on the alarm sometimes encourages watch-standers to neglect the screen.

Without radar, it takes training and much

"eyeball experience" to determine your distance off. Especially at night, depth perception is severely limited. Although it leads to some sleepless nights for us, if there is no radar aboard we ask inexperienced crew to wake one of us if they see any lights. We stress that crew shouldn't hesitate to call just because they think we need our sleep, or if they think we'll think less of them for having to call one of us. Despite our constant admonitions to the crew about not hesitating to wake us, John once had a real heart stopper:

Once in the Gulf of Panama I was off watch and sleeping when I heard the engines change RPM slightly. I flew out of bed and ran up three decks to the bridge. My sleepy eyes were greeted by a frightened-looking crewmember and the sight of two huge range lights and well-separated red and green lights bearing down on us amidships. We were about to be center-punched by a large freighter.

Fortunately we were on a sportfisher with huge engines and we had been traveling at a slow 10 knots to conserve fuel. I instantly jammed the throttles all the way forward. We went from 10 to 25 knots in a few heart-stopping seconds and got out of harm's way. Had we not been on such a fast boat, I doubt we could have avoided a collision by changing direction alone.

Training Night Watch Standers

The possibility of collision or grounding is greatly increased at night. Because of this you should train your night watch standers in at least the basics of lights and relative motion. Even though you may give them specific instructions to awaken you so you can take the appropriate action, some emergency might happen so quickly that they will have to take immediate action.

It's a good idea to train watch standers to understand ships' headings according to range lights, because this is so important in avoiding collisions or emergency maneuvering with large ships. Later in this chapter, we explain how to determine relative motion by radar and visual bearings. The Rules contain many other lights, day shapes, and sounds, so we urge aspiring skippers and anyone handling boats to learn and understand them thoroughly.

Range Lights

All vessels more than 50 meters long are required to have two range lights separated by a distance at least a quarter of the length of the vessel, the aftermost light being higher than the forward one. The separation and relationship of these lights to one another will tell you the vessel's heading. Since they are white and higher than the colored sidelights, they are visible for a much greater distance.

Figure 10-5 shows the legally required placement of range lights on a ship. The fore-

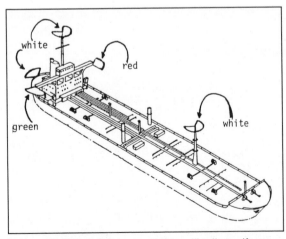

Figure 10-5. A ship's range lights will tell you if you are on a collision course.

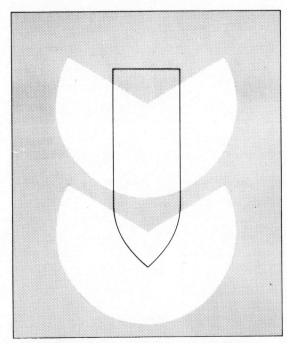

Figure 10-6. A ship's range lights and combined side lights have the same areas of visibility.

ward one is lower than the after one. We tell new crewmembers to imagine that this light pattern is defining a wedge. Whenever they see this wedge on a black sea, they can see that the ship is moving in the direction the wedge is pointing. A fat, short wedge is more likely to mean a close ship than a small ship.

Figure 10-6 shows their *arcs of visibility,* which are the same as the combined arcs of the red and green sidelights. This means any ship's range lights are visible only from forward of its bow to slightly aft its beam. If no range lights are visible, you will see only its stern light. Then the vessel is not an immediate threat unless it slows as it crosses your bow or if you are traveling at a greater speed than it is and plan to run over it.

Figure 10-7, A–E are the most commonly seen arrangements of range lights. A's forward (lower) range light is to the right of the after

(higher) range light, and the lights are well separated. This vessel is travelling from left to right in relation to your vessel, and you're looking directly at its starboard beam. Be careful of mistaking one close ship for two at a distance, or conversely, mistaking two distant ships for one close ship.

B's forward range light is far to the left of its after range light, so it's heading from right to left.

Vessel C shows the range lights directly in line, meaning the vessel is headed directly at you. If you also observe both its sidelights (as in Figure 10-8) then the vessel is quite close and you'd better do something about it quickly.

Vessel D's forward range light is to the right of its after range light, but they are not as well separated as in A. This vessel's course forms an oblique angle relative to you, and it is heading from left to right.

Vessel E's forward range light is to the left of its after light. It is on an oblique heading from right to left.

Figure 10-7 illustrates how you can determine a large vessel's heading long before you can see its colored sidelights. All of these vessels could be crossing your bow.

We haven't shown vessels from abaft their beams. Technically speaking, if the other vessel is overtaking you, you have the right of way and it *should* take action to avoid hitting you. Practically speaking, however, that ship steaming up from behind you very likely can't see your tiny stern light, low to the water as it is. Also, most yachts simply don't make a significant blip on civilian radar screens. Also, ships are routinely in a hurry. Because of all three unfortunate facts of life at sea, we allow for the "Right of Weight" rule: If he weighs more than we do, he's probably going to take the right of way. Don't argue with the big guys, and keep looking over your shoulder.

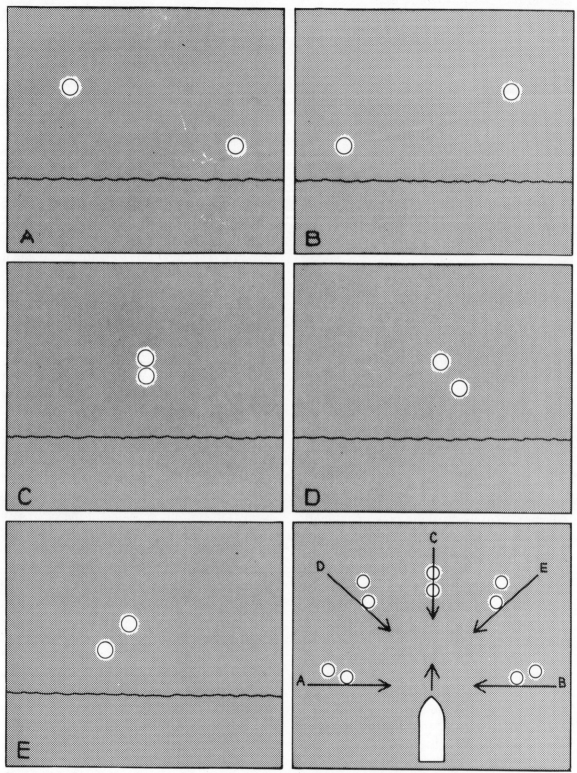

Figure 10-7. Can you read these range lights? (A) Ship is traveling from left to right. (B) Ship is traveling from right to left. (C) Ship is heading straight for you. (D) Ship is heading at an oblique angle from left to right. (E) Ship is heading at an oblique angle from right to left.

Figure 10-8. When range lights and side lights appear head on, collision is imminent unless evasive action is taken.

Figure 10-8 is the most threatening aspect of a ship you can see at night. If his range lights are directly in line and you see both running lights are well separated, you are close and directly in his path.

Figure 10-9 shows five nearby vessels on different headings. Depending on the combination of your speed and the speed of the other vessel, vessels A, E, and C are posing threats of collision. If B and D continue at course and speed, they are not threats.

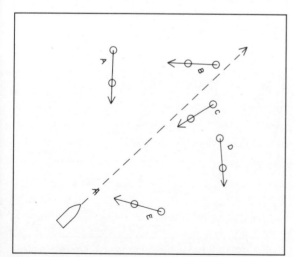

Figure 10-9. Of these five vessels on different headings, only A, C, and E pose threats of collision.

Radar

Radar's greatest advantage is in collision avoidance. Radar schools for mariners are springing up all over the country with short courses for yacht cruisers. We encourage pleasure boaters to find a good radar course near them, but for professional yacht deliverers, it's imperative.

Here's how you can use radar to determine the *relative motion* of another vessel, without going into the complex graphic solutions taught in radar school.

First, when you detect the blip of a ship on the scope, turn the movable bearing line (a straight line from the center of the screen to any point on the perimeter of the screen) so that it lies right across that blip. Now you know its bearing from your course.

If you can switch to a closer range without losing the blip off the edge of the screen, do so now. Once the movable bearing line is laid on your blip, it will follow you up or down the scale of ranges, and it will remain accurate until the blip moves off to one side or the other.

Second, note the blip's distance off and write down the exact time. You can find distance off two ways: If your model of radar has a variable range marker (VRM), slide the VRM in or out from the center of the screen until its line also lies atop the blip. This will form something like an "X" on the blip. Somewhere on the side of the screen you'll see the exact distance the VRM is denoting. Without a VRM, just interpolate between the stationary rings of that particular range. Note whether the rings signify one-mile, five-mile or eight-mile increments of distance off for that screen's range. Now you know its range and bearing.

Continue to monitor the blip's position as it changes on the scope. In Figure 10-10 the vessel is staying on the movable bearing line and getting closer. This means there is going to be a collision unless somebody does something

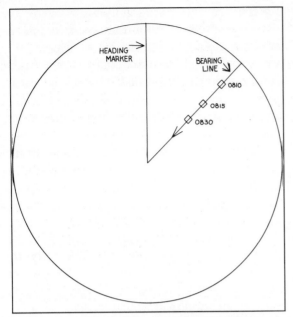

Figure 10-10. This radar screen shows another vessel on a constant bearing at a decreasing range. Collision is imminent unless evasive action is taken.

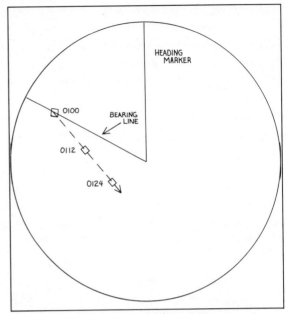

Figure 10-11. If the other vessel's speed and heading and your speed and heading remain the same, the other vessel will pass astern of you.

about it. Remember this rule: CONSTANT BEARING AND DECREASING RANGE MEAN COLLISION.

In Figure 10-11 the blip is moving off to the left of the movable bearing line, as it was laid on the target when it first appeared on the edge of the screen. If the other vessel's speed and heading AND your speed and heading remain as they are now, it will pass astern of you.

The vessel in Figure 10-12 is passing to the right of the movable bearing line and will pass ahead of your vessel, unless it slows or you speed up.

Some of the newer, more expensive model radars have a *plot mode,* which records the vessel's path across the screen by leaving a shadow or trace pattern. This is a history of its relative motion. Plot modes are marvelous devices, and when understood and used properly, they are an invaluable aid in preventing collisions and groundings. You can do the

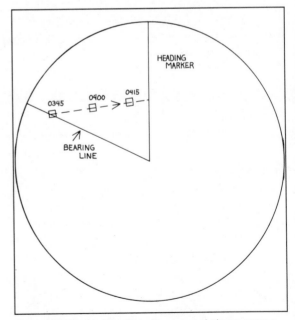

Figure 10-12. Unless the other vessel slows or you speed up, it will pass ahead of you.

same thing manually on a radar without plot mode by periodically marking the target's position directly on the radar screen with a grease pencil.

Visual Bearings

Without radar, you still can determine the risk of collision by using a hand-bearing compass. When you first sight the object, take a bearing on it and note the time, then take bearings on it at frequent intervals and note those bearings and times. If that bearing is not changing, or changing insignificantly, and if the object is getting nearer, then you are on collision course. Without radar, you can't immediately determine its exact range, but its lights will be getting brighter, details of the vessel will become sharper. The only exception to this is a ship travelling on the same course, at the same speed, and keeping the same distance off.

Note from the bearings and times in Figure 10-13 that the converging vessel will pass safely ahead. Figure 10-14 shows the sighted vessels will pass safely astern. In Figure 10-15, however, a constant bearing and decreasing range will result in collision.

Crew Training

Once you have gone over all this information with your crew, perhaps as you set night orders your first night out, the opportunity to further instruct them on "Rules of the Road" will arise soon enough.

If you gave them instructions to wake you when a vessel approaches, this provides an opportunity to quiz them on what they think they see: What is the other vessel's relative heading? Did they determine that from both radar plotting and observation? What might its speed be? If you don't collide, how close will you come? How much change of your own speed or direction would be needed to avoid colliding?

Then, as you take the appropriate action, tell the watch stander exactly what you are

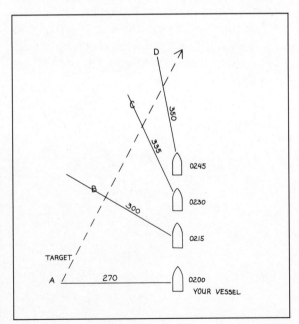

Figure 10-13. The converging vessel will pass safely ahead.

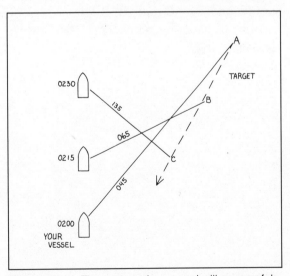

Figure 10-14. The converging vessel will pass safely astern.

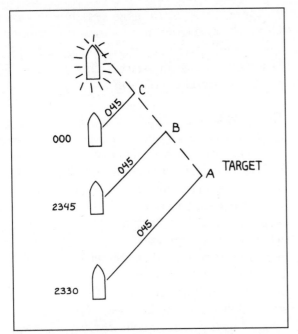

Figure 10-15. The converging vessel has a constant bearing and decreasing range. Collision is imminent unless evasive action is taken.

doing, how you are doing it and why. This is not a time for committee decisions, and crew should never argue about how or why navigation decisions are made. However, they should understand their instructions and be capable of handling their watch-standing responsibilities.

Crew training during night watches is mutually beneficial. The crew member gains hands-on experience that can only be found under live-fire situations, while the captain may rest better with more confidence in the crew.

Our relationship with crew during this type training has been overwhelmingly favorable. If it weren't, we'd have changed careers long ago and taken up growing papayas on the side of a Costa Rican mountain. However, no matter how hard we've tried to pick good crew and to train them, we have occasionally found the proverbial "rotten apple."

Such crew are just plain resentful of being told what to do, sometimes thinking they know more than the captain, and occasionally they'll deliberately fail to follow orders, which in turn can endanger lives, property, and careers.

The best policy is to hand-pick your crew carefully; don't let someone else choose them for you. Get to know them and have a good idea of their experience and qualifications before getting under way. At sea, you'll get to know one another's quirks and habits awfully well; so the time to be selective is before you leave the dock.

CHAPTER 11
COASTAL NAVIGATION

A yacht delivery captain wears many hats: ship handler, mechanic, meteorologist, translator, accountant. Above all, he must be a navigator *par excellence*. Faulty navigation is the single greatest cause of shipwreck. Therefore, captains should never totally relinquish navigation duties to crewmembers, but should ensure that they know the basics.

This chapter is intended to help crewmembers stand a better navigation watch. In it, we share techniques that we use, point out some

Sailboats such as this Peterson 44 generally have better organized, sit-down navigation areas than do powerboats.

Effective navigation demands that one area near the helm be devoted exclusively to navigation. Lack of a workable navigation station becomes a problem on some deliveries. Powerboats frequently lack a surface for chartwork and log keeping on the bridge. This Defever 54 is an exception, allowing crewmember Mike Burke to make his hourly log entry without diverting his attention from the lookout.

common errors that beginners make, and offer advice.

A revolution in the miniaturization of electronics has brought sophisticated radar, Satnav, and Loran into an affordable price range for many cruising skippers. That's good news and bad. The unfortunate effect is that many skippers are learning to navigate solely with electronics, then are helpless when their machines fail.

Our insistence on knowing non-electronic navigation is not a matter of tradition; it's a matter of safety. You must know what to do when the machine quits because eventually it will. Three times, on three different vessels, in three different parts of the world, we have lost all navigation electronics in midocean.

On one such trip, we were beating into the winter trades from Panama to the U.S. Virgin

Islands in a 65-foot motor sailer and we'd intended to do this last leg non-stop. Half way across the Caribbean the Satnav, the only electronic navigation device on board, went down, and we also lost use of one of the two engines, the leeward one. On this particular vessel, we would have risked damaging the remaining (windward) engine had we run it alone on that tack. It was a long way to anywhere if we changed tacks, so we needed to put into port for repairs.

Haiti's southwest coast was nearest, some 300 miles abeam, and we could make it by the next day. But trouble comes in threes, or so it seems. BBC radio revealed that all Haiti was writhing in bloody riots, having deposed "Baby Doc" Duvalier that very morning amid jeers of "capitalist pig, imperialist puppet." We suspected that our rather ostentatious yacht might be unwelcome there, so we had to devise a Plan B.

We could bear away for Jamaica, but this would mean we'd have to thread our way around and through the notoriously low-lying Morant Cays and the Pedro Cays. We already had broken out the sextant, but now accurate navigation would be critical. Fortunately, some good rounds of star sights carried us safely into Port Royal, Jamaica, where we made repairs.

Though we are not "old salts," we both had the fortune to begin navigating before the electronics revolution, and we both learned the solid fundamentals of traditional navigation methods. Although we use Satnav, Loran, and radar as much as anyone, we continue to practice and use our non-electronic navigation skills.

We strongly urge that you learn these traditional methods before you put to sea. Take navigation courses and practice in familiar home waters where you can double-check your accuracy by using your electronics. Develop the habit of "over navigating," spending more time at it than you know is necessary. Keep your position up to date, so that if an emergency arises, you'll know exactly where you are and what your options are. You can't know what to do if you don't know where you are.

Coastal navigation, also known as piloting, is well defined by Bowditch in the *American Practical Navigator,* the bible of navigation:

> It is navigation involving frequent or continuous determination of position or a line of position relative to geographic points, to a high order of accuracy. It is practiced in the vicinity of land, dangers, aids to navigation, etc, and requires good judgment and almost constant attention and alertness on the part of the navigator.

Beginning navigators tend to be in a hurry to study celestial navigation, but that's putting the cart before the horse. The effects of faulty navigation are minimal while you're far offshore, away from rocks and shoal water. If you've made a mistake, you can sort it out and correct it sometime the next day, perhaps, with very little consequence. In coastal waters, however, the effect of a sloppy fix may wreck your vessel within minutes.

Airplane piloting students spend 95 percent of their time practicing take-offs and landings, the most dangerous part of flying. Unless they can learn that part very, very well, there's no point learning to fly straight and level. Sure, Dutchman's rolls and controlled spins are loads of fun, but sooner or later that plane must land, and hopefully in such a manner that it can take off again.

Nautical piloting is similar; unless you first get the hang of coastal piloting, you won't have the skills for celestial navigation. No matter how intelligent, clever, or technically inclined you are, you can't get out to the open ocean without first going through the dangerous shallows.

Dead Reckoning

The term *dead reckoning* (DR) is a corruption of *deduced reckoning*. It is the basis of all navigation, both coastal and celestial. When you dead reckon, you determine your best-guess position by advancing a known position, based on the course you think you've made and the distance you think you've travelled since that last known position. Because of the effects of current, leeway, imperfect steering, compass error, and inaccurate speed measurements, a DR position is only an educated guess of position. We hesitate to use the term "position" in the same paragraph as "DR." However, until the navigator can update his position by calculating a fix from known landmarks, stars or satellites, the DR position is his best guess.

Figure 11-1 shows a DR plot based on course and speed with a course change. Notice the standard labeling. Above the course line is a "C" for course, and below the course line is the "S" for speed. A position is drawn as a small, uniform circle around the pencil mark signifying the exact position of the vessel at exactly 0900; this is the "0900 fix." The 1000 position is labeled as a dead reckoning position (DR). The 1100 position is differentiated as a square and labeled as an *estimated position* (EP).

Because he was near a navigational hazard, the navigator estimates the effects of current on his position, based either on local data from a *Tidal Stream Atlas* or on the discovered effect of current on his last few fixes.

Beginning navigators often err by not updating their DR plot often enough. This should be done at least hourly in coastal waters, and as often as every few minutes

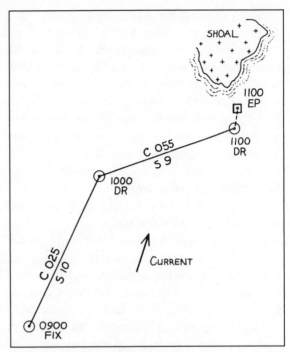

Figure 11-1. Dead reckoning plot.

when close to hazards. Whenever you change course or speed, update the DR.

Tools Used in Dead Reckoning

Charts. Nautical charts are used to plot position relative to shore. The latitude scale is printed on the right- and left-hand borders. The longitude scale is on the top and bottom. The unit of measurement of distance is the nautical mile (6,076 feet or 1.15 statute miles.) Conveniently, one nautical mile equals 1 minute of latitude, measured vertically on the *latitude* scale. The most common mistake a beginning navigator makes is to measure distance on the *longitude* scale. (Only exactly on the Equator is a minute of longitude equal to one nautical mile.) *Always* measure nautical miles on the latitude scale, the vertical one.

Compass. The magnetic compass shows the vessel's magnetic course. Unknown inaccuracies in the compass or improper plotting of the course will harm a DR position.

A magnetic compass points to the earth's magnetic pole, which is not the same as true north. The difference between magnetic north and true north is called *variation* and you will find it noted on your nautical chart. Figure 11–2 shows a typical *compass rose* found on coastal charts. Use the *outer* ring for plotting *true* courses and bearings, and the *inner* ring for determining *magnetic* courses. Notice that the variation for that particular area is printed in the very center of the rose.

Novice navigators often mistakenly plot a magnetic course as a true course or vice versa. This happens either from using the wrong ring of the compass rose, or from a mistake while correcting for variation and deviation.

Magnetic compasses rarely point directly at magnetic north, because of the influences of ferrous metals or electric currents on board the vessel itself. This difference between mag-

netic north and what the compass reads is called *deviation*. A common mistake underway is to lay the binoculars or a flashlight next to the compass. The metal in the binoculars or the current from the batteries tugs on the magnets in the compass and causes deviant course readings.

Unfortunately, many boat owners neglect to swing their main steering compass. *"Swinging the compass"* is a process used by professional compass adjusters to determine the exact degrees of deviation inherent in each point of the compass and to reduce this error as much as possible. Professional navigators should know how to determine deviation for themselves. (See Chapter 12.)

Because faulty application of deviation and variation is so common, one little memory aid has been used for generations of navigators: Timid Virgins Make Dull Company—Add Whisky. Because of her Norwegian ancestors, Pat rewrote history with her substitute: True Viking Maidens Demand Compensation— After Wedding. Memorize whichever one you like best, the point being the initials, **TVMDC-AW.** They stand for (**T**)rue, (**V**)ariation, (**M**)agnetic, (**D**)eviation, (**C**)ompass, (**A**)dd, (**W**)est. Write them in a column like this:

T
V
M
D
C
A
W

Here's how to convert a *True* course to a *Magnetic* course. The True course we wish to steer is 300°, the variation we get from the chart is 14° West, and our compass deviation card (supplied by the compass adjuster) says 5° East next to the heading of 314°.

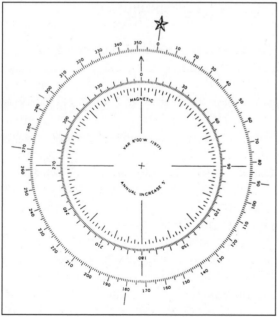

Figure 11-2. The compass rose used on charts gives true course (outer ring), magnetic course (inner ring) and variation.

T	300°
V	+14°W
M	314°
D	−05°E
C	309°

Add *West* means to add West deviation or variation to the True figure and subtract east from it when going from True to Compass. Here you are converting 300°T. Since (**V**)ariation is 14°W, add it (like adding whiskey) and come up with a (**M**)agnetic course of 314°. (**D**)eviation is 5° East, so subtract 5° from 314° to come up with 309° (**C**)ompass. On a chart you would plot 300°T as your course but steer 309° by your ship's compass. *Always plot using true courses and bearings* to avoid confusion.

Let's do the opposite, convert from a Compass course to a True course. We are steering 189° by compass and our deviation card tells us we have 3° West deviation. Our nearest compass rose on the chart says variation is 5° East. We are moving *up* the column.

T	191°
V	+05°E
M	186°
D	−03°W
C	189°

Because we are moving up the column, in the opposite direction from the previous example, and converting from Compass to True, the signs are reversed. Add east and subtract west going from Compass to True up the column. Subtract 3° West deviation from the compass course of 189° to arrive at a 186° Magnetic, and then add 5° East variation to the magnetic course to arrive at 191° True. You plot a course of 191°T on the chart and you steer 189° by your ship's compass.

Conversions are an indispensable part of

dead reckoning, whether you imagine Timid Virgins or True Viking Maidens.

Speed Logs. Faulty speed measurements are another source of error in dead reckoning. Speed logs tell you the boat's speed through the water, and, if not calibrated correctly, will give you a false reading. If you haven't already left civilization in your wake, find a measured mile and run it now. You can easily calibrate the log according to the manufacturer's manual. This will pay dividends when you approach a harbor entrance some foggy night.

Modern speed logs are notoriously unreliable. They're one of the first instruments to quit from electronic failure or, most commonly, from a fouled impeller. Although many logs are designed so you can remove the impeller housing for cleaning from inside the boat, water gushes in. This happens between the time you pull out the impeller housing and push in a bung of the correct size, and again as you remove the bung and reinsert the cleaned impeller. Be prepared for an unnerving feeling, and try to do it right the first time. Even after cleaning, marine growth immediately starts on the impeller and begins to adversely affect the speed reading.

Once we sailed non-stop from San Diego to Bora Bora with no electronics at all. The brand-new log failed before the San Diego harbor entrance fell below the horizon. We became good at estimating our boat speed for a 24-hour period, usually estimating with a margin for error of five miles over a 150-mile run. A three-percent error is not bad on a sailing vessel whose speed varies constantly with wind strength. Guessing is okay for offshore work, but close inshore it is dangerous. Do it only if you have no other alternative.

Unlike electronic logs, Walker rotating taffrail logs are highly accurate and reliable. They use simple technology that has been with us

Speed logs are notoriously unreliable, but there are exceptions, like the Walker log, a simple and accurate device that has been with us for more than a century. The rotator "fish" is towed astern, counting up RPMs that are translated into knots. Pat modified this one to keep hungry predators with sharp teeth from biting through the rotator's leader.

for more than a century. The Walker log's only drawback is that the rotator, the metal "fish" that's towed astern, occasionally is lost to large predatory fish. Spares are getting costly, so Pat Nicopressed on a steel leader wire that even barracuda couldn't bite through. It's also a good idea to paint the rotator flat black to make it less attractive to fish. Pull in the trailing line and rotator periodically and clear it of any weed that might foul it.

The speed of power vessels can accurately be determined by the RPM of their engines. Run the measured mile at a given RPM in both directions and then average the results to counter the effect of any current or windage. Do this at several different RPM settings so you can construct a speed table.

In addition to steering, compass, and log errors, other factors that cause dead reckoning positions to differ from true positions are windage and current. Currents can be non-tidal (such as the Gulf Stream) or caused by the rise and fall of the tide. Be sure to have tidal atlases on board and know how to use them.

Fixes. The longer you run a DR plot, the less accurate it becomes. You can fix your position by sailing past some known object, for instance a day mark that you identify on the chart. Floating objects are less accurate than stationary ones, because they may have drifted off their charted position somewhat.

Another method for increasing the validity of your DR is to take bearings on known objects. If you have good visibility all around your vessel's main steering compass, you can take bearings by sighting directly over it. But a *hand-bearing compass* is best for this purpose.

John prefers using a hand-bearing compass like the one pictured on page 38. It's compact enough to take along wherever we travel, easy to use and easy to read. It hangs from a sturdy lanyard around the neck so it's always handy. At night, a tiny tritium-radon light illuminates the card without needing batteries or bulbs. The compass in the photograph has given excellent service for 12 years, and the light still works, despite receiving zero maintenance. To use, sight across the top of it. The compass card shows through a prism and magnifying glass, giving very accurate bearings.

Figure 11-3 shows a fix that was obtained by taking bearings on three objects. When plotted, each of these bearings gives a *line of position* (LOP). A single LOP only tells you that your are somewhere on that line. When you plot the bearings of three objects well distributed around the compass, you can get a very accurate fix. The smaller the triangle formed by the intersection of these three LOPs, the more accurate your fix.

In Figure 11-3, the difference between the DR and the fix can be accounted for by *set and drift*, which are the direction and speed of the current in combination with leeway and steering error.

You may get by with a two-bearing fix, but

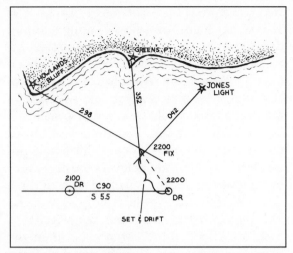

Figure 11-3. This position fix was obtained by taking bearings on three objects.

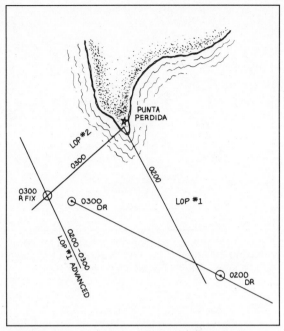

Figure 11-4. A running fix allows you to get a fix on one object.

the closer these objects are to 90 degrees apart, the more accurate the fix will be. If they are only 30 degrees apart, the fix will be less accurate.

Though three bearings result in very accurate fixes, often you will only have one object on which to take a bearing. This happens when you are paralleling the coast at night and see only one lighthouse. Figure 11-4 shows a commonly used technique called the *running fix,* which allows you to get a fix on one object.

First you take a bearing and plot it on the chart. Then you wait until the bearing changes appreciably, take another bearing and plot that LOP on the chart. Then take LOP #1 and advance it on your course heading, the distance that you ran between LOP #1 and #2. The intersection of the advance LOP#1 (a dotted line) and the LOP #2 is your running fix at the time of LOP #2. The influences affecting its accuracy are steering error, log error, any current encountered between LOP #1 and #2, the difference in angle between 1 and 2, and your accuracy in taking and plotting the bearings. Remember the running fix, because

it is the workhorse of celestial navigation when using only the sun.

Figure 11-5 shows a commonly used variation of the running fix. By doubling the angle of the first bearing, your distance away from the object you're taking a bearing on is equal to the distance you've run. When done with LOP #1 bearing 45 degrees relative to your bow, and then again when the object bears 90 degrees (directly abeam), your distance off the object (abeam) equals your distance run since LOP #1. This simple method requires very little chart work and has been used by thousands of unlettered masters of coasting vessels for centuries.

Here's a very practical and simple trick for getting a good, solid fix, not just a running fix, from one single object. You need a sextant and you need to know the height of the object.

Imagine that you are making landfall on an island and you spot its peak just above the ho-

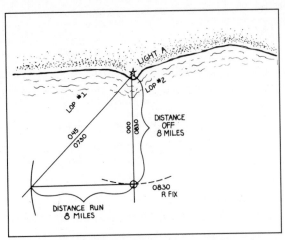

Figure 11-5. In this variation of the running fix, by doubling the angle of the first bearing, your distance off the object equals the distance you've run.

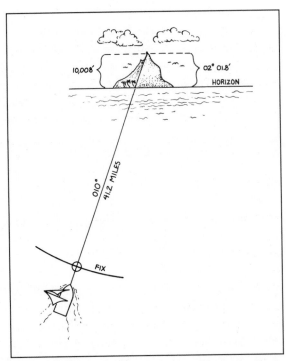

Figure 11-6. You can determine your distance off an object of known height by measuring its altitude with a sextant.

rizon (Figure 11-6). The chart shows it is 10,008 feet high. You take a bearing and plot the LOP. Then you measure with your sextant the angular distance between the mountain top and the horizon. For this to work, the horizon must be between you and the base of the object, as it would be when first making a landfall from seaward. The angle is 2°1.8' (2 degrees, 1.8 minutes). Correct this for the index error (+ 1.0') and height of the observer's eye above the ocean (8 feet). The result is 2 degrees. Now turn to Table 9 of Bowditch's *The American Practical Navigator* (Fig. 11-7), look up 2° and the difference between the height of the object and the height of eye (10,008 − 8) = 10,000. According to the table, you are 41.2 miles off that object. Take a pair of dividers with a pencil lead in one end and swing an arc 41.2 miles from the mountain peak. This arc is known as a *circle of position* (COP), meaning that you are somewhere on that arc. Exactly where the arc intercepts the LOP of your bearing is your fix.

In pre-electronic days, we used this method often, especially when coming north from Costa Rica, approaching Guatemala from well offshore. Guatemala's 12,000-foot volcanos were sometimes visible 100 miles away, and we could get very fine fixes, sometimes 60 miles offshore.

So we don't have to pack the heavy copy of Bowditch along with us for every delivery, we photocopied Table 9 and inserted it in our travelling copy of the *Nautical Almanac*.

Fujinon makes a model of binoculars with a built-in hand-bearing compass and light. These are very useful for picking out distant objects that are difficult to see unaided. The binoculars also contain a built-in height-measuring device, along with a circular slide rule printed around one of the lenses to calculate distance off. These are worthwhile, dual purpose binoculars. However, the sextant is much more accurate for such measurements.

TABLE 9

Distance by Vertical Angle

Angle	Difference in feet between height of object and height of eye of observer												Angle
	6,800	7,000	7,500	8,000	8,500	9,000	9,500	10,000	10,500	11,000	11,500	12,000	
° ′	Miles	Miles	Miles	Miles	Miles	Miles	Miles	Miles	Miles	Miles	Miles	Miles	° ′
0 10	84.3	85.7	89.0	92.3	95.5	98.5	101.5	104.4	107.3	110.1	112.8	115.4	0 10
0 11	83.3	84.6	88.0	91.3	94.4	97.5	100.5	103.4	106.2	109.0	111.7	114.4	0 11
0 12	82.2	83.6	87.0	90.2	93.4	96.5	99.4	102.4	105.2	108.0	110.7	113.3	0 12
0 13	81.2	82.6	86.0	89.2	92.4	95.4	98.4	101.3	104.2	106.9	109.6	112.3	0 13
0 14	80.3	81.6	85.0	88.2	91.4	94.4	97.4	100.3	103.1	105.9	108.6	111.2	0 14
0 15	79.3	80.7	84.0	87.2	90.4	93.4	96.4	99.3	102.1	104.9	107.6	110.2	0 15
0 20	74.6	76.0	79.3	82.5	85.6	88.6	91.5	94.4	97.2	100.0	102.6	105.3	0 20
0 25	70.3	71.6	74.9	78.0	81.1	84.1	87.0	89.8	92.6	95.3	98.0	100.6	0 25
0 30	66.3	67.6	70.8	73.9	76.9	79.9	82.7	85.5	88.2	90.9	93.5	96.1	0 30
0 35	62.6	63.9	67.0	70.0	73.0	75.9	78.7	81.5	84.2	86.8	89.4	91.9	0 35
0 40	59.2	60.4	63.5	66.5	69.4	72.2	75.0	77.7	80.3	82.9	85.5	88.0	0 40
0 45	56.0	57.2	60.2	63.1	66.0	68.7	71.5	74.1	76.7	79.3	81.8	84.2	0 45
0 50	53.1	54.3	57.2	60.0	62.8	65.5	68.2	70.8	73.3	75.8	78.3	80.7	0 50
0 55	50.4	51.6	54.4	57.2	59.9	62.5	65.1	67.7	70.2	72.6	75.0	77.4	0 55
1 00	47.9	49.0	51.8	54.5	57.1	59.7	62.3	64.7	67.2	69.6	72.0	74.3	1 00
1 10	43.5	44.6	47.2	49.7	52.2	54.7	57.1	59.5	61.8	64.1	66.3	68.6	1 10
1 20	39.7	40.7	43.2	45.6	48.0	50.3	52.6	54.8	57.0	59.2	61.4	63.5	1 20
1 30	36.5	37.4	39.7	42.0	44.2	46.4	48.6	50.8	52.9	55.0	57.0	59.0	1 30
1 40	33.7	34.6	36.7	38.9	41.0	43.1	45.1	47.2	49.2	51.2	53.1	55.1	1 40
1 50	31.2	32.0	34.1	36.1	38.1	40.1	42.1	44.0	45.9	47.8	49.7	51.5	1 50
2 00	29.1	29.9	31.8	33.7	35.6	37.5	39.3	41.2	43.0	44.8	46.6	48.3	2 00
2 15	26.3	27.0	28.8	30.6	32.3	34.1	35.8	37.5	39.2	40.9	42.5	44.2	2 15
2 30	24.0	24.7	26.3	28.0	29.6	31.2	32.8	34.4	35.9	37.5	39.1	40.6	2 30
2 45	22.1	22.7	24.2	25.7	27.2	28.7	30.2	31.7	33.2	34.6	36.1	37.5	2 45
3 00	20.4	21.0	22.4	23.8	25.2	26.6	28.0	29.4	30.8	32.1	33.5	34.8	3 00
3 20	18.5	19.0	20.3	21.6	22.9	24.2	25.5	26.7	28.0	29.3	30.5	31.8	3 20
3 40	16.9	17.4	18.7	19.8	21.0	22.2	23.4	24.5	25.7	26.9	28.0	29.2	3 40
4 00	15.6	16.0	17.1	18.2	19.3	20.4	21.5	22.6	23.7	24.8	25.9	27.0	4 00
4 20	14.4	14.8	15.9	16.9	17.9	19.0	20.0	21.0	22.0	23.0	24.0	25.0	4 20
4 40	13.4	13.8	14.8	15.8	16.7	17.7	18.6	19.6	20.5	21.5	22.4	23.4	4 40
5 00	12.6	12.9	13.8	14.7	15.6	16.5	17.4	18.3	19.2	20.1	21.0	21.9	5 00
5 20	11.8	12.1	13.0	13.9	14.7	15.5	16.4	17.2	18.1	18.9	19.8	20.6	5 20
5 40	11.1	11.4	12.3	13.1	13.9	14.7	15.5	16.3	17.1	17.9	18.6	19.4	5 40
6 00	10.5	10.8	11.6	12.3	13.1	13.9	14.6	15.4	16.1	16.9	17.6	18.4	6 00
6 20	10.0	10.3	11.0	11.7	12.4	13.2	13.9	14.6	15.3	16.0	16.7	17.5	6 20
6 40	9.5	9.8	10.4	11.1	11.8	12.5	13.2	13.9	14.6	15.2	15.9	16.6	6 40
7 00	9.0	9.3	10.0	10.6	11.3	11.9	12.6	13.2	13.9	14.5	15.2	15.8	7 00
7 20	8.6	8.9	9.5	10.1	10.8	11.4	12.0	12.6	13.3	13.9	14.5	15.1	7 20
7 40	8.3	8.5	9.1	9.7	10.3	10.9	11.5	12.1	12.7	13.3	13.9	14.5	7 40
8 00	7.9	8.1	8.7	9.3	9.9	10.4	11.0	11.6	12.2	12.7	13.3	13.9	8 00
8 20	7.6	7.8	8.4	8.9	9.5	10.0	10.6	11.1	11.7	12.2	12.8	13.3	8 20
8 40	7.3	7.5	8.0	8.6	9.1	9.6	10.2	10.7	11.2	11.8	12.3	12.8	8 40
9 00	7.0	7.2	7.7	8.3	8.8	9.3	9.8	10.3	10.8	11.3	11.8	12.3	9 00
9 30	6.7	6.9	7.3	7.8	8.3	8.8	9.3	9.8	10.3	10.7	11.2	11.7	9 30
10 00	6.3	6.5	7.0	7.4	7.9	8.4	8.8	9.3	9.7	10.2	10.7	11.1	10 00
10 30	6.0	6.2	6.6	7.1	7.5	7.9	8.4	8.8	9.3	9.7	10.1	10.6	10 30
11 00	5.7	5.9	6.3	6.7	7.2	7.6	8.0	8.4	8.8	9.3	9.7	10.1	11 00
11 30	5.5	5.6	6.0	6.4	6.8	7.3	7.6	8.0	8.5	8.8	9.3	9.7	11 30
12 00	5.3	5.4	5.8	6.2	6.6	6.9	7.3	7.7	8.1	8.5	8.9	9.2	12 00
12 30	5.0	5.2	5.6	5.9	6.3	6.7	7.0	7.4	7.8	8.1	8.5	8.9	12 30
13 00	4.8	5.0	5.3	5.7	6.0	6.4	6.7	7.1	7.5	7.8	8.2	8.5	13 00
13 30	4.6	4.8	5.1	5.5	5.8	6.1	6.5	6.8	7.2	7.5	7.9	8.2	13 30
14 00	4.5	4.6	4.9	5.3	5.6	5.9	6.2	6.6	6.9	7.2	7.6	7.9	14 00
14 30	4.3	4.4	4.8	5.1	5.4	5.7	6.0	6.3	6.7	7.0	7.3	7.6	14 30
15 00	4.2	4.3	4.6	4.9	5.2	5.5	5.8	6.1	6.4	6.7	7.0	7.3	15 00
16 00	3.9	4.0	4.3	4.6	4.9	5.2	5.4	5.7	6.0	6.3	6.6	6.9	16 00
17 00	3.7	3.8	4.0	4.3	4.6	4.8	5.1	5.4	5.6	5.9	6.2	6.5	17 00
18 00	3.4	3.5	3.8	4.1	4.2	4.5	4.8	5.1	5.3	5.6	5.8	6.1	18 00
19 00	3.2	3.3	3.6	3.8	4.1	4.3	4.5	4.8	5.0	5.2	5.5	5.7	19 00
20 00	3.1	3.2	3.4	3.6	3.8	4.1	4.3	4.5	4.7	5.0	5.2	5.4	20 00

Figure 11-7. Table 9 from Bowditch's *The American Practical Navigator* helps you find distance off.

CHAPTER 12
CELESTIAL NAVIGATION

THE IMPORTANCE OF THE STARS

Several years ago an article appeared in a monthly boating magazine that interviews professional captains. The interviewer asked the skipper of a large, well-known motorsailer questions about circumnavigation. The captain replied something to this effect: "I think it's absurd that the Coast Guard continues to require captains to pass a test on celestial navigation. Marine electronics are so reliable these days that I have taken my sextant and welded it into a lamp base on board."

Our first thought was a vision of this supposedly professional captain frantically trying to chip the welds off his delicate instrument when his "reliable" Satnav failed in mid-ocean. In late 1987 the Coast Guard made it possible for captains holding a 100-ton license or smaller to take the test for the "Upon Oceans" endorsement. This endorsement proves to the Coast Guard your abilities in celestial navigation. They don't require the endorsement, but without it you are limited to 200 miles offshore.

Among professional captains, this "Upon Oceans" endorsement separates the men from the boys and the sheep from the goats. It represents a quantum leap forward in the demonstration of navigation ability. A discerning boat owner looking for a delivery captain ought to hesitate to hire anyone who didn't have an "Upon Oceans" endorsement.

You don't have to be a mathematical genius to learn celestial navigation. The mathematics involved are no more complex than addition and subtraction. Learning celestial does require diligence and attention to detail. Our advice to pleasure-boat sailors—skipper and crew alike—is never cross an ocean on a boat that doesn't have at least one person who has a thorough working knowledge of celestial navigation and the equipment to use it.

It is not within the scope of this book to give a thorough instruction on celestial navigation. For further reading consult the reading list at the back of this book.

What You Will Need

The *sextant* measures the angle between a celestial body and the visible horizon. Like most precision instruments, a good one is expensive. Inexpensive plastic sextants are fine for learning in your home waters, and fine for a spare or back up to a good metal sextant, but don't trust your life to a lump of PVC. Plastic sextants are constantly subject to warping, especially when you carry them out on a hot (or cold) deck and then back inside. This alone destroys their accuracy. Their index mirrors need adjustment every time you use them.

Mirror adjustment is beyond the ken of many navigators. John remembers meeting two Japanese sailors who had just sailed nonstop from Japan to Mexico's Acapulco Yacht Club. Their sextant mirrors were so out of ad-

The full-size metal Tamaya (upper right) is large and heavy, though extremely accurate. It is a favorite for serious cruising. For yacht deliveries, we prefer the half-size metal Watanabe (lower), because it is smaller, lighter, and far easier to protect while carrying it on and off airplanes as we travel to and from our work. Never rely on a plastic model (upper left) as your only sextant, because they are prone to warping. Limit its use to backing up your high-quality metal sextant, or as a learning tool.

justment that they had a 20-minute index error. Twenty minutes could equate to a navigation error as great as 20 miles. Their only common language was Spanish, so John taught them to adjust the mirrors in that language. Bowditch and Dutton both have instructions on mirror adjustments, in English.

The favored *sight reduction tables* among pleasure boaters is *H.O.-(U.S. Hydrographic Office) 249*. Air navigators use *H.O.-249* primarily because it meets their demands of limited space in the aircraft cockpit, and for speed of usage, since aircraft travel so fast. *H.O.-249*'s abbreviated method costs some accuracy, less than a mile, but considering the inherent inaccuracy caused by taking a sight on the moving deck of a small boat at sea, the cost is insignificant compared to the advantages. Even in moderate seas, you're more likely to "catch" a wave top than the true horizon, so there's no point using a sight reduction method more accurate that your ability to take an accurate sight.

The Navy and Merchant Marine use *H.O.-229*, as opposed to *H.O.-249*, and therefore applicants for an "Upon Oceans" endorsement must pass a test using *H.O.-229*.

H.O.-229 was born during the Great Depression, conceived by the U.S. government and a huge group of unemployed mathematicians who were hired to devise a highly accurate sight reduction method. To keep themselves employed for as long as possible, the math wizards came up with what many now think is an unnecessarily complex form. For instance, *229* measures the azimuth of a body to within 1/10 of one degree, an accuracy level that's impossible to attain from the deck of a ship. You would have to have accurate surveying instruments planted firmly on dry land to ever measure azimuth that closely.

H.O.-249 is our personal favorite. It comes in paper-bound volumes, so is cheaper and lighter to carry around than the leather-bound *H.O.-229*.

Taking a *noon sight* gives you latitude only, but it requires only the *Nautical Almanac*; no additional tables. Many skippers end their celestial knowledge right there. You compute longitude by plotting several sights to determine the exact time of local apparent noon, yet you still can be off as much as 15 miles. That simply is not accurate enough, though it is a good method to know for emergency navigation.

If the sun is your only celestial body, all you can ever get are running fixes. Most of our navigation students are taken aback after they complete their first sight reduction and we plot the LOP. After all that work, they expect to have both latitude and longitude, and all they have is one measly LOP. To get a fix from the sun, take your first sight and then wait until the earth revolves enough to give you an angular separation, enough so that when you advance the first LOP, it crosses the second. Often this interval is about three hours.

Figure 11–4 in the coastal navigation chap-

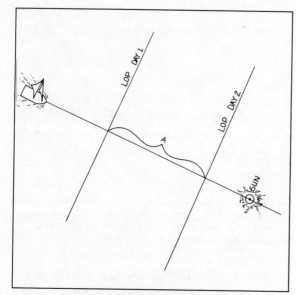

Figure 12-1. Any celestial body sighted directly off your bow or stern will give you an LOP that is perpendicular to your course.

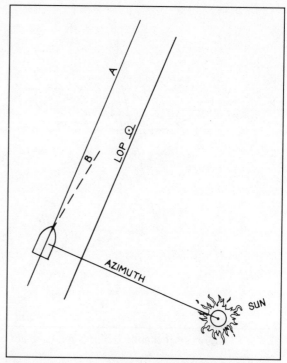

Figure 12-2. A celestial body sighted on your beam gives you an LOP parallel to your course.

ter explains the running fix. Advance your LOP# 1 along your course steered for the distance run. The intersection of the advanced LOP# 1 and LOP# 2 gives a running fix.

Here's an easy method of celestial navigation that involves taking only two sun lines a day, making maximum use of the information contained in each LOP. Any celestial body sighted directly off the bow or stern while steering your intended course will give you an LOP that is perpendicular to your course (Figure 12–1). This single LOP will tell you your distance run and speed of advance (A) when compared with your last fix.

A body sighted on the beam gives you an LOP parallel to your course, as in Figure 12–2. This tells you if you're to the right or left of course. In Fig. 12–2 the LOP is to your right, showing that you are drifting or steering to the left of your intended course (A) and will have to compensate by steering a course (B) to the right.

This method is available most of the year and in most portions of the globe. In deep

ocean, far from navigation hazards, these sights alone are sufficient. But during the last couple of days before you approach land, you should refine your position with as many rounds of star sights as you possibly can.

Star sights are simpler to reduce than are sun sights, yet few navigators know how to use the stars. Fig. 12–3 is a "round of stars," a series of simultaneous sights that give you a very accurate fix. This is not a running fix, but a real fix and the tighter the triangle formed by their crossing LOPs, the more accurate your position. Even in midocean we take at least one round of star sights per day, usually in the evening. We take four sights, because one of them will often be inaccurate. Common sources of inaccuracy are mistaking a reading from the sextant arc, incorrectly reading the time, looking in the wrong column of the *Nautical Almanac*, or making simple math errors. We

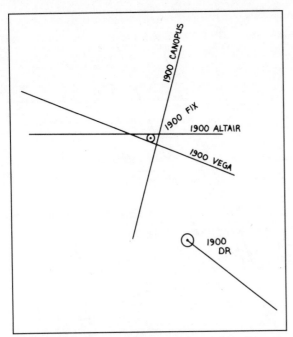

Figure 12-3. Three simultaneous star sights give an accurate fix.

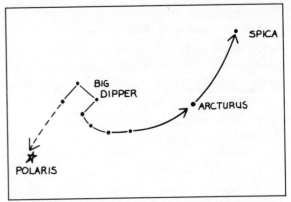

Figure 12-4. The pointer stars of the Big Dipper lead to Polaris, while the arc of its handle sweeps to Arcturus and on to Spica.

work out all four sights, but throw out the least accurate one, leaving three good lines.

If the reduction of star sights is so easy, why don't more people do it? It's a matter of star identification. Many people don't know how to locate and identify the stars that will give a good fix.

When primitive man first looked toward the sky, his imagination grouped the stars into constellations and named them according to his mythology. Many books on star identification are published for general audiences, and it's a good idea to learn the major constellations before you go to sea.

The best idea is to use the star maps in the *Nautical Almanac* or Bowditch since, as a navigator, you should own these anyway. These books emphasize the 57 stars used for navigation. The star diagrams group the constellations and use certain star pointers to show groups of navigational stars. As shown in Figure 12–4, the most famous are the

"pointers" of the Big Dipper, which direct your eye across the heavens to Polaris. Following the ARC of the Big Dipper's handle, you come to ARCturus and then to Spica.

Go out on a clear night armed with a flashlight covered with red cellophane to read your identification book. Look into the cosmos and teach thyself. If you have children, take them along; they'll love you for it and will learn something valuable that they won't forget for the rest of their lives. In town, star gazing is best if you get away from the nearest bright lights. Find a vacant lot, park, or school yard where can see enough of the major constellations and brighter navigation stars to be useful. Local planetariums have programs to teach the positions of the stars, and you can learn them in the comfort of an auditorium.

If you already are at sea, you have the perfect platform to learn while passing the hours of your night watch. All you have to do is look up. Knowing the major constellations will help you locate specific navigational stars.

The best time for taking star sights is twilight, when the brighter stars are visible and the horizon is still clearly defined. This period lasts about half an hour, just before sunrise or after sundown. (Thus the traditional navigator's watch is 0400–0800 and 1600–2000.)

When the moon is up you have more time. A full moon illuminates the horizon so you can shoot stars all night long, providing it doesn't wipe out the stars you want. Steve Dashew describes this in his book *The Circumnavigator's Handbook*.

In the South Pacific there is a strange rumor concerning a cult of moon worshippers in the cruising fraternity. Entire anchorages in the Marquesas and Tuamotus become restless on the approach of a full moon. Tension rises perceptibly in these yacht-filled anchorages, and then, as the full moon approaches, the yachts vanish. They are taking advantage of moonlight for making star fixes during the evening, and for better overall visibility to get a start on their next passage.

Select a few well-placed stars at the beginning of your voyage. If you choose well, you can travel great distances under the guidance of these familiar stars.

There are other methods to aid in star identification, and the best is *H.O.-249, Volume I*. By precomputing the time you will be making your sights, Volume 1 (shown in Figure 12–5) gives you seven selected stars, their azimuths and altitudes. Any three of these will give you a fix. First you compute the *local hour angle* (LHA) of Aires from the *Nautical Almanac*, then consult Vol. I with the LHA and your DR latitude. When the stars first come out, you can identify them by setting your sextant at the star's indicated altitude and then taking a compass bearing (corrected to true bearing) to the indicated azimuth. Your chosen star should fall right into your viewfinder. You may have to move the sextant arm slightly up or down and scan the horizon a few degrees to find it, but it will be there.

Sometimes you can't identify particularly bright stars when they first come out in the evening because there aren't enough neighboring stars to put them in their proper constellations. Take the star sights anyway, and identify them as soon as the other stars come out.

The Tamaya Astro-Navigation Calculators have a program for star identification. You shoot the star as you normally would, but then, through a reverse sight reduction, you come up with its *sidereal hour angle* (SHA) and *declination*. By scanning the *Nautical Almanac's* list of stars, you can identify the star whose SHA and declination match your computation. You'll find more on calculators in the next chapter, with electronic navigation.

COMPASS DEVIATION AT SEA

A very handy side benefit of knowing celestial navigation is that you can determine your compass's deviation even though you're in the middle of the ocean, far from terrestrial ranges commonly used for this job.

Each vessel has its own magnetic field that affects its compasses, but this field can change significantly during a long voyage due to nothing more than the hull's friction when moving through the water.

We were delivering a steel boat on an offshore voyage, when, well into the trip, our celestial fixes began diverging from our DR position. Because we soon would be approaching land, we were greatly concerned and had to figure it out quickly. Current might have caused the discrepancy between the DRs and fixes, but this area was not known for heavy current. Another cause could have been steering error, but by paying closer attention to our course, we decided nothing was amiss in that department. We checked around the compass to see if someone put any hunks of metal or electronics nearby, but they had not. By the process of elimination, we began to suspect that the compass was in error. I took a

LHA ♈	Hc Zn	Hc Zn	Hc Zn	Hc Zn	Hc Zn	Hc Zn	Hc Zn
	♦DENEB	Enif	♦Nunki	ANTARES	♦ARCTURUS	Alkaid	Kochab
270	51 56 048	34 58 096	37 02 165	34 03 205	37 56 276	35 53 314	35 01 346
271	52 36 047	35 52 096	37 16 166	33 40 206	37 02 276	35 14 314	34 48 346
272	53 16 047	36 46 097	37 29 167	33 16 207	36 07 276	34 35 314	34 34 345
273	53 56 046	37 40 097	37 41 168	32 51 208	35 13 277	33 56 314	34 20 345
274	54 35 046	38 34 098	37 51 169	32 25 209	34 19 277	33 17 314	34 07 345
275	55 14 045	39 28 098	38 01 170	31 59 210	33 26 277	32 38 314	33 52 345
276	55 52 045	40 22 099	38 10 171	31 32 210	32 32 278	31 59 314	33 38 345
277	56 30 044	41 16 099	38 17 172	31 04 211	31 38 278	31 20 314	33 24 345
278	57 08 044	42 09 100	38 24 174	30 35 212	30 44 278	30 41 314	33 10 345
279	57 46 043	43 03 100	38 30 175	30 06 213	29 50 279	30 02 314	32 55 344
280	58 23 043	43 56 101	38 34 176	29 36 214	28 56 279	29 23 314	32 40 344
281	58 59 042	44 50 101	38 37 177	29 05 215	28 03 279	28 44 314	32 25 344
282	59 35 041	45 43 102	38 40 178	28 34 216	27 09 280	28 06 314	32 10 344
283	60 11 040	46 36 103	38 41 179	28 01 216	26 16 280	27 27 315	31 55 344
284	60 46 040	47 29 103	38 41 180	27 29 217	25 22 280	26 48 315	31 40 344
	DENEB	♦Alpheratz	FOMALHAUT	♦Nunki	ANTARES	♦ARCTURUS	Kochab
285	61 20 039	22 37 067	11 10 130	38 40 182	26 56 218	24 29 281	31 25 344
286	61 54 038	23 27 068	11 51 131	38 38 183	26 22 219	23 35 281	31 09 344
287	62 27 037	24 18 068	12 32 132	38 35 184	25 47 220	22 42 282	30 54 343
288	62 59 036	25 08 068	13 12 132	38 30 185	25 12 220	21 49 282	30 38 343
289	63 31 035	25 58 068	13 53 133	38 25 186	24 37 221	20 56 282	30 23 343
290	64 01 034	26 49 069	14 32 133	38 19 187	24 01 222	20 02 283	30 07 343
291	64 31 033	27 40 069	15 12 134	38 11 188	23 24 223	19 09 283	29 51 343
292	65 00 031	28 31 069	15 51 134	38 03 190	22 47 223	18 16 283	29 35 343
293	65 28 030	29 21 069	16 29 135	37 53 191	22 10 224	17 23 284	29 19 343
294	65 55 029	30 12 070	17 07 136	37 42 192	21 32 225	16 31 284	29 03 343
295	66 20 027	31 03 070	17 45 136	37 31 193	20 53 225	15 38 284	28 47 343
296	66 45 026	31 54 070	18 23 137	37 18 194	20 14 226	14 45 285	28 31 343
297	67 08 025	32 46 070	18 59 138	37 04 195	19 35 227	13 53 285	28 15 343
298	67 30 023	33 37 071	19 36 138	36 50 196	18 55 227	13 00 285	27 59 343
299	67 50 021	34 28 071	20 12 139	36 34 197	18 15 228	12 08 286	27 43 343
	♦DENEB	Schedar	Alpheratz	♦FOMALHAUT	Nunki	♦Rasalhague	VEGA
300	68 09 020	31 37 038	35 20 071	20 47 140	36 18 198	53 29 257	67 38 313
301	68 27 018	32 10 038	36 11 071	21 22 140	36 00 199	52 35 258	66 58 312
302	68 43 016	32 43 037	37 03 071	21 57 141	35 41 200	51 42 258	66 18 311
303	68 57 014	33 16 037	37 54 072	22 31 142	35 22 201	50 49 259	65 36 310
304	69 09 012	33 49 037	38 46 072	23 04 142	35 02 202	49 56 260	64 54 309
305	69 20 010	34 22 037	39 38 072	23 37 143	34 41 203	49 02 260	64 12 309
306	69 29 009	34 55 037	40 29 072	24 09 144	34 18 204	48 08 261	63 29 308
307	69 36 007	35 28 037	41 21 072	24 41 145	33 56 205	47 15 261	62 46 307
308	69 42 005	36 01 037	42 13 073	25 12 145	33 32 206	46 21 262	62 03 307
309	69 45 003	36 34 037	43 05 073	25 43 146	33 07 207	45 27 262	61 19 306

Figure 12-5. *H.O. 249*, Vol. 1 gives you seven selected stars, their azimuths and altitudes.

bearing on the sun directly on our course line and found that we had developed a 20-degree compass deviation since we'd been at sea. We would have made a very sloppy landfall, especially in the fog, had we not discovered the deviation.

Cruising skippers and yacht delivery captains alike must know how to determine compass deviation. While prepping the boat, the skipper is under pressure to get started as quickly as possible and often he has no time to have the compass swung by a professional compass adjuster. The skipper doesn't necessarily need to know how to adjust the compass, but he should know how to determine its deviation.

A compass adjuster (usually a captain tired of going to sea) tries to eliminate as much deviation as possible, but there is usually a minor amount on certain courses that he can't adjust out. These small deviations must be dealt with in the same way that large ones are. If you can determine on your own the amount of deviation for various points of the compass, even if the deviation ranges from two to 20 degrees east or west, you still can steer a correct course.

How do you determine deviation without using objects on shore? Each celestial sight reduction results in an azimuth. You can compare this azimuth with your compass heading to determine the deviation. You can do it without using a sextant by sighting across the compass at the sun. This works best with sun elevations below 30 degrees. At the exact instant you are on your course, mark the compass bearing of the sun and the GMT.

Work through the sight reduction. You can do this quickly, because you don't have to do those portions dealing with HS or HO. Just come up with an azimuth and compare it to your compass heading. Use the mnemonic device, Timid Virgins Make Dull Company—Add Whiskey, further described in Chapter 11.

An example: The ship's heading is 135° by compass. The sun's compass bearing was 214°, the variation as shown on the chart was 5°E, and the azimuth from the sight reduction was 200° True. What was the deviation on this heading?

T	200°
V	–5°E
M	195°
D	+19°W Down Add West
C	214°

First determine what the sun's magnetic bearing is. Since we are going down the column, we add west, which is the same as subtracting east. Subtracting 5° from 200°, we arrive at 195°. This is the magnetic bearing, which is what the sun's bearing would be if there were no deviation. Continuing down TVMDC, the difference between magnetic and compass is 19°. We must add 19° to magnetic to arrive at a compass heading of 214°. Therefore, the deviation is west. Our result: On a compass heading of 135°, the compass's deviation must be 19° West.

On the high seas, the success of this method depends on how calm it is. The more you roll, the more difficult it is to determine deviation with accuracy. Even so, you can easily determine gross errors, like our 20-degrees discrepancy, from the DRs. You can refine this accuracy by taking several sights and averaging the results.

In ports of call or before you begin the delivery, you can use a similar and easier method by using ranges marked on shore. Look at Figure 12–6. By sailing across this range on a variety of courses equally spaced around the compass, you can come up with your own deviation table.

Celestial navigators who rely too much on electronic navigation tend to get rusty in

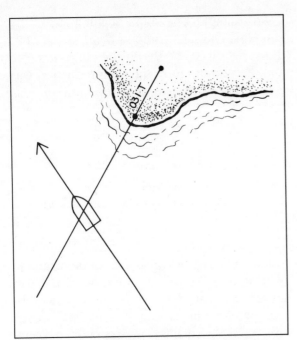

Figure 12-6. To determine your boat's deviation, find a range marker on shore and cross this bearing on a variety of courses equally spaced around the compass.

doing sight reductions. The best way to overcome this is to have the navigator give classes while underway to teach celestial to crewmembers. Besides oiling up a rusty navigator, these classes fulfill several important func-

tions. First, sights from the classes can be used to verify the ship's electronic position. Second, the navigator can develop able assistants to share some of his work load. Third, it trains crewmembers so they have the ability to make port if something happens to the navigator.

Lastly, giving onboard classes in celestial navigation builds excellent crew morale. Most crewmembers who already show an aptitude for coastal navigation are more than willing to learn celestial, but we don't force them to learn if they don't wish to. Onboard classes are a time of crew togetherness, and the crew is well aware of the classes' importance to their education and to everyone's safety.

In the field of yacht delivery, crewmembers often sign on—knowing the low wages prevalent in the profession—for the exciting adventure, the hard-to-find experience, and to learn something. When the captain teaches them navigation, particularly celestial, it is a major form of compensation, it lifts their spirits, and it keeps them from thinking the captain is a skinflint.

CHAPTER 13
ELECTRONIC NAVIGATION

Both ashore and at sea, this is the age of the electronics revolution. While early electronic navigation equipment was viewed with skepticism, its impact over the past decade has been astounding.

Those boat owners who purchased the high-priced, first-generation electronic widgits were in effect repaying the pioneer manufacturers for their costly investment in research and development. When sales picked up, prices began to come down. As more manufacturers appeared in the field, competition forced prices down again.

The first satellite navigation computers of the late seventies cost around $15,000; now you can buy one for as little as $1,000. Today's Satnavs are much smaller, thanks to microcircuitry. They offer step-saving features that are virtually foolproof, and they draw far less power than their ancestors. All of this brings them within the grasp of pleasure boat owners who plan to venture beyond their own coastal waters.

Earlier, we stressed the importance of knowing traditional coastal and celestial navigation methods and not becoming overly dependent on electronics. As Freeman Pittman, co-author of *Straightshooter's Guide to Marine Electronics,* says:

> The microchip offers us entirely new ways to look at getting a boat across the water quickly and safely. But these electronic black boxes demand more knowledge on our part, not less.

The professional mariner cannot afford to be a hardcore traditionalist who scorns the use of electronics. These marvelous gadgets increase safety and free up an enormous amount of time. If Christopher Columbus had had a Furuno depth sounder, you can bet he would have used it.

The array of navigation electronics available is truly vast. Each manufacturer has several types of instruments, each type has several models, and each model requires a different set of instructions to use. It can be mind-boggling.

We'll discuss major navigation electronics in the order of their importance: depth sounders, radar, Satnav, and Loran. Navigation calculators are infinitely handy, but since they're not considered a major electronic instrument, we've put them last.

DEPTH SOUNDERS

Depth sounders are high on our priority list, and it's rare today to find an offshore boat or a cruising vessel without one. Budget permitting, a back-up depth sounder also should be carried. Even with a second sounder, all boats should carry a lead line in case of power failure.

A good electronic array on a 90-foot trawler: closed-circuit television for the engine room, satellite communication system (SATCOM) terminal (voice and telex), weatherfax, two VHF radios, two SSB radios, two Satnavs, two Lorans, one digital depth sounder, and one recording fathometer.

The sounder gauges the depth of the water by emitting a sound pulse directed towards the bottom and measuring the time it takes to reflect back to the boat. Because the speed of sound in water is a known quantity (800 fathoms per second), it converts this time into distance—as feet, fathoms, or meters. Meters eventually will be the international standard of measurement, and U.S. chart agencies are beginning to print charts with depths in meters. It is helpful to have a sounder that reads in meters, feet, and fathoms, since you will soon have more charts that use meters. Such sounders automatically do the conversion for you.

Maximum depth is the greatest variation among sounders. Many cruising boats carry sounders whose range is only a couple hundred feet. That's adequate to measure the depth of an anchorage and to help you judge how much scope to put out, but such limited depth is not much good for navigational use.

It's preferable for sounders to reach at least 100 fathoms, because the 100-fathom curve is all-important in coastal navigation. Most off-lying rocks and navigational hazards lie within

it. A good night order for a captain to set with the crew might be, "Do not come within 60 fathoms. If you do, wake me."

Many sounder models have a built-in alarm that can be set to go off whenever the bottom shoals up to the selected depth. This makes night orders easier. Depth alarms can be handy at anchor, since their beeping indicates that the boat has swung or dragged its anchor into shallower water.

Depth sounders use several different ways to display depth. The older models used a flashing rotary display, newer models have a direct digital readout. We prefer the digital display, though it is sometimes helpful to have both for comparison.

Recording depth sounders are more expensive, but they give you a record on paper of the depths you've covered. For navigational purposes, the recording sounder can verify whether you've crossed some ridge or seamount, for example. This is handy if you're short-handed and don't have someone monitoring the sounder and manually recording depths. Paper-recording is useful for fishing because schools of fish will show on the paper.

The newer models record the depth on a monochrome or color video screen, rather than on paper. The color models display different colors to distinguish certain bottom characteristics, red showing the hardest bottom. This is almost like lowering a color TV camera underwater. These are especially useful for fishing.

Forward-scanning sonar is at the high end of the price spectrum, but it has grown more reasonable in the past few years. We've delivered luxury yachts and sportfishers with this equipment. Sonars use the same echo-location principle to look forward and off to the side, which is a tremendous advantage when piloting in coral. You can see reefs far

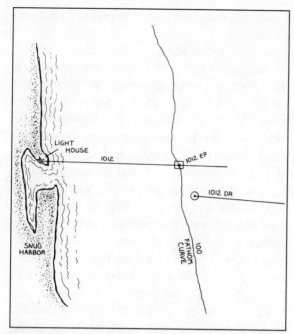

Figure 13-1. A depth sounder can be used to give you an estimated position (EP).

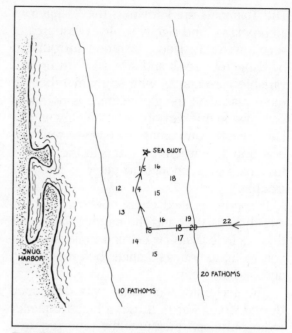

Figure 13-2. A depth sounder can help you make landfall in fog.

enough ahead to change course. It's handy for fishing, too. A limitation of the conventional depth sounder is that it measures the bottom only directly underneath the vessel.

How is a depth sounder used in navigation?

The 100-fathom curve is useful for getting a line of position (LOP) and an estimated position (EP) when making an approach to land. In Figure 13–1 your vessel is coming into a harbor from offshore. At 1012 your sounder shows you have crossed the 100-fathom curve, but your DR posiiton does not. You get a bearing from a lighthouse on shore. Where that bearing crosses the 100-fathom curve is your EP. It's not quite as good as a fix, but nearly so.

In limited visibility such as fog, the sounder becomes very valuable when trying to make a harbor entrance. Find the depth of the sea buoy. Deliberately head for one side or the other of it, so you will have no doubt which side you are on. In Figure 13–2 you chose the

left. When you reach the same depth as the sea buoy, make a right-hand turn and stay in the same depth of the water until you find the sea buoy.

RADAR

Why would anyone choose radar over Loran or Satnav as second in importance? Because knowing your exact position well offshore is not that crucial, since you are well away from danger and you can use celestial navigation. Making landfall brings you closest to danger. Radar shows a graphic display of all the "hard spots" around you—on land and sea, day and night, and in all conditions of visibility. Loran and Satnav only tell your position.

Let's say you intend to cruise from the Marquesas to the Tuamotus in the South Pacific.

The Tuamotus are known as the "dangerous archipelago," and rightly so. It's a vast area of very low coral islands, each one surrounded by dangerous reefs and swept by strong and variable currents. As with so many other remote places on the globe, there is no Loran coverage in this part of the Pacific. If you only have Satnav, you commonly have to wait several hours between fixes, and in the Tuamotus, that's long enough to get you into real trouble.

Properly adjusted radar, however, will detect these islands and the barely-awash reefs that encircle them far enough in advance for you to make course changes before you run aground on them.

The technology of radar was developed during World War II. It uses a high-frequency radio pulse and measures the time required for that pulse to travel to a "target" and return, and then converts this to an accurate representation of distance on a screen. Radar also provides bearings—but with far less accuracy, as we'll discuss. It effectively paints a picture of everything around you.

Recent advances have reduced a radar unit's size and power drain so much that radar is now common on yachts, even on sailboats. Another advance is the *raster scan,* a digitally processed video output also known as "bright screen." Unlike the first generation of radar screens, the new bright screens are meant to be used on a bridge in daylight without the need of the hood to shield ambient light from your eyes. The only exception to this is direct sunlight.

Several years ago, a lovely, new custom sportfisher we were about to deliver was coming from the builder equipped with a then-new raster scan radar built into the console of the fly bridge, and we were excited about getting to try it out. Unfortunately, the owner did not want a bimini top on his open fly bridge. This meant we were going to have to make the entire 6,000-mile delivery exposed to the sun all day.

As soon as we left the coastal clouds astern, we learned a valuable lesson about raster radar. Accurate and advanced as it was, we simply could not read the too-well lighted screen in broad daylight. And this particular model had no dimmer adjustment. Hastily, we made a hood by cutting a hole in the bottom of a plastic bucket, and tied it near the radar screen. After sunset, the screen was so blindingly bright that even a swift glance destroyed your night vision. It seemed an impossible situation until we taped a square of cardboard over the screen, making a "peek flap." Only with our hilarious adaptions could we use this $5,000 piece of equipment.

The addendum to this story is that, within months, technological improvements made that early model obsolete.

Bright-screen radar is available in either color or monochrome. With color, an internal computer chip determines the "hardness" of various targets and then paints them different colors, according to their hardness. On most machines, red is hardest, meaning it's the densest or strongest radar return. Other colors may be gradations running from orange to yellowish green for weaker targets. A large ship will show as a red shape made up of many red and orange grains or dots of light on the screen. Sometimes a cruise ship's twin stacks even show up separately. A steep cliff may be a long sweep of red grains. A small sailboat might show as a single yellow-orange grain. A gently sloping beach in front of the steep cliffs may be a thin line of yellow.

The main disadvantage of color becomes apparent when you're trying to pick out a ship engulfed in a rain storm. Once the human eye is educated by many hours of staring into a monochrome radar scope, it can differentiate rain from a ship much better than a computer chip can.

Pat was alone on the bridge one night, just after we'd transitted the Panama Canal and were heading south to clear Punta Mala. On the color radar, she was tracking two oncoming freighters, doing 15 and 20 knots, and two aimlessly drifting rain squalls. Everything was fine and she'd just calculated that in about six minutes we should alter our course for the freighters.

Suddenly, our autopilot croaked and we plunged into a hard right turn, directly for the rocks of shore. She got us back on course quickly, but when she went back to the radar screen, both rain clouds had merged into one, which was now drifting across our path, and neither ship was to be seen. Obviously the ships were engulfed in the rain squall, but so too would we be by the time our planned course change would have occurred. After some quick calculations, she advanced the position of both freighters and ourselves, and corrected our course ahead of time, just to make sure.

Just then, the next watch arrived on the bridge and began to make jokes about dodging rain showers. Deciding not to turn over the watch, Pat kept the con until all three ships had emerged from the squall, and she'd put us back on course, clear of Punta Mala and the traffic lanes.

Color radar is a handy option, but not a necessity. We are not alone in this belief. The Panama Canal is only nine degrees north of the Equator, and therefore has a major visibility problem with the frequent and intense rain squalls. Of the many Panama Canal pilots we've interviewed aboard our delivery vessels, virtually all agree that they can pick a ship out of a rain cloud much more easily with monochrome radar than with color.

Radar Fixes

Radar can give very precise fixes. Whenever we're sailing close enough to shore for the ra-

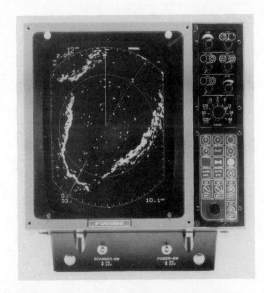

Furuno's Digiscan radar. One of its advanced features is a plot mode that tracks a target's path on the screen. This is very useful for tactical decisions in avoiding collision. (Photo courtesy of Furuno, USA Inc.)

dar to paint a good picture, we choose it for fixes rather than choosing Loran or Satnav. A position fix derived from numerical latitude and longitude, as with Loran and Satnav, is subject to some degree of error, while radar gives you a graphic fix in relation to the hard spots you are trying to avoid.

Radar fixes are very accurate and can be made quickly, so whenever entering tight quarters or an unfamiliar harbor, take radar fixes almost continuously. This will leave little doubt about the effect of unknown current or your distance off hard objects. Radar is very useful for setting night orders. (See Chapter 10, page 97.)

Make a radar fix by taking three *ranges*. A range is your distance off, measured from a recognizable point ashore. Using dividers with a pencil lead in one side, draw a circle of position (COP) around each object ashore. The radius of each COP is your range from that object. If you can get only one COP, you

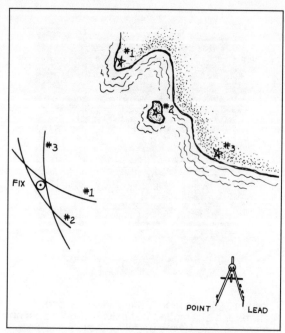

Figure 13-3. You can obtain a radar fix by taking the ranges of three objects ashore and drawing three circles of position. Where these three circles intersect is your fix.

know only that you are somewhere on the perimeter of the circle. Where the three COPs intersect is your fix. (See Figure 13–3.) The smaller the triangle, the more accurate your fix.

The variable range marker (VRM) makes tight triangles possible. Older models or radar without the VRM are slightly more difficult to use for this kind of fix. You must interpolate the range of any target lying between "non-variable" range rings, using the old eyeball method, which is fraught with inaccuracies.

Using the computer-generated VRM, you move an electronic ring either in or out from the center of the screen, which is your position, until it lays directly across the object you're measuring. A digital readout tells you the radius of the COP, which is the distance between you and the object. VRMs are accurate to within 0.1 mile.

While two or three COPs give ideal fixes,

they aren't always available. Single bearing fixes (Figure 13–4) are easy with radar. Where the range (distance off) and bearing (relative to your bow) intersect is the fix. Radar ranges are very accurate, but radar bearings are not. You can use an additional hand-bearing compass to increase the accuracy of a single-object radar position. This works best with clearly observable, well-located objects like a lighthouse, or in daylight when you can visually see the object beyond your hand-bearing compass.

Even the older radar units have a mechanical means of finding an object's bearing. It is a thin plastic cursor line that you rotate around the screen until it's directly over your target. The target's relative bearing can then be seen at the top of the plastic ring around the screen. Remember, this is a relative bearing, not a True or Magnetic one. It is also not the other ship's heading.

Newer radars have one or two electronic bearing lines (EBLs), which electronically measure the targets' relative bearings.

Distance off the beam is a common method of radar positioning with one object. Figure

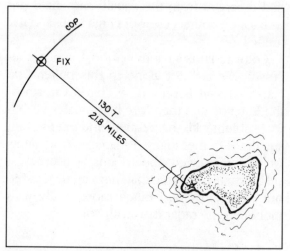

Figure 13-4. A single-bearing radar fix can be obtained by finding the range and bearing of an object. Where they intersect is your fix.

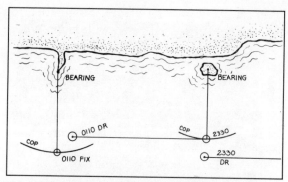

Figure 13-5. When paralleling the coast, a radar fix is obtained by measuring an object's distance off when it is directly abeam on the radar screen.

13–5 shows a course that's basically paralleling the coast, but how do you know how close inshore you're getting set? When the lighthouse is directly abeam, measure its distance off in the radar scope. Go to the side of the chart and adjust the dividers so you describe that distance. Now, lay out that distance on a line perpendicular (90 degrees) to your course line. To do this, some people use a protractor's right angle with the dividers. Your position fix is where the range and bearing (90 degrees) intersect. It's likely you'll need to redraw your course line parallel to the first one. The lighthouse hasn't moved; you have.

While skirting the infamous and windy Gulf of Tehuantepec with one foot on the beach, we shoot a continuous series of these fixes. It's a handy method for running down a coast filled with prominent headlands and lighthouses.

Fog and darkness do not affect radar in the slightest, so it is invaluable for avoiding collisions. When you first sight a ship on radar, place the bearing cursor over it and put the VRM over it and note its range and bearing. Then, every few moments, note the change in its position relative to the original range and bearing. Constant bearing and decreasing range mean collision is imminent. If the object marches down the bearing line, you need

to take appropriate action. Change course and/or speed to avoid collision. (Also see Chapter 10, Figures 10–9, 10–10, and 10–15.)

Newer and more sophisticated color radars have a plot mode, a separate function overlaid on the scanner, in which the computer memory actually paints a picture of a target's progress across the radar scope over a period of time. Fig. 13–6 shows the plot mode as a dotted line depicting the path of the vessel's relative motion as it safely passes ahead. Plot modes sometimes use blue tracer shadows to designate the plot of anything moving in the screen. Of course, shorelines appear to move too, as you pass along them. With only a little practice, you can distinguish relative motion from actual motion in the plot mode.

The radar alarm is another aid in collision avoidance. You can preset the alarm to beep when you have targets in a certain sector of the screen or when targets are a specified distance off. The beeper alerts the watch-stander.

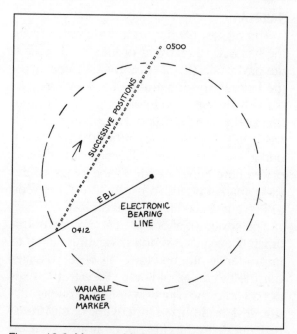

Figure 13-6. More sophisticated radar units have a plot mode that tracks a target's progress across the radar screen (dotted line).

We fear that radar alarms may inspire overreliance on them rather than on one's own eyes, and therefore generate a lackadaisical approach to watch-standing. Prudently used, the alarm can be helpful.

The *racon* is a radar beacon with a Morse code identifier that appears on your radar screen. Racons are often located on sea buoys at the entrance to busy harbors, such as Boston. They are great aids to making landfall. When approaching a busy harbor from weeks of passagemaking, a common sea buoy is often indistinguishable from the tangle of other radar targets. The racon clearly flashes its Morse code signal radiating from its center in the direction of its bearing. As you move, so too does its angle of radiation. For example, the racon at Boston's harbor entrance flashes its welcoming "B" or "dash, dot, dot, dot" across the radar. We look forward to an increased use of these helpful devices.

SATNAV

The biggest revolution in blue-water cruising has been the advent of inexpensive satellite navigation (Satnav) receivers. Satnav fixes the latitude and longitude of a vessel very accurately by receiving information from one of five satellites in earth orbit. Merchant shipping has used this system for more than 20 years, but it has been only relatively recently that prices have fallen to within the range of the yachtsman's budget. You can spend between $1,000 and $5,000 for a Satnav system.

The advent of affordable Satnavs has unfortunately encouraged non-navigating sailors to imprudently attempt long offshore passages outside the range of Loran. Though the fixes are reliable, the Satnav system is prone to failure. It is made up of a network of electronic machines based in the upper atmosphere, on shore and on your boat. To rely solely on Sat-

Affordable Satnav has revolutionized cruising and these machines are now found on many smaller boats. (Photo courtesy of Furuno, USA Inc.)

nav is a mistake. We urge passagemakers to know celestial navigation as a backup.

Satnav reception normally is available worldwide. Unlike celestial navigation, the accuracy of Satnav fixes is unaffected by weather or visibility. Satnav also releases the navigator from hours of daily work required for precise celestial navigation.

One of Satnav's big disadvantages is that it does not give a continuous fix as do Loran and Omega. Only when a satellite is high enough above the horizon can a fresh fix be made. Depending on your location, the interval between fixes can vary greatly. You may get three good fixes in one hour, but then have none at all for the next 10 hours. However, even at its worst, Satnav exceeds the frequency of fixes you can obtain by using celestial. Satnav can dead reckon (DR) for you between fixes with either manual or automatic inputs of course and speed.

If you use manual inputs, you first determine your speed and course and enter them into the Satnav computer, which then continuously updates your latitude and longitude until another satellite pass fixes your position precisely. Everytime you change course and speed you must make a new entry into the machine. By use of a flux-gate compass and speed sensor, the computer can receive these inputs automatically. This is accurate if you calibrate the instruments correctly. It is especially useful for a sailboat whose speed varies continuously with wind strength, point of sail, and constant course changes from tacking.

The Satnav computer goes a step further in increasing the accuracy of a dead-reckoning position by automatically calculating the effect of set and drift. It compares the dead reckoning to the actual fix to determine set and drift and applies this new correction to the dead reckoning course and speed. The computer combines all this information to give your estimated speed and course over the ground.

A frequent problem is that Satnav users with manual inputs forget to turn off the automatic set and drift, and they forget to set the manual speed to zero when they arrive in port. Thus the computer keeps telling itself that the hull is moving. Then, when the fresh satellite fixes and the dead-reckoning positions disagree by a certain number of miles, the computer begins rejecting the fixes.

You can cure this by reinitializing the machine. Enter the present position, turn the speed setting to zero, and shut off the automatic set and drift. After the next satellite pass, the Satnav computer is back to normal.

Waypoints

A useful planning feature of Satnav is the ability to program the latitude and longitude of several waypoints. The computer can then tell you the range and bearing from your present position to a waypoint, stated either as rhumb line or great-circle course. Using this waypoint data and whatever speed of travel you input, the Satnav can tell you your estimated time of arrival. Waypoint data is helpful for pre-trip planning of the various legs of your delivery. The computer will tell you how many days and hours the trip will take at the speed you input. Of course, you should double-check the accuracy by manually laying out your course on the charts.

The use of electronic devices has changed the way we navigate. John explains how we use Satnav, but we caution you to be ready to revert to manual dead reckoning and coastal and celestial position fixing.

A divergence I make from traditional navigation routines is to draw a course line from my departure point to my first waypoint. Most orthodox navigation textbooks will tell you not to do this because you draw a new course line from each fix. With my method you draw a line between waypoints. As you begin the first leg, you steer the course for that waypoint by figuring it out from the chart and also double-checking that course from the bearing of the Satnav. (Figure 13–7.)

I set up a navigation log for the watch to use. Every hour the watch stander enters the Satnav latitude and longitude in the log and plots it on the chart. I also have him enter the dead-reckoning time in the log, which he gets from the Satnav. This tells me the amount of time that has elapsed since the last satellite fix, which directly bears on fix accuracy. A Satnav DR that is several hours old and in an area of heavy current is getting unreliable.

Figure 13–7 shows, after the first few fixes, that we are tracking to the left. The Gulf Stream is carrying us sideways. I alter course 5 degrees to starboard to compensate. After several hours I see that 5 degrees is not enough and I alter another 5 degrees to starboard. Several fixes later I see that we are coming back toward our rhumb line. This method of fixes at short intervals allows us to march down the rhumb line, like Pacman eat-

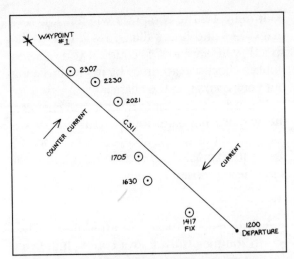

Figure 13-7. By drawing a course line from your departure point to your first waypoint, you can plot Satnav fixes along the way and tell at a glance whether you're to the left or right of the rhumb line.

ing up the dots. Always calculate the effect of set and drift so you can convert to manual if the machine fails.

You can use Satnav's *range-and-bearing-to-waypoint* function to compare its bearing with your original heading. Also check your speed, range and ETA from your chart work, just as you would without the Satnav. All automatic, electronic position-finding devices (Satnav, Loran, and Omega) tempt you into chartless navigation. Resist the temptation; only by plotting on the chart can you see how close you are to hazards to navigation.

At the beginning of an ocean crossing, I take a round of star sights the first day out to check if the Satnav is working. Then, often, in midocean I'll take another round. Just before landfall, I always take a round of star sights to make doubly sure we're making landfall on the right continent. During the time just before landfall or approaching a critical waypoint, I also check the future satellite menu to see how updated our position will be. In certain tricky conditions such as approaching a harbor entrance at night in the fog, I might

consider laying to and waiting until a satellite pass gives me an accurate fix before proceeding.

Occasionally the use of electronics will give you a scare. They sometimes paint ghost targets which aren't really there. As we approached our landfall on Cabo San Lucas from Hawaii on *Andaleena,* I double-checked the Satnav with a round of star sights and the two positions coincided. Then, 180 miles out I began to see on the outer limits of our 48-mile radar what looked like land. It wasn't a hard target but rather a soft fuzzy area such as you might see if there was high land many miles behind a low-lying coast. That's what exists at Cabo, a 10,000-foot mountain peak several miles inland. But I couldn't possibly see land at 48 miles when my Satnav and my trusty sextant said 180 miles.

Radar is notorious for giving "ghost" images. Sometimes ghosts are caused by reflections off your own masts and sails, but these usually stay at the same spot on the scope despite vessel movement, or they are so erratic in their nature that it is obviously interference. But the fuzzy mass off Cabo was growing closer at the same rate as our forward speed. It gave every indication of being a landmass, except that as we drew close, it never became a strong or "hard" target. I began to doubt the Satnav, my sextant, and my ability as a navigator.

I took another round of sights, which put me right where I thought we were in the first place—well out of radar range of the coast. During that day we had unlimited visibility. As darkness fell we were almost upon the mass on the radar, but we still hadn't seen anything. Then, with the ghostly radar target only three miles off, I began to get soundings on the fathometer. They were erratic but decreasing in depth.

As an experiment I set the depth alarm. Sure enough, when the readings came up, the alarm sounded. What was going on? The chart said we were in water four miles deep. I nearly panicked and stopped the boat. But no, we pressed onward on the calculated assumption that it had to be some freak meteorological condition.

Just as we entered the edge of the mass on radar, the whole mass disappeared from the scope, as did the soundings. I was much relieved but still puzzled and went on to make a textbook landfall on the tip of the Baja Peninsula.

What caused this mysterious ghost? My conjecture is that the electronic readings were somehow related to the abnormally high barometric pressure that prevailed at the time. High pressure can cause an inversion layer, and this may have caused the radar to detect land that was yet over the horizon.

To the best of my knowledge, atmospheric inversion layers do not penetrate below the surface of the ocean. So that doesn't explain the depth soundings. However, extreme differences in water temperature may deflect a depth sounder's pulses. It seemed too great a coincidence for both conditions to occur simultaneously, but I have no other explanations.

Ancient mariners had their sea monsters to contend with, and so, too, do we modern mariners. Ours are just more high-tech.

Global Positioning System

The inability of Satnav to give continuous, instantaneous fixes created the need for a new system. The *Global Positioning System* (GPS) is the answer. When fully implemented, GPS will have 18 satellites in orbit, at least four of which will always be "visible" to earth stations. These visible satellites will give constant latitude and longitude and are capable of such a high degree of accuracy that they will deliberately transmit to civilian users a small, pro-

grammed degree of inaccuracy. The U.S. military doesn't want to give its enemies free precision positions.

GPS gives position in latitude, longitude, and altitude. Beyond its obvious use for aircraft, Pat thinks that a recording device for this third dimension, altitude, will be of great value to flamboyant mariners who tell tales of surviving 30-foot seas and of whales that leap over their bows.

Since the Challenger space shuttle accident, GPS has fallen far enough behind its original deployment schedule that it may not be fully operational until the turn of the century. Meanwhile, some electronics firms have already manufactured GPS receivers. As with the early days of satnav, these GPS units are quite expensive. As the system is implemented and sales of individual units increase, their prices will no doubt fall.

LORAN

Loran-C yields an accurate, constant position, but its present reception is limited to the coastal regions of North America, Europe, and Japan. Although the technology has been with us for nearly a half century, Loran-C has been used by private yachts for only the last decade.

In 1974 the U.S. government established

Global Positioning and Navigation System (GPS) will replace the current transit satellite system (Satnav) before the end of the century. The front of Magnavox's GPS is only slightly different from its Satnav.

In areas where you can receive strong signals, Loran is a marvelous instrument that continuously gives your latitude and longitude, speed and course over the ground, as well as other useful planning functions.

Loran-C as the principal electronic navigation system for coastal navigation. It was meant to cover waters from the shoreline out to 50 miles or the 100 fathom curve, whichever was farther. In reality, Loran is useful under certain conditions out to 1,200 miles from the Loran station, but with decreasing accuracy.

For qualified yacht deliverers, Loran's limited range has been a blessing in disguise. Owners who would move a boat themselves in areas of Loran coverage will sometimes hire a professional to move the boat in areas without Loran coverage, where a high degree of navigational expertise is required. We have delivered several boats that routinely were run by paid captains who were unable to navigate outside of Loran range—another example of overreliance on electronics.

The Loran system consists of a master and four slave stations that transmit short, timed pulses near a frequency of 100 kHz. The time difference (TD) between the signals sent by master station and any one of the slave stations, computed in millionths of a second, gives a line of position (LOP). The government publishes charts that are overlaid with these TD LOPs. The TDs from other slave sta-

tions give different LOPs. The intersection of these LOPs gives a fix. As with all LOPs, the closer to 90 degrees they intersect, the more accurate the fix.

Most Loran receivers automatically convert TDs into latitude and longitude, in a foolproof digital display. However, if you can plot with TDs directly on your charts, you'll not only have greater accuracy, but you'll also be able to return to the same spot on your charts. Such "repeatability" is imperative to lobster fisherman who have to find that exact spot to retrieve their anchored traps.

True course and speed over the bottom is an optional mode offered by many Loran receivers, but it only operates if you have a strong signal. This mode is extremely valuable when operating in areas of heavy current. In the Gulf of Mexico we have often been able to set the autopilot to steer a course direct to our waypoint by looking at the true-course-over-the-ground display on the Loran. We were able to do this in spite of the strong lateral set caused by the Gulf Stream.

Another Loran feature is preprogrammed waypoints, similar to Satnav, but Loran sets can have as many as 99 possible waypoints. From the waypoint information comes course to steer, whether you are right or left of course, and ETA at present speed.

Loran navigation methods are the same as Satnav. Plot your position on the chart hourly or more often when close to hazards. Loran is not accurate enough for use in harbors, and to discourage its misuse this way, the Hydrographic Office does not print TDs on harbor charts. However, Loran is accurate enough to get you to the sea buoy in a dense fog.

John offers this example:

I made my first trip from Hawaii to the West Coast aboard a 40-foot sailboat with Loran and radar. Throughout the rough passage all the electronics worked flawlessly. I had Loran coverage for a few hundred miles outbound from Hawaii, and when it faded I resorted to celestial navigation. We left the radar off during the day and on standby during the night to conserve power. There wasn't much to look at out in the middle of nowhere. After 27 days at sea, we closed with San Diego and it got foggier and foggier. Then, when we most needed it, the radar quit. We proceeded in severely restricted visibility using the Loran and the depth sounder. At 0200 we practically ran over the sea buoy at San Diego's harbor entrance, right on schedule. It was the first aid to navigation we had seen in almost a month. We then navigated into the harbor by dead reckoning from buoy to buoy down the channel until were safely tied up in our slip.

Fringe areas of Loran coverage offer the true test of the navigator's abilities. Some Loran sets are better at receiving weak signals than others. A few older sets have the ability to control manually the Loran's functions and are much better in fringe areas than the newer sets in which the Loran computer automatically controls these functions. The old Northstar 6000 has manual controls, and for this reason many are still found on fishing vessels whose navigators prefer them over the new automatic models.

The manufacturer's manual shows the set's long-range capabilities. Look up the dynamic range and acquisition/signal noise ratio (SNR). A good set has a dynamic range of 120 db, while 110 db is considered average. An acquisition SNR of -18 db to -20 db is good, and average is from -10 db to -15 db. These better numbers are usually found in the more expensive sets.

Antenna installation affects performance. Place the Loran antenna well away from radio-transmitting antennas. Before final installation, move the Loran antenna around the boat to determine where the set gets the best SNR.

For operating outside of normal Loran range, you will need to get special *Loran plotting sheets* at a chart store. These have TD lines drawn on them beyond the range of the regular charts. As you leave an area of strong coverage, the first automatic function to disappear is the latitude and longitude converter. It will begin to give false numbers and then fail completely. Pick TDs with the strongest SNRs and crossing angles closest to 90 degrees. Plot them on the sheets to come up with a fix.

A *baseline extension* is a line drawn from one Loran master transmitting station to one of its slaves. These lines are shown on Loran charts, and operation anywhere close to them causes you to lose the ability to use that TD.

When signals are weak, you may find only one line that has a strong enough SNR to use. This one line can be very useful, as shown in Figure 13–8, where we intend to pass between two low-lying reefs well offshore. The one TD that still is strong (29810) passes right between the reefs. By following it we will keep clear of danger. To further fix our position we can choose a celestial body with an LOP that has a good crossing angle. Here we shoot Polaris, which gives us latitude and has an LOP crossing angle of nearly 90 degrees for an accurate fix.

As you go farther away from the transmitting stations you pick up *sky-wave signals,* signals that have bounced off the ionosphere rather than been transmitted directly by ground wave along the earth's surface. Sky-wave signals are incorrect. They have traveled farther, so have taken longer to arrive at your location. You can apply sky wave corrections to these TDs, but don't rely on weak Loran signals. At some point on the fringe area, the

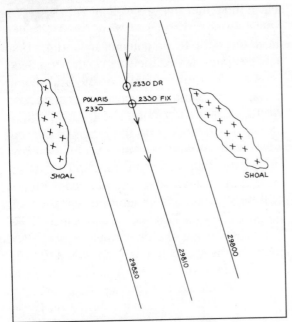

Figure 13-8. In an area where Loran signals are weak, one strong TD (29810) can give you a safe course to steer and, if crossed with another LOP, a fix as well.

Loran machine will degenerate into a random number generator, and you will have to turn to some other means to fix your position.

Omega

Omega is similar to Loran except that it is a worldwide navigation system. In practice, Omega has proved less than satisfactory, and since the advent of small, inexpensive Satnav units, Omega is seldom used aboard yachts. Unlike Loran, you must know your position to within five miles before you start. If for some reason you lose power or, as often happens, one of the Omega stations goes off the air, you will be unable to recover your position unless you again fix it to within five miles by some other means.

The best system we have seen aboard a yacht was a combination Omega and Satnav, by Tracor. The Omega gave constant position information between satellite fixes and the satnav served as the controlling unit and would update both systems when it obtained a satellite fix. This way the Omega could never get off track, but it was an expensive system.

When the GPS system is fully in place, Omega may become a thing of the past.

CALCULATORS

The first hand-held calculators became available to the general public in the early 1970s. Since then great advances have been made in their capabilities, and their price has fallen so that some of the advanced navigation calculators cost under $100. In order to save the navigator time, the machine should be programmable and be able to handle trig functions. If it can't hold the program in memory when you turn it off, you will have to re-program it every time.

Some use programs written on a card. You buy a card with a specific navigation program already written for you and insert it in the calculator. Others are "hard wired" with the program built in.

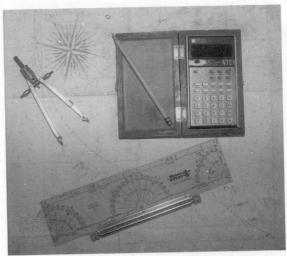

Navigation calculators save the navigator many hours of routine computation. This Tamaya NC-2 has served reliably for over a dozen years.

Even the cheaper calculators can relieve you of time-consuming addition, subtraction, multiplication, and division calculations for problems of speed, time, and distance and fuel consumption. On a higher level, more expensive calculators can do vector problems such as computing true wind speed and direction from apparent wind.

The best navigation calculators can even solve course and distance problems that normally require chart work. For example, by measuring the latitude and longitude of a departure and a waypoint you can arrive at a course and distance rather than having to lay it off from a chart. This is especially useful on ocean crossings. After computing a latitude and longitude for your daily fix and placing it on your plotting sheet, instead of transferring the fix to a large general coverage chart showing your next waypoint a thousand miles away, you simply plug the position into the calculator and it presents your course to steer and distance.

Their greatest time-saving advantage is for the celestial navigator. Most of the advanced nav calculators work directly from a dead reckoning position (DR) rather than from the assumed position (AP) as required by *H.O. 229* and *249*. This saves the drudgery of plotting the DR and the AP only to erase the latter. It also reduces the error involved in plotting long intercepts from an assumed position.

Preprogrammed calculators that do celestial sight reductions generally are one of two types: those with a built-in perpetual almanac and those without. Those with the almanac need no *Nautical Almanac* or sight reduction tables at all, and thus save enormous amounts of time and opportunity for error.

How much time do they save? It takes us about 15 minutes to manually reduce a single sight to an LOP using tables. With the calculator we can do it in about five minutes. Since a navigator's routine requires several sight reductions each day, you can see that a calculator saves hours of manual work.

Good navigation calculators are very reliable. We've had our Tamaya NC-2 for 12 years, and it still computes flawlessly. However you must avoid learning celestial using only the calculator. When the machine gets drowned or the batteries die, you should be able to do the math longhand.

Dutton also offers a word of caution in *Navigation and Piloting*:

It is emphasized that the only safe way to use an electronic calculator for the solution of navigation problems is with a full knowledge and understanding of the basic equations. Blind reliance on programs prepared by other people, or on purchased prerecorded magnetic cards or plug-in modules, can only lead to disaster in emergency situations. Calculators can be a great help, but the only "brain" available to solve the problem is the gray matter in the navigator's skull.

We think this applies to all marine electronics.

CHAPTER 14
WEATHER

Nothing affects the operation of a vessel at sea so radically as does the weather, so any skipper who ventures offshore needs to know as much as possible about how weather develops and how to handle immediate weather conditions. His life, the lives of his crew, and the safety of the vessel depend on his ability to interpret weather information and to draw appropriate conclusions.

Cruising boaters can limit their exposure to bad weather simply by planning to cruise during seasons of benevolent weather, and by moving on as the season changes. Delivery captains can't afford that luxury. In fact, we are asked to move boats during bad weather so often that off-season passagemaking is a large part of our business. Vessel owners who might move their own boats in favorable seasons often will hire a professional captain just during the rough season.

For this reason, the delivery captain must be able to make sound weather judgments. There are certain times when making a certain voyage is close to suicidal, such as going far offshore through known hurricane tracks during the height of hurricane season. If we are to stay alive to deliver yachts in the future, we must know when to say, "No way, Jose!"

John remembers a friend who once had been a seaman aboard a large, passenger-carrying square-rigger. He told a harrowing tale of getting caught in back-to-back hurricanes:

The vessel loaded her paying passengers in a northern Mexican port in mid-July, destination Tahiti. About one week out they were hit by the full fury of a hurricane. They survived, but only barely. Crew and passengers were bailing with buckets, but they suffered so much damage that they had to put out a distress call. A freighter diverted from her route and took them in tow back toward Mexico. The second hurricane ran them down en route, and the freighter had to cast off the tow line and stand by while the square-rigger again fought for her life.

No lives were lost, and they eventually made it back to their port of departure, but the vessel's owners were tied up in litigation for years by the unhappy passengers.

I told my friend, "I think the captain was at fault for leaving port for Tahiti at that time of year. All you have to do is look at pilot charts for July and August to see that the vessel's track to Tahiti crosses many hurricane paths, and the storm frequency is so high then, that it would have been a miracle if they hadn't tangled with a hurricane. Had anyone been killed, it would have been the captain's fault."

"Now wait a minute," he said in a defense of

his former captain. "The owners ordered him to go. If he hadn't gone, he would have lost his job."

This story illustrates the crucial decision that a master must make about weather. This captain would have been better off either to have refused to make the trip and lost his job, or to have tried to convince the owners of the voyage's folly. In the long run, everyone would have been better off to have stayed in port. The owners wouldn't have been involved in expensive litigation with disgruntled passengers and salvagers, and the vessel wouldn't have required expensive repairs.

John has encountered remarkably little bad weather in his career. Much uncomfortable weather mind you, but very little dangerous weather. He attributes this to three things: the formal study of meteorology, his habit of constantly monitoring the weather underway by the best available means, and taking *calculated,* but not unnecessarily high, risks.

Anyone planning to venture offshore for an extended period would benefit from taking a class in general meteorology. The one-semester course John took through a community college was designed for anyone with a general interest in weather. It has proved immeasurably valuable in boating over the years. Check with your local community college. It will pay big dividends.

You should also have a personal library of publications for study, reference and planning purposes. Our choices:

1 *Weather for the Mariner,* by Kotsch. A good overall study of meteorology. Read it and learn.

2 *Planning Guides,* U.S. Hydrographic Office (H.O.) Publications Numbers *140* and *152* and *130.* These are sailing directions planning guides for the North Atlantic, North Pacific and Mediterranean respectively, containing very detailed and extensive meteorological data. Such guides are also available for the Far East, South Pacific, South Atlantic, and the Indian Oceans.

3 *Atlas of Pilot Charts* for specific delivery areas.

4 U.S. Hydrographic Office *Sailing Directions* for specific delivery areas. (Each segment has a regional weather summary.)

5 *Ocean Passages for the World,* published by the British Admiralty Hydrographic Department.

6 *Atlas de Huracanes,* published by the Mexican Hydrographic Office. Available at the Map Center, 2611 University Ave., San Diego, CA 92104. This is a 25-year study of hurricanes in the western Atlantic/Caribbean and eastern North Pacific. Its charts are invaluable and well worth the price. If you read Spanish, its explanations of hurricane formation are very useful.

7 *World Wide Weather Broadcasts.* A listing of times, frequencies and modes of weather available throughout the world for voice, teletype, Morse code, and weatherfax. An absolute must.

8 *A Mariners Guide to Radiofacsimile Weather Charts,* by Dr. Joseph M. Bishop.

9 *World Cruising Routes,* by Jimmy Cornell. An excellent summary of popular yachting itineraries. It lists the best times of year for making passages in popular cruising areas and routing. It takes a necessarily conservative approach and the cruising sailor should follow this valuable advice. The professional mariner often will, with calculated risk and much care, extend the times listed.

WEATHER REPORTS

You must know where to get the most recent weather reports. Always check the weather just before leaving port. This is also important for the casual sailor going out for a day sail on the bay. Underway, listen to or watch the weather at least once a day—in times of bad weather, several times a day.

VHF Radio

Because of VHF's limited range (usually less than 100 miles), its forecasts are necessarily coastal in nature, generally no farther than 250 miles offshore. As you travel along the coast, you must keep changing frequencies to pick up the next VHF weather station.

Station reports are just as important as forecasts, because they let you know what is presently going on around you. Most reporting stations are on land. If they are close to the shoreline, their reports are valuable, but land tends to modify the weather.

In recent years NOAA (the National Oceanic and Atmospheric Administration) has installed a series of automated offshore weather buoys, varying from close inshore to several hundred miles offshore. Their reports are dispensed over VHF and are updated every few hours. They consist of wind direction and strength, swell height and period, and barometric pressure. We listen closely to these station reports.

Let's assume you are running between Astoria, Oregon, and Seattle, Washington. The forecast calls for an approaching front from the Gulf of Alaska with calm winds for the next 18 hours, then wind shifting to southerly at gale force. You have a "window" and you want to get as far north as possible before this bad weather hits. So you head out.

Throughout the day, VHF weather gives shore reports showing calm winds along the coast, and this coincides with your actual conditions underway. Later in the day, the report from the automated weather buoy 300 miles offshore shows the barometer dropping, the wind shifting to southerly and increasing in strength. That verifies the earlier forecast and you know you only have a few more hours to seek shelter.

If your trip is beyond the range of a single VHF weather station, you need to get an overview of the weather along the entire coast. Likewise, when you venture offshore beyond the range of VHF or into foreign waters with no VHF broadcasts, you must resort to other ways of receiving weather information. The best source is marine SSB transmissions on a variety of frequencies listed in *World Wide Marine Weather Broadcasts*.

The best weather stations for offshore waters of the western Atlantic, eastern Pacific, and South Pacific are the USCG stations at Norfolk, Virginia (NMN), San Francisco (NMC), and Honolulu (NMO), respectively. They broadcast for these diverse areas on the same frequencies, but at rotating times as listed in Weather Broadcasts. The Coast Guard uses computer-synthesized voices which may lend some humor to your day, but at least they enunciate the report so slowly and clearly that you can copy it easily. Each USCG station has its own format, so after listening to the station a few times, you will discover what information is given when and how. In fringe areas with poor reception, you may wish to tape record the broadcast so you can replay it if you aren't sure you got it all the first time.

The FCC requires Public Correspondence Stations such as WOM Miami, WOO New York, and KMI San Francisco to give weather reports several times a day on several frequencies as a public service. Unfortunately, these reports are given at a much more rapid speed than are the U.S.C.G. reports. As a result they are sometimes difficult to copy. Fortunately, they are

Pat checks the latest incoming weatherfax picture. "Fax" is a marvelous tool, but having one on board does not automatically guarantee you will avoid bad weather.

broadcast each day at the same time as the radio traffic list. This is a roll call of all vessels that have shore-to-ship phone calls waiting for them with the offshore radio operator. If someone wants to get in touch with you at sea (such as an owner who wants to know where his boat is), tell them you'll be standing by for the traffic list at a specific hour every day. Thus the weather report becomes a daily routine along with a communication schedule. Pat calls KMI, WOO or Whiskey-Oscar-Mike to re-

quest a repeat of the last weather broadcast, whenever other ship traffic delays it past her watch schedule.

WeatherFax

Onboard weatherfax, the electronic miracle of receiving printed weather charts and satellite pictures, has become the rule among well-equipped boats, rather than the exception. Fax is becoming more common on even the smaller yachts. As with most items in the elec-

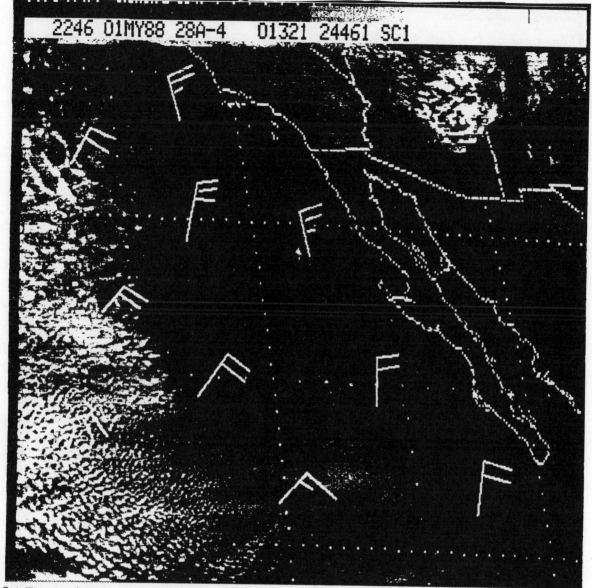

`2246 01MY88 28A-4    01321 24461 SC1`

Satellites can focus on the full disk of the earth or on specific areas such as this 1000-mile stretch between Pt. Conception and Cabo San Lucas. This picture was down-linked from a satellite to NWS, then retransmitted and received on a shipboard weatherfax printer.

tronic revolution, prices and sizes are coming down to within range of even cruising boats on a tight budget.

Weatherfax is the best available onboard tool for weather reporting and forecasting. It gives you the big picture, graphically, of high- and low-pressure zones, wind patterns and strengths on the surface and at upper levels, and satellite photos of cloud cover.

Miraculous as it is, weatherfax's usefulness

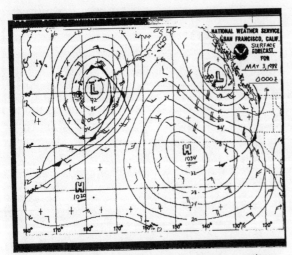

The National Weather Service broadcasts weather charts via weatherfax. These charts give mariners the "big picture," so we can draw our own forecasts and plan accordingly. Some NWS charts require study and experience to read correctly.

is limited by the amount of meteorological knowledge of the person interpreting its charts. We know many professional captains who can't tell the difference between charts of upper-level winds and those of surface conditions, or who don't know how to tune in particular charts they need. Therefore we recommend that you read and study John Alden's *Weather Facsimile*.

Having one of these miracle machines on board doesn't ensure that you are immune to all bad weather. Even if you can see storms approaching, there are certain regions where you can't operate without danger during seasons of foul weather.

For example, the owner of a large, expensive motor yacht called us to deliver it from the Caribbean to the U.S. West Coast in August and September. This meant we'd have to traverse the hurricane belts of two oceans during the peak hurricane season in each ocean. John said, "Sorry sir, you have a fine boat for the trip, except it's the wrong season. I fear for my life."

His reply was, "Young man, haven't you ever heard of Weatherfax?" His implication was that having one on board would simply steer us around any hurricanes, or make us invisible, or beam us out of danger, million-dollar yacht and all.

One of the major problems that no amount of weather savvy or machinery can help with is that some areas are veritable seed beds for hurricane formation—that is, tropical depressions that gave birth to full-blown hurricanes actually form right on top of your head. As sophisticated as satellite imagery is, it still can't instantaneously determine which cloudy patches are generating into depressions and which will remain no more dangerous than bands of squalls and intense thunderstorms. They sometimes take a day or two to make up their minds.

Several times, we've had tropical depressions form right over our heads, only to discover them reported on the fax 36 hours later, after we'd already been pasted. If luck exists, it has a lot to do with avoiding bad weather, but so does wisdom.

Well, that disgruntled boat owner eventually found someone else to deliver his boat during hurricane season, and although that captain was a habitual risk taker, he made it safely. That time. Less than a year later, however, the captain's short career ended in disaster when he drove a multi-million dollar yacht on the rocks.

Two-Way Radio

In many corners of the globe, weather reporting is very sparse, because there are almost no reporting stations. Weather reports are made from satellite pictures and computer-generated models. Actual conditions may vary greatly from the report. It is invaluable to be able to contact other vessels that will give on-site weather reports within a several-hundred-mile radius.

For instance, on the Pacific coast of Baja,

vessels equipped with Marine SSB often leave their sets on Channel 12-A (12.4292 MHz). Vessels underway along the 750-mile-long peninsula exchange weather reports and then report to their base stations in Southern California. By monitoring 12-A around midmorning you can get a very accurate picture of the weather along this rough stretch of coast.

In some very remote areas, ham radio becomes the only means of getting the weather. The South Pacific is a good example. Ham radio nets invite ham-equipped boats to check in with weather reports. Even if you don't have a ham license, just listening in on these nets will give you valuable information. (See the section on ham radio nets in Chapter 15, pages 161–163.)

TV and Newspapers

If you don't have weatherfax, you can track the weather while in port by watching TV weather and by clipping weather charts in the newspaper. This way you'll know when or when not to leave port and what to expect for the next few hours when you get out there.

Reporting quality varies enormously. While local TV often offers nothing more detailed than yesterday's temperature and precipitation, most fishing and boating communities have locally produced weather reports on TV and radio that are quite sophisticated.

New Bedford, Massachusetts, is a prime example. It's been a fishing port since colonial days, and it has a 24-hour cable TV channel devoted to wonderfully detailed weather reporting for the fishing fleet.

The best TV weather reporting we've ever seen was in Eureka, California, where weather conditions are generally blustery, changeable and plain lousy. The entire local economy is based on fishing, agriculture, and logging, all highly dependent on weather.

All big-city and national newspapers give synoptic charts, satellite pictures, and reprints of the coastal and offshore National Weather Service (NWS) weather reports. Most have brief regional forecasts, too, but they are frequently limited to onshore or the coastal margin.

For a personalized forecast, you can call on a private company like Weather Services Corporation. They use European, Japanese and U.S. weather satellite data plus historic records to come up with their analyses and 48-hour forecasts pertaining to your exact route and days of travel. Contact can be made just prior to departure, and once at sea, via SSB ship-to-shore voice links. With any ASCII computer, you can receive onboard charts of worldwide weather. This type of service is commonly used by hot-air balloonists and long-distance racers, and it's excellent for yacht deliveries outside U.S. waters.

PLANNING AND TACTICS: A CASE STUDY

The tale we're about to relate is of one of those borderline deliveries we're frequently asked to make. From our experience, we hope you'll absorb lessons in the planning stage that analyzes the weather prognosis; the decision-making process of whether to accept the trip or not; weather-monitoring methods underway; the occurrences of freak weather; and finally, the traditional and nontraditional tactics of tropical storm avoidance.

In the middle of July, an owner contacted us about a trans-Atlantic passage to the Mediterranean. He wanted us to deliver a motorsailer from Mystic Seaport, Connecticut, to Mallorca, Spain, departing around August 1. This is late in the season, as August 15 is generally considered the very latest cutoff date for making a west-to-east crossing, but we checked all our planning publications and charts.

Satellites are a tremendous aid in gathering world-wide weather information, and in disseminating it instantly to ships at sea. On this day (August 7, 1980) Hurricane Allen is making a bee line for the Texas coast. In the Pacific, Hurricane Howard heads for the Mexican coast. (Photo courtesy of the National Weather Service, San Diego.)

Figure 14-1, *H.O. 140* for August, shows the average isobars (lines of equal barometric pressure) around the North Atlantic High to the southwest of the Azores. The general flow across the Atlantic is clockwise around this high, making the wind mostly from the southwest to west in the first half, shifting to northerly as you approach Europe. It looked like a favorable reach the whole way.

Figure 14-2 is an inset from the Defense Mapping Agency *Pilot Chart* for the month of August. The tracks in the lower right hand corner (T) are the average storm tracks for hurricanes. The probability of gales formed by tropical weather was greatest close along shore, since the storm track generally followed the warm path of the Gulf Stream. The inset does carry this warning: "These tracks

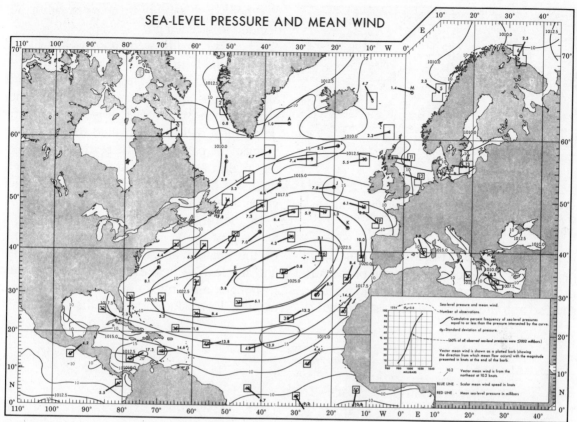

Figure 14-1. Weather map for the North Atlantic, August, shows the flow of air moving clockwise around the Atlantic high.

represent averages. Movements of individual systems may vary widely." The numbers in each 5-degree square show the average percentage of ship reports in which winds of at least Force 8 have been reported. There are 1's close to shore, but they drop to zero in the middle. Not a bad picture, statistically speaking.

As shown in Figure 14-3, we would be crossing the Gulf Stream fairly close to shore and end up south of it as it swings to the northeast. Since the vast majority of these storms are formed in the Caribbean, we would have plenty of time to track them, and if all was clear, we would be able to get well out into the Atlantic before a new one could form. Once we made it clear of the coast, the

probability of gales in the central Atlantic was zero, according to the chart, and the rest of the trip posed no major problems.

The boat itself was the other major consideration in deciding whether to do the trip. *Bird of Passage* was a 50-foot, double-ended, ketch-rigged, pilothouse motorsailer. A noteworthy vessel, she had been conceived by a former commodore of the New York Yacht Club, designed by Sparkman and Stephens, and was featured in Robert Beebe's book, *Voyaging Under Power*. She was a very stout vessel that had already proven herself during two Atlantic crossings in high latitudes, and by cruising near Ireland, Norway, and the Baltic.

Particularly important was the fact that she could easily make eight knots under power, at

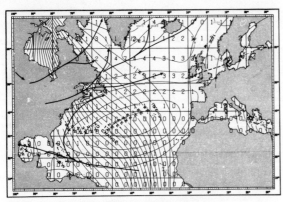

Figure 14-2. North Atlantic Pilot Chart for the month of August shows hurricane tracks and incidence of gale-force winds.

least to the Azores. This would enable us to motor clear of the coast to get out of the hurricane track. If we did encounter bad weather, she had a stout rig that could be shortened to

give her good stability in heavy weather. We decided to give it a go.

When we finally went aboard her in the boatyard in Mystic, it was obvious much more time was needed to get her ready for the Med. Modifications were being made to suit her charterers in Mallorca. The work had to be done, yet it had to be finished in time for us to make the passage and be ready for the charter in Europe. The schedule was extremely tight. We began to worry about the weather cutoff date of August 15.

By the time the *Bird* was ready to leave, it was August 14. We'd been keeping a close eye on the weather, and when we left it was with an "all clear"—meaning no tropical weather forming at all. Only 24 hours out, however, a tropical depression formed in the Gulf Stream

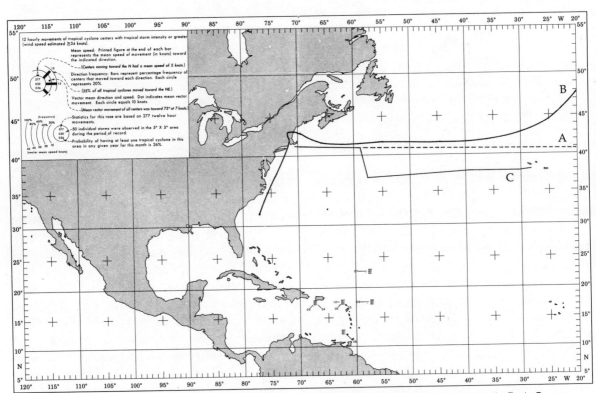

Figure 14-3. Track of *Bird of Passage*. Path A was our planned route; Path B, the storm's track; Path C, our actual route.

just off Savannah, Georgia. This was an oddity in itself, since most storms form well south of there. We continued on our course due east.

According to the *Pilot Chart,* the storm would most likely move north and then slam into the coast, but we would be well out into the Atlantic by then, out with all those "zeroes." Sure enough, the storm quickly formed into Hurricane Charlie and true to form, it moved north and slammed into Cape Cod.

By then we were 600 miles into the Atlantic. The night Hurricane Charlie hit Cape Cod, it was quickly down-graded to no storm at all. We both went off watch thinking that was the end of it.

When we got the next morning's weatherfax chart from Halifax, Nova Scotia, we learned that the storm had taken a radical turn to the east, and had moved back out to sea. It was intensifying and was headed our way. It was technically no longer called a hurricane, but rather a massive and very strong "extra-tropical cyclone."

No matter what it was called, we had to get out of its way. With its present course and speed, it would overtake us in about three days. We had intended to cross the Atlantic at latitude 42° North to take advantage of stronger favorable winds and then gradually curve south towards Gibraltar about due north of the Azores.

What were we to do now?

Tropical Storm Avoidance

The *American Practical Navigator,* commonly known as Bowditch, gives the best advice on how to avoid tropical storms. In the following explanation, the directions refer to the Northern Hemisphere. In the Southern Hemisphere, directions are exactly opposite.

First, steer a course to position the boat in the storm's *navigable semicircle,* as shown in Figure 14-4. The other side of the storm circle

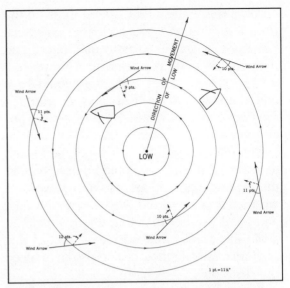

Figure 14-4. If caught offshore when a tropical storm hits, the skipper should maneuver to avoid the storm center.

is more dangerous, because the wind speed is augmented by the forward motion of the storm, and hence it is known as the *dangerous semicircle.* The wind and sea will carry the vessel right into the storm's path.

When the boat is facing into the wind, the storm's low-pressure center will be to starboard in the Northern Hemisphere and somewhat to the rear. A plot of successive positions of the storm center will show you the semicircle in which the vessel is located.

Here's a general rule of thumb for safety: Mariners in the dangerous semicircle should put the wind on their starboard bow and make all speed away from the storm center. Those in the navigable semicircle should put the wind on their starboard quarter and, again, head away quickly.

Do not try to pass ahead of the storm center if there is any other action possible. If you must heave to in a sailing vessel in the dangerous semicircle, try to do so on the starboard tack.

All of this made a lot of sense to us on the *Bird.* Even though it was no longer an official hurricane, it was circular in nature and had many of the same characteristics. However if we had followed this tactic, we would have ended up way too far north, and according to the *Pilot Chart,* we'd have been in iceberg territory.

The *Pilot Chart* told us if we dipped south to avoid the storm, we should be heading into the Atlantic high and get into more favorable weather. And so we did. We had enough time and good weather to get far enough south to avoid the worst of the weather. The fact that *Bird* was a strong motorsailer also influenced our decision.

We would not have been able to head southeast on a regular sailboat, because it was taking us into a head wind and we wouldn't have had the power to punch into it.

As the storm overtook us, we started off with east winds building from 17 to 21 knots, or Force 5. We were uncomfortable bashing into it, but we were just glad to be getting south of the storm track. We battened everything down in preparation for bad weather, and put on the storm shutters.

The storm kept building in intensity and size and continuing due east on a steady track at Latitude 42°North. As we monitored the radio constantly, we learned that all commercial shipping in the North Atlantic was diverting to south of the storm track.

The wind slowly shifted from the east in a clockwise direction. When we were at 37° North (300 miles south of the storm center), the wind finally came around to the southwest and built to gale force.

At this point we had intended to heave to, simply park the boat on as comfortable a heading as possible, let the storm rage on around us until it passed, and then get underway again. Much to our surprise, the *Bird*

simply wouldn't heave to. Try as we might, we merely succeeded in blowing out the mizzen sail, and having the autopilot succumb to the overpowering seas.

Then we thought we would run off with it on a broad reach. This would keep us at least parallel to the storm's path, not closer to it. But our forward speed in the same direction meant we'd remain under its fury longer. But then again, we'd be headed straight at our destination. At this point, we had few other choices.

On a broad reach with reduced, sail we still made four knots. Though the motion was uncomfortable it was not dangerous. There wasn't a spare second to step away from the wheel, of course, or we would have risked broaching. The wind built from Force 8 (34–40 knots) to Force 9 (41–47 knots), accompanied by lead-gray skies and heavy rain squalls. We were surfing down awesome 20-foot seas. As the storm center passed closest to us, it was 20 millibars lower than when, as Hurricane Charlie, it had slammed into Cape Cod.

It was here in mid-Atlantic that we became fans of canoe-sterned vessels. The *Bird* rode well in these conditions, which continued for six long days and nights. Her tall canoe stern gracefully parted a thousand, monstrous snarling seas that passed under us. We're sure that a flat-transom vessel encountering those overtaking seas would have been shoved around far more than we were, which would have increased the likelihood of broaching.

We were not alone out there. Occasionally we would see ships on the radar screen. Visibility was reduced to zero at times by blowing spray and by rain, but still we would strain to see these ships. Even at five miles, it was impossible to see them in the boiling seas. Only when both of us happened to be on top of an exceptionally large wave could we see them. Even 400-foot ships looked like toy boats, plunging up and down at unbelievably steep angles. We knew they were drier than we were, but with their bridge decks so high above the tossing seas, it didn't look like they were having any more fun than we were.

By the seventh day, the wind began to subside until we were in totally flat seas with zero wind. We motored the rest of the way on into the port of Horta in the Azores to refuel.

The storm had wreaked havoc on the islands and washed out many roads clinging to the sides of the steep cliffs. Another vessel arrived the next day. She had crossed in the same direction as we had, but had stayed at 42°North instead of dropping south as we did. Her crew encountered Force 11 conditions (56–63 knots) when the storm passed over them.

On the local news we heard that Charlie smashed into Ireland, causing great damage and went into their history books as one of the worst storms ever at that time of year. Some trips are like that: tough going every inch of the way.

After licking our wounds in the Azores, we took off for Gibraltar and finally Mallorca. We had light easterlies again, building to gale force on the approach to Gibraltar. The wind dropped but did not shift in the straits. It stayed a *levanter* (the local name for east wind) and consequently blew on the nose all the way to Mallorca.

We hope this weather case study has shown you the planning stages of a trip, how tactics develop during heavy weather, and how you have to be flexible enough to not always go by the book.

CHAPTER 15
RADIO COMMUNICATION

In emergencies, radio is a boat crew's vital link to shore and to other boats. It's foolish to go to sea without radio capability to reach help.

In the Azores we met a liveaboard family who'd sailed there non-stop from South Africa, without a radio. The traditionalist skipper told us, "I go to sea to get away from it all. I don't like listening to the chatter on the radio, and I don't want people to worry about me if they don't hear from me."

If you don't want to listen to the radio, turn it off. Having a radio available for emergencies is one of those basic responsibilities a captain has for his crew, and that a parent has for his family. Folks ashore are going to have concern for loved ones cruising off the edge of the Earth whether they hear from you or not. But the amount of time they actually worry will be far less if they hear from you on a loose schedule, like once a month or so. Shunning radio doesn't keep anyone from worrying about you. And everyone who's ever drifted in a life raft has wished they had a radio.

Of course we go to sea as self-sufficiently as possible, but situations can develop beyond our control. For this reason, we take our own VHF, SSB and ham radios along on deliveries if the vessel doesn't already have them. We maintain regular radio schedules, so that someone always knows approximately where we are. If they don't hear from us, they know where to ask around. Maybe we were unable to reach them and left messages elsewhere. If no one has heard from us, maybe we had radio trouble. Only after a few more days do they begin to worry. After awhile they'll contact the Coast Guard.

To keep a regular schedule requires a certain amount of discipline, depending on how often you set up your contact schedules. If you get lazy or just forget, people will worry unnecessarily.

If the radio quits, they'll wonder what's up until you fix it and get back on the air. Modern solid-state radios are very reliable, but they're known to blow a fuse from time to time. Fuses are easily replaced. If you lose your antenna or tuner, it can be jury-rigged or bypassed with simple knowledge and common tools on board. Each year, there are fewer and fewer reasons to shun radio.

VHF

VHF (very-high-frequency) radio is the everyday work-horse in coastal waters. It is a form of line-of-sight communications, meaning that if you are over the horizon from the station you are calling, or if there's an obstruction like a high island between you, then you cannot communicate. VHF either works well or it doesn't work at all. When two talking stations are within range of one another, the reception is clear. As they move over the horizon it quickly fades to nothing.

Besides ship-to-ship communication, VHF is useful for ship-to-shore contacts. "Marine Operator" is a system of public correspondence companies that manage certain VHF frequencies, allowing ships at sea to link into the telephone system on shore, for a price of course. The National Weather Service also broadcasts its area forecasts over certain VHF frequencies. The Coast Guard monitors and uses VHF channels for emergency communication.

A VHF operator's license is very easy to get. All you have to do is fill out a simple form, send it to the FCC, and they send you a license.

For a delivery or pleasure cruise within coastal U.S. waters, within VHF range (60–80 miles offshore), a vessel equipped only with VHF radio gear is adequately covered.

Yacht delivery captains often must deliver brand-new boats that aren't yet fully commissioned and have no radio on board. For such cases we take along two of our own hand-held VHF radios, which are adequate as long as we're not too far offshore. You must realize that a hand-held VHF only operates on 3–5 watts of power (as opposed to the 25 watts of a built-in set), and that the tiny 'rubber ducky' antenna is no match for a masthead antenna.

We normally take our hand-helds on all deliveries, since they can back up the ship's own radio in an emergency. Mainly, they serve as time-saving portable units, allowing crewmembers ashore to communicate with the boat.

SSB

Marine Single Sideband (SSB) is termed high-frequency (HF) radio, and is the workhorse for long-range communications up to several thousand miles. Like VHF, SSB also designates frequencies or channels for ship-

to-ship calls and Coast Guard frequencies for emergencies and weather.

Reception over SSB can vary from strong and readable voice signals to "I know that's him but I can't understand what he's saying."

The high-seas operator and other public correspondence stations on SSB also tie boats to the shoreside phone system, but it is more expensive than VHF, about $5 per minute with a three-minute minimum. Our phone bills for business calls after a long trip are sometimes astronomical. But it beats no communication at all.

SSB is not cheap. Complete installations begin at about $3,000. The advantage is long-range capability with idiotproof technology. Budget permitting, however, SSB should be on board any long-distance cruising boat.

Getting the license to operate on SSB (Marine Radio Operator Permit) is slightly more involved than getting one for VHF, but the process is as simple as the SSB radios are to operate. The short test given by the FCC covers the rules of radio/telephone procedure. (If such testing were an FCC requirement for VHF operators, much of the rude, improper usage you hear on summer weekends would be eliminated.)

SSB ship-to-ship channels can get chaotic since there are no controls. Channel 12A is a good example, because it is used for ship-to-ship calls by yachts and commercial vessels along the entire Pacific Coast and Mexico. In spite of FCC rules, few operators wait their turn, and instead they start transmitting on top of others. Whoever has the strongest signal wins.

AMATEUR RADIO

Amateur radio, also called ham radio, is more widely used among the cruising fraternity than is marine SSB, because ham is much less expensive to buy and install. A cruising boat can be set up with an efficient ham rig for less than $1,000. Making marine SSB "idiotproof" requires an expensive automatic antenna tuner, but ham rigs are tunable with inexpensive manual equipment. While ham is more complicated to operate, it is more versatile.

The best setup is an FCC-licensed marine SSB radio that combines both ham and marine frequencies. Such radios are expensive, and the cheaper models are awkward to use on the ham mode. The costlier models are easy to use in both modes. Many cruising boats are equipped solely with ham radio as their only means of long-range communication, even though their owners may not have a ham operators license. Monitoring is completely legal, and the many weather broadcasts are a safety feature to long-range cruisers. Then, if an emergency arises, transmitting for help on the ham bands is permissible, license or no license.

The number of legally licensed operators is on the increase. License holders who were diligent enough to do their homework enjoy the full benefits of two-way communication.

What makes ham radio so useful for yacht deliveries and cruisers alike are the controlled frequencies run by the maritime mobile networks.

A maritime mobile net is a network of amateur radio operators who meet on a regular schedule on a given frequency. Their specific purpose is to aid "maritime mobiles"—boat-based stations underway. Each session of a "net" has one person designated as the "net control," who moderates the flow of calls with the help of several "net assistants." The net controller opens the net by calling for all other operators who wish to speak to "check in" with the net, and he then determines in what order each will talk. This structure elim-

This directional-beam ham antenna atop Ft. Loma in San Diego operates a powerful relay station on the Maritime Mobile Net (14.313).

inates tremendous confusion. The net control and assistants are usually land-based stations with powerful amplifiers and directional antennas. They can more easily pick up the maritime mobiles (MMs) whose signals are necessarily weaker because of the limited power supplies available on board and less efficient antennas.

Radio nets provide clear calling frequencies on the otherwise crowded ham bands in two ways. First, because the control stations are so strong, they can overpower interfering stations. Second, non-participating hams stay clear of these well-known, time-honored net frequencies during their regularly scheduled times.

Hundreds of regular hams just monitor the maritime nets, even if they never check in, because the service such nets provide to ships at sea and in exotic, remote corners of the globe is valued and famed worldwide. It's one of the most exciting events in the day of a ham operator.

This clear frequency allows boats to call for other boats or shore-based stations. Once contact is made and they link, they then shift off to another frequency to begin their conversation, known as traffic.

This is much the same way you use Channel 16 on VHF radio, the difference being the controller. Some nets allow you to pass short messages directly on the net, making it unnecessary to shift off to crowded frequencies where it is sometimes difficult for weak stations to make contact.

The designated assistant net controllers are scattered as evenly as possible around a large geographical area, extending the umbrella coverage of the net. When two stations can't hear each other well enough due to poor propagation they often are able to relay their messages through whichever assistant net control they can hear best.

Ham radio's most important use is for emergencies. When a vessel in distress sends a Mayday over the ham band, chances are excellent that someone will hear him somewhere in the world. Usually, many will hear in several places. All other radio operators will yield their conversations in order to give the Mayday vessel a clear frequency.

Hams have been trained to do this and will often help the distressed yachtsman in any manner they can—including linking him by telephone directly to the Coast Guard. The net controls of the various maritime mobile nets are more experienced in handling emergencies than you would like to think.

Medical emergencies arise thousands of miles out to sea or in remote anchorages far from medical help, but the maritime nets have instant contacts with many doctors and direct telephone links with hospitals. For instance, the Long Beach (California) Hospital routinely accepts long-distance collect calls from hams who are relaying details of a medical emergency. Within minutes, a professional medical diagnosis and step-by-step advice can be received aboard a small boat in mid-ocean. Many lives have been saved by this feature of ham radio.

What initially got John interested in ham radio was its usefulness in gathering weather information. Current weather information for less populated corners of Oceania is pitifully sketchy, broadcast mainly via U.S. Coast Guard stations in the vicinity, if there are any. Their data originate with the National Weather Service, whose principal source is satellite pictures. While this information is useful, it covers such a large area with so few reporting stations that local conditions may vary greatly from the forecast.

Fortunately, some maritime mobile nets issue their own weather forecasts for specific areas. These forecasts are a compilation of data from commercial weather broadcasts plus actual on-sight weather reports from many MM stations. As they check into the net from their various and scattered locations, each boat makes a detailed report of the current weather conditions in its vicinity.

Weather gathering via radio has become an important scene in the daily life of yacht delivery and passagemaking. We either begin the watchday with a steaming hot mug of coffee, or take a break from other tasks to huddle around the radio to see what the weather has in store.

Maritime mobile nets also aid in the exchange of cruising information between boats. Any participant can ask the net for information about his next port, its clearance procedures, where to anchor, etc. Skippers who check in constitute many eyes, ears, and mouths, scattered over thousands of miles and this creates a vast information resource. They have even found stolen boats.

Licensed operators are able to keep in contact with family and friends via free phone patches courtesy of amateur operators in their local calling zones. This is all legal in the U.S. as long as the caller does not discuss business. The nets enhance this ability to link with the phone lines by providing a forum for connecting shore stations with phone patch capabilities to vessels wishing that service. Ham operators on both ends of phone patches are conscientious and self-policing about the abuse of this non-business rule for fear that the FCC will take the privilege away.

MAJOR AMATEUR RADIO MARITIME MOBILE NETS

Amateur radio nets are created informally, and they come and go with the needs of the participants, though some of them have been on the air for many years. There are dozens of maritime mobile nets scattered around the world. They pick times and frequencies that cover a geographical area of interest to particular groups. The following is a list by frequency band of some of the primary maritime mobile nets, including descriptions of the areas they cover and how they operate.

20 METERS
(14.175–14.350 MHz)

Of all the frequency bands allotted by the FCC to amateur radio, the 20-meter band is best for all-around propagation. It is also the most crowded. Twenty-meters has good propagation for most boat radio installations for three to four thousand miles during daytime hours and, depending on the sunspot cycle, into the early evening hours. It is normally dead during the night.

MARITIME MOBILE SERVICE NET
(14.313 MHz)

This is the largest and most widely used of them all. The net operates 24 hours a day around the world, with the net controls shifting west with the sun, as the net fades out in the darkened portions of the world. As it shifts it also calls itself by different names: the Coast Guard Net, Intercon Net, Seafarers Net, etc.

Its net controls are very adept at handling emergencies. They have close ties to the Coast Guard and hospitals for medical emergencies. "Break break" is a special emergency term used on the nets. Any station with an emergency, calling these two words, will get priority and immediate attention. We have had cause to use this term and got an immediate response with the frequency cleared of all other traffic.

Because of the large number of hams listening to 14.313 MHz all over the world (particularly in the U.S.), anyone shouting "Break break" into the mike on this frequency, even with low batteries, has a very good chance of being heard. For this reason, in the Western Hemisphere we leave our radio on this frequency all day, so that the set is ready for anyone to pick up the mike and shout for help.

This net is the most businesslike of all, with very little idle chitchat between stations. The net control calls for check-ins while slowly swinging his beam antenna in a complete circle, listing them in order, giving priority to maritime mobiles, and then having them call their "traffic." Traffic means what or whom they are looking for, be it a certain station or a phone patch into a particular location.

The most useful part of this net in the Pacific begins at 0430 Zulu (GMT). The net control usually centers in Hawaii with net relays in Alaska, the continental U.S., Guam, and New Zealand, virtually covering the Pacific Ocean. As with many of these nets, the control starts with a round-robin call among the net relays for any emergency traffic. After the controller and each of his relays ask if there are any emergencies, they listen for a few seconds to provide a clear frequency for any weak stations. The net control then calls for previously checked-in vessels that are underway. The vessels respond with information presented in the following format.

1 Latitude and longitude.

2 Course and speed.

3 Wind direction, speed, swell height and di-

rection, percentage of cloud cover and barometric pressure.

4 Any requests of the net.

The net control plots their positions and tracks their progress on voyages between ports in the vast regions of the Pacific.

With weather reporting so scanty in the Pacific, these reports, combined with regular Coast Guard weather broadcasts, give the best weather information available in the Pacific.

UNITED KINGDOM NET
(14.303 MHz at 0800 and 1800 GMT)

The U.K. net airs once in the morning and once in the evening with good propagation to Europe from the mid-Atlantic through the Mediterranean. Vessels underway check in with weather reports. This net also dispenses weather for the offshore and coastal waters of the eastern Atlantic and for the western Med. We've found this broadcast very useful, since Europe does not have commercial voice broadcasts of offshore weather. Unless you have weather facsimile or can copy Morse code at 20 words per minute, this U.K. net is your only weather information source in the area.

MAÑANA NET
(14.342 MHz at 1900 GMT)

This is the foremost ham net for the cruising fleet in Mexico because it covers the entire west coasts of Mexico and the U.S. Powerful net control stations and relays are located in San Diego, Seattle, and Albuquerque.

15 METERS
(21.225–21.450 MHz)

You can use 15 meters during daylight hours, when it offers even longer range communication than 20 meters, is less crowded and has less atmospheric noise. However, it fades out completely at night and didn't work at all during the depths of the last 11-year sun spot cycle. This constantly fluctuating cycle regulates the quality of radio propagation all over the earth. Fortunately, propagation began improving in 1987.

PACIFIC MARITIME MOBILE NET
(21.404 MHz at 2230 GMT)

This net centers in Hawaii with reasonable propagation throughout the Pacific basin and rim. Amazingly, we have even been able to check in with this net in the Caribbean and along the U.S. East Coast. As an example of how far you can talk on 15 meters, we once made a phone patch to friends in Hawaii from a boat at sea near the Virgin Islands by using another ham on the island of Oahu. All for free!

HALO NET
(21.390 MHz at 2100 GMT)

This net is run by and oriented toward missionaries, mostly in South America and Africa, to share logistical information between missions of various religions, and to talk with their families back in the continental U.S. They don't do business over the air, so don't be afraid they'll try to convert you. And because of its broad geographical range and loose structure, this net is often used by maritime mobiles. The Halo net has a designated controller for about an hour each day, around 2100 GMT, so many stations use 21.390 MHz for a clear calling frequency throughout the day, switching off to other frequencies to converse.

40 METERS
(7.225–7.300 MHz lower sideband)

The 40-meter band has a limited daytime range, but it builds to several thousand miles at night. Since these nets operate at a time of day when their range is about 1,000 miles, they have a more regionalized focus. Participants are often close friends and so generate a relaxed, chatty atmosphere. These nets are excellent for localized weather and regional information.

CALIFORNIA BAJA NET
(7.2385 MHz at 0800 Pacific Standard or Daylight Time, lower sideband)

The net control is in Southern California with relay stations as far south as Guaymas, Mexico. Because of the frequency and the time of day, its range is what its name implies, California and Baja. This net's most useful feature is the weather forecast at 0815, which is the most complete and accurate weather information available to boaters in Mexico.

WATERWAY NET
(7.268 MHz at 0800 Eastern Standard or Daylight Time)

This net covers the entire eastern seaboard, Gulf Coast to Maine, Cozumel to the Bahamas. On it, vessels underway give weather reports and shore stations relay Coast Guard weather reports. It also allows vessels to file their float plans, after which the net controller checks their daily progress until safe arrival in port. Though the net runs for about an hour on each side of 0800, many stations leave their sets on this frequency throughout the day.

GUARDING EMERGENCY FREQUENCIES

Several emergencies at sea have taught us the value of leaving a high frequency (HF) radio tuned in to a well-used frequency. We pick a frequency appropriate to the time of day and our distance from the transmitting station. We leave the volume turned down so we don't have to listen to the chatter, but we leave it in the "standby" position. In case of emergency, all anyone onboard has to do is turn the volume up and start talking.

In the offshore waters of the eastern Pacific and the western half of the Atlantic, we leave the radio on 14.313 MHz for the Maritime Mobile Net. Our rationale is that there are so many radio operators monitoring this net and scattered over a wide area, that our chances of anyone hearing us are greater than on the Coast Guard frequencies.

At night we generally leave the set on 8765.4 MHz, a Coast Guard frequency, because there are no nighttime maritime mobile nets on the lower frequencies needed for nighttime propagation. John learned this the hard way. He recalls:

We were delivering a 90-foot trawler to Hawaii from San Diego. At 0330 on the third night out, the high-water bilge alarm went off. My watch partner ran into the engine room to check it out, and phoned the bridge to tell me that water was coming in quickly from the port side. We started up the emergency bilge pump and called all hands. Mike, who worked on the boat full time, ran into the engine room that he knew so well. He called to the bridge to say that we had broken a stabilizer and that the shaft had dropped out and we had a 2-inch hole in the bottom of the boat.

I decided it was time to call the Coast Guard. I didn't want to put out a Mayday, but I did want them to know we were having serious trouble, and to know our position and status while we worked on our problem. I could talk on the radio and still watch what was going on in the engine room on the closed-circuit television. The water was so high down there that as the ship rolled, seawater reached the belts on the engine and splashed water all over the engine room. If the water got much higher we would lose our engines, then eventually our battery power and ability to transmit on the radio.

I had left the radio on 14.313 MHz during the night because earlier I had been making a phone patch home. It was a new model of radio to me, and since it was early into the trip

I wasn't all that familiar with all its functions. I knew no one would hear me on 14.313 MHz at that time of night. Because I didn't know by memory the Coast Guard frequency, I would have had to look it up in the book. So I plugged in a KMI frequency (San Francisco's ship-to-shore station) that I knew would work. Within seconds I got KMI who immediately patched me through on the telephone to the Coast Guard Search and Rescue in San Francisco.

We were very lucky. There have been incidents of yachts sinking within minutes of striking submerged objects in mid-ocean. In such a case, we would have sunk long before we could look up a frequency, tune up the radio, and then transmit our distress and position.

However, our condition was shaky. We needed to cap the hole, but it was located awkwardly beneath the ship's stabilizer motor and electronics. We had a ready-made cap to fit over the hole, but there was only a tiny space to get at it from the side, and the tremendous amount of water gushing in under pressure made working conditions worse. Our pumps were slowly losing ground.

We knew we wouldn't sink because the engine room was a watertight compartment; once the water level got to the floor of the watertight door, we would close it off. We would continue to float, but we would have no propulsion or electricity and would be condemned to drift around helplessly 600 miles from land.

We had five crewmembers. Two continued to work in the engine room, one served as a runner to communicate between the bridge and engine room, and the other helped me to prepare to abandon ship. We didn't think it would come to that, but we got out the lifejackets, made sure the life rafts were ready to launch, and prepared EPIRBs and other survival gear to go into the raft with us. The Coast Guard had diverted a merchant ship about 200 miles away toward our position and was preparing to launch an aircraft.

After our initial contact on KMI, and when we knew we weren't going to sink immediately, we shifted to 4428.7, the Coast Guard frequency, and maintained direct radio contact rather than through the KMI phone link.

After an hour of touch-and-go, Mike managed to get the cap in place and the water pumped out. The Coast Guard canceled their aircraft launch and ship diversion but maintained contact with us over the next few hours, until it was apparent we were back to normal.

The crew did their job very professionally throughout the emergency; no one freaked out and they all remained calm. All we lost was an air-conditioning pump that drowned from saltwater. I learned my lesson and have since left the radio on Coast Guard frequencies at night.

GETTING A HAM RADIO LICENSE

Obtaining an amateur radio license does not require great intelligence, but you need the desire and some self-discipline. Amateur radio is an important tool to have both for cruising and for delivering yachts. It takes a certain amount of self-discipline to set aside time to study for the ham license.

The first two grades of ham license are Novice and Technician. They are of little value to the mariner as operators with these classes of license are not permitted to operate on maritime mobile nets.

The General Class license is the much-sought-after entry level into voice communication on the Maritime Mobile frequencies.

For most, the Morse code requirement of 13 words per minute is the biggest stumbling block in obtaining a General Class license. However, the need to know code is very defendable because of its use in emergencies.

Morse code transmits more clearly and over greater distances than does voice. If the ship's batteries are not kept completely charged during voice transmission, the voice becomes garbled. Morse code continues to transmit, albeit progressively weaker, until the batteries are completely exhausted. Anyone who knows code can also send and receive flashing light signals. The ability to receive and send Morse code by radio and light has saved many lives.

The most readily available method of learning code is to listen to Gordon West's prepared cassette tapes, which you can buy at Radio Shack. These take you progressively up in speed. Since the test is for receiving only, you do not have to know how to send.

In the initial stages of learning it is important to keep thinking in auditory and not visual terms. The temptation is to write down the dits and dashes. Avoid doing this. Instead, repeat their sound in your mind or vocalize them. Do not write them down. The human mind processes auditory and visual inputs differently, and visualization can lead you down a false path.

The key to passing the code test is regular study. By studying two hours each day, you could go from 0 words a minute to the required 13 words in about 6 weeks.

In addition to the code test, you must pass a theory test. Passing this test is probably easier than in past years because the FCC publishes a list of all the questions for the test. Most ham exam study guides list all the possible questions and give you the answers. Passing the test means only memorizing several hundred answers. In the memorization process you learn a lot, and the pass rate is quite high using these study guides.

A contingent of old-time hams feels that this is not quite fair, but the main point is for radio operators to get legally licensed. If you'd like a full explanation of each FCC answer, a thorough study guide is available from the American Radio Relay League, the ARRL.

Using fake or foreign call signs isn't a very successful trick, because the maritime mobile nets are so tightly self-policed. Pirates (those using call signs not listed in the yearly published *Call Book* of General Class or higher) are quickly discovered on the air and loudly given the cold shoulder. The only way to get full advantage of ham is to bite the bullet and get the license—before you go to sea. Don't leave home without it.

TEMPORARY RADIO INSTALLATIONS

We take along a compact ham/marine SSB radio on any vessel we're delivering long range, if it doesn't already have a radio with ham capabilities. Typically, radios are scarce on new boats that aren't fully commissioned, and on older boats that are for sale or "between owners." Offering to provide our own radio has helped us to land some deliveries, and it assures us we'll have a good radio we're familiar with.

John's radio is a ham transceiver capable of transmitting on any frequency from 2 MHz to 30 MHz. This means that besides using it as a ham radio, we can listen to weather on any frequency, pick up weather fax signals, Voice of America (VOA) or British Broadcasting Company (BBC) news broadcasts. In an emergency we can transmit on regular marine SSB frequencies, like the Coast Guard's and make duplex ship-to-shore telephone calls. The complete setup, including radio, manual tuner, coaxial cable, and a dipole antenna, costs about $1,000. A similar marine SSB would be at least $3,000.

Several models offer these features, but they come from the factory disabled of their abilities to transmit on any but ham frequencies. They are easily modified. On the ICOM 720A all John had to do was lift the top access panel and clip an easy-to-find blue wire, just as they told him in the store where he bought it.

Since many of our deliveries either begin or end with an airplane ride, we carefully pack all our radio gear in a hard, locked Samsonite suitcase, well padded with styrofoam and bubble plastic.

To temporarily install a ham rig, first find a place to pick up 12-volt DC current. You should do this with the cable supplied by the manufacturer and go directly to the batteries, observing the correct polarity. The cable is usually no longer than eight feet, so if you can't go directly to the batteries, you could pick up the 12 volts from a buss bar or very heavy-gauge wire running directly from the batteries.

This is important, because voice communication disappears when voltage drops much

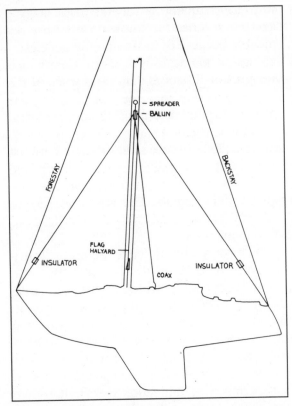

Figure 15-2. Dipole antenna.

below 13.6 volts, which is a fully charged condition. If the pickup wire is too thin or too long, there is too much voltage drop. Also, such heavy resistance means you'll have to charge your ship's batteries whenever you try to transmit for more than a few minutes.

Mount the radio and the tuner in a convenient location, securing them for a pitching sea, and connect the coax cables (see Figure 15-1).

Find a place to run your coaxial cable outside, possibly where other wire bundles pass through the deck or coach roof, in order to feed the dipole antenna. Cut off the coax connector from one end, snake it through the wire run, and then resolder the connector. A dipole antenna is shown in Figure 15-2.

Hang the dipole antenna on deck so that it

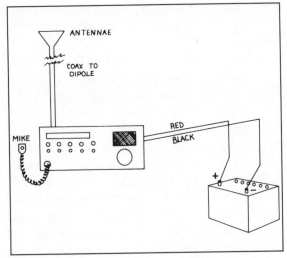

Figure 15-1. Temporary radio installation.

won't touch any other wires (such as rigging), and it isn't in the way of rotating radar antennas, swinging booms or any other normal goings-on. Connect the coax to the center insulator.

The beauty of a dipole antenna for a temporary installation is that it is a "balanced" antenna and does not need to have a *ground plane,* which is difficult to construct for temporary use. The dipole antenna is efficient, cheap, highly portable and easy to make; it consists of two pieces of wire and a center insulator. You should take one along anyway as an emergency backup to your primary antenna.

It usually takes about half an hour to make such an installation. Then we are ready to talk to the world.

CHAPTER 16
SAFETY AND EMERGENCIES

SAFETY AT SEA

We will focus on two aspects of safety: first, an underlying attitude or awareness of how to live on board, doing normal shipboard activities safely; and second, specific safety procedures. You can learn both.

If any one of your crewmembers doesn't have a firm foundation in safety—that is, if he or she hasn't finished some sort of marine course in firefighting, lifeboat launching, first aid, CPR, etc.—then it's up to the captain to instill in them the essential information they need to know, and to make sure they practice it.

While taking safety classes or training in emergency procedures, people learn more than just the specifics they're tested on. Submersion in an atmosphere of emergency preparedness brings the students' attention around so much to those adrenaline situations, those horror stories we hope will never occur, that a deeper sense of awareness develops within them.

This deeper safety awareness is a pervasive alertness to all the potential hazards found on all boats, and a quiet confidence about dealing with emergencies successfully. Ideally, this safety awareness becomes instinctive and remains with the crewmember back out in the real world.

The antithesis of the prudent seaman is the blissfully ignorant crewmember who steps blindly over each potential danger (the lazy sheet that snaps up or trips him, the burned-out bulb on the high-water alarm, the poorly tuned radar screen), then freezes in sheer panic when he is the one standing nearest to the man overboard pole.

Having a regular set of crewmembers that you know is trained, that you have trained yourself, and that you have observed under

Figure 16-1. Don't give accidents a place to happen. Safety drills and regular exercise help crew members stay alert and agile during long passages.

fire is the best way to assure that everyone will do their normal jobs to your standard of safety. They won't let obscure little hazards turn into real emergencies. And if disaster develops, they'll at least have some idea of how to react. This is exactly why we try to retain a cadre of experienced seamen to choose from for each delivery.

Mellow personalities are delightful at sea, but a mellow attitude toward safety is dangerous. It's not cute, it doesn't show how cool a person is, and it doesn't equate to being an optimist or a positive thinker.

Now let's get into an emergency.

EMERGENCIES

You cannot learn from a book everything to do in an emergency, whether it's fire, high water, collision, capsize, man overboard, illness, or mutiny. Each emergency has dozens of contributing aspects, many of them changing quickly, which you must assess as you take action.

You can learn from a book what emergencies you might anticipate and how to drill for a few of them. But that's a lot if it helps you through your next emergency.

It's been said that seamanship is anticipation. If you can anticipate what often goes wrong on boats, you probably can prevent many emergencies. Heed Murphy's Law, which says that whatever can go wrong will go wrong, and at the worst possible time. This would be a horrible creed to follow throughout life, but just for a few hours before each voyage, you should scrutinize the vessel, crew, itinerary, and weather conditions through the fatalistic filter of Murphy's Law.

If fuel fumes overpower you when you lift the engine shroud and the engine isn't even running yet, then visions of an onboard fire, a poisoned coral reef, or at least an expensive

Coast Guard citation should pop into your noggin and inspire you to fix the fuel leak.

If your course is going to take you into shipping lanes or traffic separation zones, you should imagine sweating through three consecutive four-hour watches on the bridge with less experienced crew. This might turn your thoughts toward increasing your radar visibility, checking your running lights, binoculars, and helm response, testing your VHF on Channels 16, 13 and 63, scheduling the watch around peak traffic, and perhaps hiring more experienced crew.

If the float switch on the main bilge pump has been stuck in the up position for two weeks, then nightmares of floating in your bunk should haunt you relentlessly, until you pick up all those plastic wiring ties and wood scraps that slosh around down there, or until you replace the pump motor.

If squalls, gales, or hurricanes ever occur in the waters you're about to enter, then you should anticipate the worst they might dish up, multiply it by three, and then plan on streaming the sea anchor, running under reefed sails or bare poles, heaving to, and maybe taking a knockdown or capsize. Have you tested the sea anchor? Are the reef ties long enough if you haven't got all day? What would happen to the knives, glass, and batteries if the boat turned upside down for a few seconds?

As these examples show, it doesn't take much practice examining your upcoming trip through the Murphy's Law filter to spot all the potential emergencies. Only by planning on disaster, by preparing for the absolute worst that could happen, can you gain a slight advantage when emergencies arise. *When,* not *if,* because emergencies are a fact of life. No one can afford to adopt an it-won't-happen-to-me attitude, because the longer and farther you go to sea, the greater your risk of encountering an emergency. The degree to which you are *not* prepared for an emergency becomes the degree of severity of that emergency.

Here are some tips for anticipating the most common emergencies. We also practice drills for some. (See Chapter 17.)

Fires often start in the engine area or near the stove, but they also can start in frayed wiring hidden behind paneling or in oily rags in the bosun's locker.

Failed through-hull fittings, underpowered, faulty, or clogged bilge pumps, and flimsy deck hatches are the main culprits in high-water situations that lead to sinkings. There are more sinkings in coastal waters due to these three failures than there are sinkings at high sea due to boarding waves.

Collision should be anticipated and avoided by the person keeping the lookout. That's your legal responsibility 24 hours a day. Watch orders should include the Closest Point of Approach (CPA). (See Chapter 10, Watch Standing.) If anything "hard" enters your chosen safe perimeter, you should anticipate collision and do something quickly to avoid it.

General Rule of Collisions Number 1 says that when another vessel's range is decreasing but his bearing off your course remains the same, then you are on a collision course.

General Rule of Collisions Number 2 says that you should turn to starboard, enough to starboard so that the other guy can see you have turned, and do it far enough in advance so that it keeps your courses from intersecting. If everyone approaching the collision turns to starboard, they will not collide, at least in theory.

A truly seaworthy sailboat should be built with the intention of surviving a 360-degree roll, even if you lose the mast. Unfortunately, many boats the delivery skipper takes on are designed for cocktail parties, or at best for coastal marina-hopping.

If deck hatches, portholes, and passageways through watertight bulkheads are left open or unsecured in turbulent weather, it's not the builders' fault if the boat turns upside down, takes on enough water to prevent its momentum from carrying it through the complete roll, and it therefore sinks.

Powerboats usually fare worse in capsize situations, so the best you can do is to anticipate: If I turn this boat on its beam, what is going to go flying? How much damage could it do as a "loose cannon?" If the sofa is not through-bolted to the cabin sole, it could smash through the cabin side if the boat broaches. If the cabin side is smashed open, the boat could sink.

Glass, knives, books, batteries, tool boxes, and canned goods do much damage during and after capsize. Can you imagine those lovely, sliding mirrored doors on closets in big boats? Many builders are still using glass instead of plastics. (See Chapter 9—Securing for Sea.)

When assembling your medical kit, anticipate specific maladies based on your route and on crewmembers' medical histories.

Tropic routes call for salt tablets, sun screen, and sunburn remedy, water purification treatment, and mosquito repellant and mosquito netting for use in port.

Heat stroke, also called sun stroke, is a serious medical emergency that can cause brain damage and even death. The acute stage begins when sweating stops. Heat exhaustion is less serious, but at the onset of both conditions, the symptoms are similar. Rapid and severe loss of salt and water (ironically) from the body induces heat stroke and heat exhaustion, so keep fluids flowing and salt tablets handy.

Everyone on board should be instructed to recognize the difference between heat stroke and the less severe heat exhaustion, and how to treat both. At the onset of both maladies, sweating is common and the victim may lose consciousness. Drag him to the coolest shade.

If sweating stops, it's heat stroke, and it's serious. The only way to tell if or when sweating stops it to continually wipe off the previous perspiration. If sweating stops, you must chill down the torso, neck and head immediately. Use shade, a tub of ice water, wet blankets, air conditioning, fans, or whatever is available. Bring the body temperature down quickly, but don't allow it to fall below 101°F. or 38.3°C. Keep it down until you reach port, which should now be your top priority

Read the U.S. government publication *The Ship's Medicine Chest and Medical Aid at Sea,* Number HSA 78-2024, or the American Red Cross's *Standard First Aid,* or Dr. Peter Eastman's *Advanced First Aid Afloat.*

Frost bite and hypothermia are higher-latitude problems you want to anticipate in your emergency drill routine. Briefly, hypothermia requires rewarming as soon as possible, but cardiac arrest is possible during the rewarming, so know how to administer CPR. (See CPR chart, page 182). Frostbitten parts should never be rubbed, only rewarmed slowly once the danger of rechilling is completely past.

Seasickness is the most common malady in boating. If you brag that you never get seasick, it might just mean to everyone that you haven't been to sea long enough. Unfortunately, that queazy stomach doesn't automatically relieve anyone from their responsibilities for standing watch, working in the engine room, or cooking meals for others.

Soda crackers and bread soak up stomach acid. Avoid dairy products, which sour in the seasick stomach. Practice deep breathing slowly in the fresh air while focusing on the horizon, even if it's lumpy.

Seasickness medications that induce drowsiness can be dangerous, because you must be

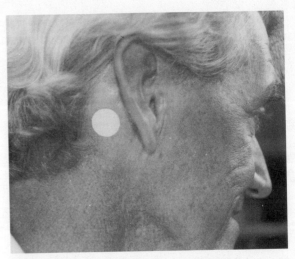

These adhesive patches allow seasickness medication to be absorbed without causing drowsiness.

fully alert in order to stand a proper watch on the helm or bridge. Small details that a doped-up sailor misses in the engine room can develop into big problems. And anyone working with a hot stove, knives, glass, and hot liquids can't afford to be groggy. Eight hours is the normal duration of medication-induced drowsiness, and that doesn't fit into many watch schedules.

We have prescriptions for "transderm" scopalomine that doesn't make us drowsy. The drug is slowly absorbed by the skin through a stick-on patch placed behind your ear. It should be removed or replaced after three days. Fortunately, we've never needed to use them that long, but I have seen people get slightly cross-eyed while wearing the patch for just one day. We recommend that each crewmember secure his own prescription and be well familiar with the drug's possible side effects.

The notion of a mutiny aboard evokes some dramatic images. In the delivery business and aboard cruising yachts, true mutinies are almost non-existent. Polite creatures that we are, we'd all rather just put up with the miserable offender until we can make a crew change during the next port call.

Pat recalls an awful delivery with a mutinous crew member:

Four of us were six days into a 20-day ocean crossing aboard a small sailboat when the owner's wife became paranoid about being beyond the sight of land and refused to stand her watch. Whether to turn around was no easy decision for her husband since we were hand-steering with just three watch standers in the huge following seas of the trade winds. "Press on," he said.

No amount of consolation could keep her mental state from deteriorating, until, on day eight, she grabbed a kitchen knife and threatened to "get" us, including her husband, if we didn't turn the boat around and return to California.

I hid all knives except for the one she kept in hand. Tension on board was horrid, as she repeatedly threatened our lives. Sadly, secretly, we conferred about how we might be able to safely fall upon this huge woman and tie her up. We were spared acting on this when, on day 11, she retreated into the fo'c's'le with six gallons of Scotch and remained mostly sequestered there until the anchor went down in Hawaii. She and the owner were soon divorced.

Technically, when a crewmember revolts against authority, he's being mutinous. Your best defense against mutiny is to check crew references thoroughly before signing anyone on. Historically, captains took physical control of all firearms the day they stepped aboard, which is still a good idea, and they routinely shot mutinous crew. We don't recommend this. You might try talking it out first.

Seriously, if someone begins to "nut out" in deep sea, it's wise to have a mild sedative that the distraught person can take voluntarily, or that you can slip into their food. Get instructions from the prescribing doctor on how to administer it.

Now that you know the worst to anticipate, let's look at some emergency drills.

CHAPTER 17
EMERGENCY DRILLS

The reason we drill for emergencies is not to scare people; it's to prevent wasting time in a true emergency. Precious seconds are consumed while you run around like a flock of headless chickens or become paralyzed by fear.

It should be the captain's decision to call a Mayday or to abandon ship. The response to fire, man overboard, and medical emergencies requiring artificial resuscitation and CPR must be instant and spontaneous.

Assign each person on board a specific set of tasks for each emergency. Have everyone get together and rehearse their moves to assure there'll be no conflicts, duplications, or surprises, and then run through each of these drills one time before you leave the dock. You may need to replace items.

Drill again after you're underway, perhaps by springing various surprise drills. The smoother you get now, the better you'll react in an actual emergency. Surprise drills can become hilariously entertaining, but we must take them seriously.

FIRE

"Fire!" Whoever spots it must simultaneously alert someone else and begin fighting the fire. Locate all fire extinguishers, note the different types you might have onboard, and show everyone how to operate each type. Locate the fire alarm or horn. Fill a can with flour and keep it near the stove. Locate and test water pumps and hoses that could fight fire. In a deck or cabin fire, turn the boat so that the fire is downwind of the rest of the boat.

Engine room fires are very serious, even on diesel-driven boats. Hot diesel can ignite surrounding materials. Explosion is possible. If the older, toxic form of Halon fire extinguisher is automatically released in the engine room, instruct crew to evacuate the area. If CO_2 is automatically released in the engine room but the engine room exhaust fan isn't synchronized with the CO_2 release system, the crew must shut off the engine room exhaust switch. Locate it and notice how far it is from the engine room exit. Generally, fight an engine room fire from the exit so you can back out and seal the exit behind you. Don't admit air to a fuel fire if you can avoid it.

Everyone on board should fight the fire or stand by to help those who are. Meanwhile, the decision to call a Mayday lies solely with the captain.

MAYDAY

The words "Mayday, Mayday, Mayday" on the radio signify that you have a life-threatening problem on board for which you are requesting immediate help.

Delegate one person (or one from each watch) who should, upon captain's order, stop

A fixed Halon fire-extinguishing system in the engine room. Check all onboard fire systems to see that they are charged and up to date.

on these frequencies with the volume turned down.

Your Mayday drill should sound something like this:

> Mayday, Mayday, Mayday. This is *Pink Lady, Pink Lady, Pink Lady*, Whiskey Yankee Bravo Five Niner Three Seven. My position is one-niner degrees one-five minutes north, eight-zero degrees five-zero minutes west. We have fire in the engine room, growing out of control. May have to abandon ship into a liferaft and Sabot dinghy. Four persons aboard. *Pink Lady* is a 42-foot sailboat, white hull, pink trim, one mast. *Pink Lady,* standing by on four four two eight seven. Over.

Listen for someone to respond and be ready to write down instructions or answer questions. If you don't hear any response within 15 seconds, make sure you're transmitting and repeat the Mayday. Someone whom you cannot hear may be relaying your plight to others.

Each person on board should be shown how to find the vessel's most recent position, especially those who aren't regular crewmembers or watch-standers. Keep your navigation log book on the nav desk and show everyone where to look inside it for the most recent position. It should never be more than one hour old. Show everyone how to punch up the current latitude/longitude on the Satnav or Loran.

The best way to alleviate someone's "mike fright" is to have them make a calm, clear radio check on the radio before getting underway. Pat recalls the first time she had to talk on a marine radio:

> My voice sounded like someone was choking me and I didn't realize I was speaking into the back side of the mike. If anyone could

fighting the fire (or bailing, rowing, etc.) to radio the Mayday call. Generally, women's voices carry better over the air and most men make better firefighters. If you wait too long before sending the Mayday, explosion, flames or high water over the batteries may prevent you from getting the call made.

Drill for a Mayday situation with the radio or mike turned *off.* While you're coastal cruising or within sight of other boats, use VHF Channel 16. Otherwise, use SSB *and* VHF. Make a list of all SSB frequencies and their appropriate time of day for all U.S. Coast Guard and international emergency frequencies that cover your route. Keep this list near the SSB radio, even if you have to tape it to a bulkhead. We routinely leave our radios tuned read my garbled transmission, they still couldn't respond to me, because I didn't know enough to let go of the transmit key!

ABANDONING SHIP

The drill for abandoning ship should be tailored to suit each vessel and its crew. In the true emergency sequence, as many crewmembers as possible continue fighting the emergency, and when the captain orders, one person calls Mayday. The captain's decision to abandon ship may come at the same time as the Mayday, minutes later, or it may never come at all if the fire is put out. However, if possible, never abandon ship until at least one Mayday broadcast has been sent. If you have enough hands aboard, leave the radio operator broadcasting your Mayday and position for as long as is practical and at least one person fighting the fire.

Delegate one or two of the remaining crew to start the process of abandoning ship by launching the liferaft. Everyone should be familiar with this rather complicated, important task. However, because liferafts must be professionally repacked at considerable cost, you

The heart of this excellent custom liferaft-launching system is the stainless steel frame that is mounted on the side of the boat. By simply pulling a pin, the liferaft falls into the water. The EPIRB, just in front of the raft, will float free and begin to transmit an emergency signal.

can only simulate deploying the life raft in your drill.

For inflatables: (1) Lift the raft from its secured position. If it wasn't already secured to the deck, you must now tie its painter to the boat, so choose several appropriate locations. (2) Throw the raft overboard, to windward if you're on fire, otherwise to leeward. (3) Yank the inflating line, but don't sever the painter until everyone's aboard the raft and then only if you absolutely must.

Even after leaving the mother ship, you shouldn't abandon the ship's location for three days. Some boats take a long time to sink, and it's probable that it will be sighted by an airplane before your tiny liferaft is seen. Another reason to remain with the mother ship is that debris helps pinpoint your location.

Read your raft's instructions, recheck the date, distinguish which cables hold the container in place, and which inflate the raft or serve as the painter. You should never need a screwdriver or knife to free the canister from its holder, but if you do, secure a screwdriver or knife nearby before getting underway.

Launchers should notice which shrouds or lifelines could obstruct the raft's path to the

Part of the abandon ship drill is to mock-launch the liferaft. How is the canister secured on deck? Does it need to be tied to something else before tossing it overboard? What obstructions are nearby?

water, especially when the boat is awash, dismasted or knocked down. Others should don survival suits, wet suits, or long-sleeve shirts, but never waste time rummaging for personal items.

If you must leap from the boat into water covered with burning oil, leap feet first, swim to windward under water as far as possible, push away the oil with your hands as you resurface, get air and dive again. Buoyant wet suits make swimming under water more strenuous. Those already in the raft may need to help guide swimmers to the raft by shouting and shining flashlights.

We don't accept yacht deliveries unless there is either an offshore-type life raft, within date, or a stable dinghy that's quick and easy to launch *without electricity.*

Inflatable dinghies make poor life rafts, even for coastal trips. In 20 knots of wind they often blow away while being launched. They are easily punctured by severed shroud wires, they have no anti-capsize device, and without the welded-on canopy, the occupants can be washed out by each breaking sea.

For other lifeboats: If an electric crane is required to launch a hard skiff doubling as a life boat, activate it before the ship loses power. Manually-operated davits may require two crew to avoid capsizing the lifeboat while launching it. If an outboard motor is stowed elsewhere, lash it in the skiff's bottom before launching.

If the hard lifeboat can be tied alongside the mother ship while transferring crew, do so, because it may capsize more easily than the inflatable from swimmers coming up over its sides or from others leaping down into it from a distance. If threatened by fire spread or explosion, stream it away on a stout painter.

If you're relying solely on a typical hard dinghy, make up an especially complete "ditch kit" that contains at the very least everything found in a U.S.C.G.-approved life raft. (See supplemental ditch kit, below.) You will be far more vulnerable to capsize and exposure than survivors in a good inflatable life raft. If you have both, drill for launching both. Use anything additional that floats.

Douglas Robertson, in *Sea Survival, A Manual,* recommends getting injured survivors into the raft, of course, but he also suggests scrutinizing all floating debris, "regardless of their apparent uselessness at the time. . . . reserve buoyancy and waterproof container space are the castaway's two most precious assets followed by shelter and warm clothing in cold areas, shade in tropical zones. Additional water reserves are crucial in all climates."

If floating debris is "of the slightest possible use and not dangerous to the survival craft," Robertson advises either gathering it aboard or, as with a large piece of spar or hull, securing it at the end of a leeward painter so it won't chafe or puncture the raft.

Except in a case of fire, Robertson thinks there may be some protection in the lee of the mother ship for hauling in survivors. Also, if you choose the lee side, debris will float your way. If barnacles on the underside of the mother ship threaten to puncture the raft, move off a bit.

Discuss what's factory-packed inside this life raft and make up a supplementary ditch kit of your own. Between the two, you should have the following:

Ditch Kit
- EPIRB—First person into the raft takes it. Spare battery.
- FRESH WATER—Minimum of one pint per day per person for X days.
- RADIOS—Solar-powered SSB in floating case, (made by Vector Radio). Hand-held VHF.
- RESCUE GEAR—Flares and flare gun, smoke rockets, metal mirror.

- FIRST-AID KIT—Prescription drugs and glasses, pre-threaded surgical needles, antiseptic alcohol, adhesive tape, sterile pads, inflatable arm and leg casts, chemical ice packs, antiseptic ointment, eye drops, sunblock.

- FOOD—Canned juices, fruits and vegetables with juices, non-salty precooked meats. Two can openers. High glucose staples in Ziploc bags.

- SURVIVAL GEAR—Survival suits (in cool waters, each person wears one). Wet suits, fins, mask, snorkel. Solar still: new models are more efficient and cheaper. Many boats carry two or three.

- MISCELLANEOUS GEAR—Compass, sextant, binoculars, charts, flashlights, sea anchor, spear gun, fish hooks, steel leaders, sheathed filet knife, insulating cushions, plastic tarps, Ziploc bags, Tupperware lidded containers, the books *Sea Survival* by D. Robertson, *First Aid Afloat* by P. Eastman, pens and paper, light paperbacks, hair brush.

Fashionable people pay big bucks to elegant health resorts for the privilege of not eating, of fasting. A controlled fast of 25 days is considered acceptable, as long as water or juice keeps the kidneys flushing toxins out of the body. So water is more important than food. Never drink saltwater; it destroys the kidneys. You can live longer without freshwater than you can without kidneys.

Make your ditch kit by filling a duffel bag, zippered bag of soft luggage, or pillow cases with gear and food. Avoid glass. Keep it near the main companionway so you can grab it as you abandon. Otherwise, can you imagine having to dive on your submerged boat to retrieve all the gear?

If these gear items are not spares, you'll constantly be digging into your ditch kit to "borrow" them, and Murphy's Law says disaster will strike when you've forgotten to return them.

If all you have aboard are your primary sextant, binoculars, compass, medical kit and EPIRB, keep as much of this gear as possible in one bag located in one handy spot, like on the bridge where you'd use the binoculars. Food and water can be kept in a separate bag, but together they comprise your ditch kit.

If you have two EPIRBs, keep one in the ditch kit. Take the second to cannibalize for its battery. A spare hand-bearing compass, a plastic sextant and old binoculars are practical to leave in the kit. One small-scale (large area) chart that covers your entire route is more practical than a complete set of duplicates, but assign someone to grab the chart you are now plotting on.

Vector Radio's solar-powered SSB radio reaches ham frequencies where 24-hour networks stand by just for marine emergencies, plus regular U.S. Coast Guard channels in the

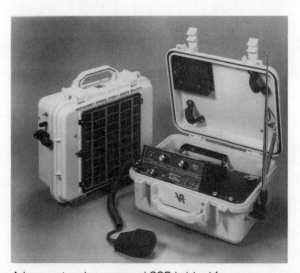

A buoyant, solar-powered SSB is ideal for your "ditch kit." EPIRB signals aren't always detected, but this little unit allows survivors to voice-broadcast world-wide from their liferaft, talking directly to rescuers and receiving medical advice while they wait. (Photo courtesy of Vector Radio, Oceanside, CA.)

HF bands. The bright-yellow watertight case floats.

As part of your first drill, make up a first-aid kit of drugs, instruments, and sterile supplies that fits into a plastic fishing tackle box or similar watertight case. Keep it in the ditch kit's gear bag. If you have no duplicates for these items in the ship's bulky medical chest, replace them now before you leave the dock. If you have time, in the real emergency take all the additional medical supplies you can carry with you.

MAN OVERBOARD DRILL

Before leaving the docks, or before too many hours have passed, gather the crew for man-overboard instructions. Here's how it should go:

1 Whoever sees the accident shouts "Man Overboard! starboard" or "Man Overboard! port" and throws the detached life ring over the appropriate side of the boat so the victim can swim to it, or at least to mark the spot. That person must keep his eyes trained on the spot where the victim was last seen, a difficult task in heavy seas.

2 The helmsman immediately halts forward progress of the boat, noting the compass course. Powerboats should make an immediate 180-degree turn, using the reciprocal compass course. If the engine on a sailboat is not running, start it and perform a power turn. If purely under sail, you may need to tack or jibe to return to the victim.

3 As crewmembers arrive on deck, one should assist the spotter, but not replace him. One crew should relay directions between the spotter and the helmsman so that neither of them has to leave his post. Any extra hands should also try to spot the victim, should throw paper cups, pages from

magazines, or other small, floatable objects to help mark their course, or should ready an inflatable dinghy or a heaving line or boarding lines.

4 Get close to the victim and throw him a line, pulling him to the boat. If you approach from upwind, you'll create a lee and can perhaps drift downwind toward him, with the engine in neutral, hopefully bringing him alongside. Be careful not to drift on top of the victim, because you cannot use the prop(s) for maneuvering. Determine if using the dinghy is practical.

5 If a crew member *must* enter the water to rescue the victim, tie a light line from the boat to his waist, which they can attach to the victim. They should wear one life preserver and carry one to the victim. (During drills, use the boat hook.)

6 If you cannot locate the man overboard, issue the "Pan-pan, Pan-pan, Pan-pan" call for assistance by Coast Guard and other vessels.

Once these instructions are understood and soon after the voyage is underway, the captain should spring a man-overboard drill on the crew. The best method is for the captain to quietly throw a life preserver overboard and then yell, "MAN OVERBOARD!" Each member of the crew responds according to where he happens to be at the time the alarm is sounded, or according to which job he's been assigned, depending on the number of crew. Perform the entire drill without the captain once, in case he turns out to be the victim. Remember, in the actual event, you'll be one crewmember short.

ARTIFICIAL RESPIRATION (AR)

When the victim isn't breathing, artificial respiration must be done quickly to prevent

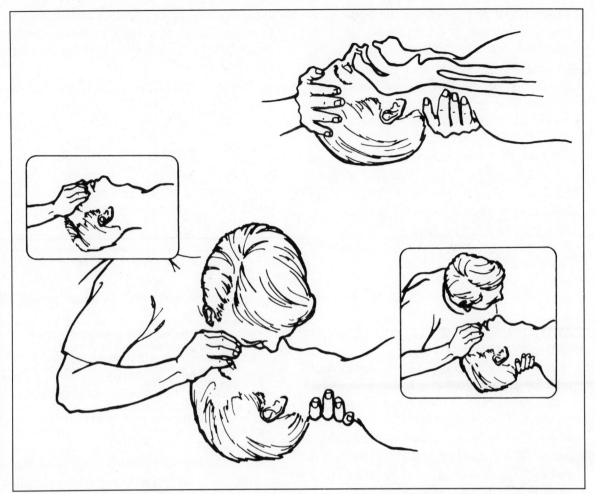

Figure 17-1. Artificial respiration. Counter-clockwise from upper right: To open air passages, hold forehead steady and lift neck. If nothing is clogging the throat, victim may resume self-breathing. If air passages are clear yet no breathing can be seen, begin artificial respiration immediately.

Pinch victim's nostrils closed with thumb and forefinger of hand holding forehead. Other hand remains under victim's neck, tilting chin up and mouth open.

Take a deep breath, form a tight seal with your open lips around the victim's open mouth, and blow assertively into the victim's lungs.

Remove your mouth, but not your hands, and allow victim to exhale passively, evidenced by a slight chest fall. Without allowing victim's lungs to completely deflate, repeat for four (4) quick breaths. Then, for not more than ten (10) seconds, check victim for carotid pulse and normal breathing. If pulse but no breathing, continue inflating lungs approximately once every five seconds, or twelve (12) times each minute.

brain damage or death. Performing it in the water is awkward, but the victim will die if he doesn't breath within six minutes. Dying is more awkward. According to the American Red Cross (See Fig. 17-1):

1 Remove water or debris from the victim's mouth and throat by suction or your fingers. If he vomits, turn him sideways so he doesn't choke on it. Don't turn him face-down in the water.

2 Open his airway by tilting the head back slightly and jutting the jawbone up. This takes two hands in the water.

3 Now seal your mouth over his and inflate his lungs three times, uncovering his mouth after each inflation to allow the lungs to expel. Maintain steady rhythm of 10 to 12 breaths per minute.

If you can't get air to go in . . .

4 Turn him sideways again, deliver a sharp blow between his shoulder blades, and try to dislodge whatever clogs his airway before resuming lung inflation.

Continue for at least 10 minutes or until he is revived.

CARDIOPULMINARY RESUSCITATION (CPR)

If the heartbeat and pulse are absent and pupils are dilated, the heart has stopped. CPR is a combination of AR plus heart massage. It must be done on a rigid floor. The CPR-giver may need to kneel beside the victim for hours to revive him. According to the American Red Cross (See Fig. 17-2):

Remember the ABCs of CPR:

A Airway open—tilt head back, jut jaw up, remove debris as in AR.

B Breathe—inflate lungs as in AR.

C Cardiac massage—place heel of one hand on lower end of breast bone, other hand atop first hand, and press down firmly and evenly by rocking forward slowly with your elbows straight.

Repeat B and C, one breath between every five heart massages (1 for 5) rhythmically, strongly, carefully, until someone can slip in

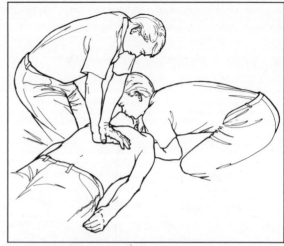

Figure 17-2. Cardiopulmonary Resuscitation. With two rescuers, give five (5) cardiac compressions to one (1) lung inflation, or 5:1. Rescuer giving compressions counts aloud, "ONE, one thousand, TWO, one thousand, THREE, one thousand, FOUR, one thousand, FIVE, inflate and, ONE, one thousand, ..." Rescuer inflating lungs interposes the full breath between the compressions of FIVE and ONE of the next cycle, but does it fast enough not to interrupt the rhythm. Beware not to compress and inflate at the same time.

With one rescuer, the ratio must be fifteen (15) faster compressions to two (2) consecutive inflations, or 15:2. That means about 80 compressions per minute. This method is extremely fatiguing.

alongside you and take over, without stopping the rhythm. CPR is taxing at this pace. Two or more CPR-givers may relay for several hours.

If no one can replace you before you're exhausted, the Red Cross says you can give two lung inflations between every 15 heart massages (2 to 15) to extend your range of treatment.

If a CPR-giver hasn't had CPR training, he should beware of breaking the victim's ribs by jerking or leaning too hard.

If you must move the victim, arrange a stiff gurney so the CPR can continue uninterrupted. If you use too soft a platform for moving the victim (such as a mattress), then most of your heart massage pressure will be lost on the springy mattress. Try a door, floorboard or table top. If you must move the cardiac victim on a mattress or seat cushion, place a stiff board, a storage bin cover or a large, hard-bound book under his back, between his shoulder blades, so that the heart massage portion of CPR can be continued effectively.

CHAPTER 18
GUNS AND BOATS

WHY GUNS?

When giving a seminar for cruisers, John always throws it open for questions at the end. Invariably, the first one asked is, "What about carrying guns aboard?" This issue concerns all of us who travel the world in small craft, but it's a highly subjective, often emotional topic with no absolute answers. While we discuss the many pros and cons, in the end, each of us has to decide for ourself.

If you have absolutely no background with weapons, yet you think you should carry guns on board, don't just go out and buy one and head to sea with it. Get some training. Whether through sport hunting or military training, many Americans, particularly men, have some knowledge of weaponry.

John cites his early background:

In my youth, I hunted in the local woodlands with a bow and arrow, graduating to shotgun and rifle. I was drafted into the infantry for two years at the height of the Vietnam War. I wasn't happy about it, but I decided to make the best of a bad predicament. My year-long weapons training focused on small arms: pistols, automatic rifles, heavy machine guns, grenade launchers, bayonets, high explosives, bare hands, etc. During the following year in the jungles of Vietnam and Cambodia, I had ample opportunity to put this training to practical use in close combat.

When the Army discharged me from action in Vietnam, I was thoroughly disgusted with death and destruction and swore I'd never carry a firearm again. Twelve years of delivering boats in various parts of the world have moderated that view.

I tremble when I recall discussions I've had with inexperienced, untrained people who believe they should go heavily armed throughout the world. They espouse the John Wayne/Rambo mentality and are dangerous to themselves and innocent people around them.

Firearms usually get you in more trouble than they could ever get you out of (unless, of course, you're in the middle of an all-out war). Introducing a gun to a volatile situation presupposes it will be used and tends to escalate the situation. Knowing when to use or not use a gun is just as important as knowing how to use it.

The opposite view can be dangerous, too. Many Americans have a naïve view of the rest of the world. Piracy, smuggling and revolution were all parts of the real world long before Hollywood romanticized them. If it were stolen and sold on the black market even our humblest of cruising boats could feed several starving villages and keep them in medical supplies for a year. It could carry tons of automatic weapons or drugs or other contraband if pirates decided they wanted it. And what a *coup d'etat* would be the liberation of that ostentatious yacht by political propagandists in the heat of a revolution. Yacht deliverers and cruisers in certain areas may be exposed to real dangers of hostile attack.

We have delivered vessels both armed and unarmed. The decision of whether to carry arms is based on the route and destination of each trip. Cruisers who prefer to sail unarmed can plan their itineraries in order to avoid areas known to have problems. Since most yacht deliverers can't afford the luxury of choosing where they'll pick up boats or deliver them to, we have to take wisdom and common sense along when we move through potentially dangerous waters. And sometimes that means guns, too.

Before you go, research the social and political stability of areas along your proposed routes. Investigative newspapers and news magazines are your best source. Cruising guides are helpful, but some mention only the good features, avoiding discussion of hot issues that could drive tourists away. A call to the U.S. Department of State will tell you those countries Americans are currently advised to avoid.

Underway, keep abreast of developments by talking with other cruisers who've visited these places recently. Pay attention to local newspapers and radio. On the radio, the VOA or BBC may tell you more than consuls in foreign countries. Long deliveries involve a mixture of friendly and occasionally dangerous areas. In some regions, social stability can deteriorate rapidly. If the good-guy port captain retires, you might find thievery rampant where it didn't exist the month before and hadn't even been heard of in years.

If you decide to carry firearms, be prepared to conform to the weapons laws of the countries you are going to visit. Check with their consulates before departure to find out their restrictions. Get written permits or embossed letters if you can.

In some countries, your firearms may be bonded aboard your boat—that is, kept in a locked compartment. Typically, the customs officer will affix tamper proof seals to the seams of the locker, which will be checked when you leave.

Many countries simply will not allow you to enter their waters with firearms aboard. Their boarding officers will politely confiscate them and lock them up in the port of entry. This can create an enormous hassle when you eventually need to retrieve your property before you leave that country. If you are travelling *through,* not *to* a country, you may need to depart from some port hundreds of miles away from wherever your gun is locked up.

It can get even worse. Some countries have laws that forbid you to travel on land with your gun. You either bring your boat back to that port of entry, retrieve your gun, and depart directly from there, or you risk illegal transportation of weapons. The alternative is to just go on without it.

An undeclared gun, if discovered, will create an enormous problem, possibly the worst problem you've ever had. For instance, throughout Jamaica the penalty for possession of an undeclared firearm is mandatory life imprisonment. If you declare your weapon upon arrival in Jamaica, the officials take it away and return it when you leave. They are courteous, and it's all very legal. They do a thorough search. Never take the chance of not declaring your weapons in places like Jamaica.

If this sounds unfair or somehow impinges on your right to bear arms, keep in mind that you're no longer in the United States and that such rights are far from universal. Foreign visitors to the U.S. aren't allowed to carry weapons either; they're put in storage just as is done in Jamaica.

John's example shows the sort of hassle attendant with carrying weapons:

I had a Mexican client who carried a pair of .25-caliber automatic pistols aboard his racing sailboat. I was delivering the boat from Acapulco up to Los Angeles, so the owner could race back down to Puerto Vallarta.

Upon entering the States from the south in his foreign-flag vessel, I had to declare the guns to the customs officers who came on board in San Diego. They put the guns in storage, and I continued on with the boat to Los Angeles, where the owner took possession and began preparations for his international race.

Unfortunately, the only way he could recover his firearms by boat was to return to San Diego and take them on board just before direct departure out of the country. Since such a stop wasn't terribly practical during a race, he had to resort to other means.

After the race, he made a special trip by plane from Mexico City to San Diego to pick up his guns. He had to hand-carry them across the border into Tijuana, where he flew back to his home in Mexico City. Such is the inconvenience of carrying firearms.

KNOW THE RULES

For the yacht deliverer, transportation of firearms is a big problem, because either the beginning or the end of your long-range delivery normally involves some air travel. If even part of your air travel is outside the U.S., then the problem is compounded.

Let's assume, for example, that you're delivering a vessel from Miami to San Francisco via Panama, and that you must fly from your home

in Boston to Miami to begin the trip, and then fly home again from San Francisco. If you decide to have your own firearms on board, you'll have to fly them with you on both ends of the delivery.

If your flights take place totally over the U.S., that's no problem. The guns must be unloaded and placed in a hard, lockable container, with any ammunition in a separate piece of luggage. Declare the firearms as you check your luggage, and be sure to lock the container when told to do so. Carry a permit with you as well. Some airlines ask you to take the gun case into a back room, open it and prove the guns are unloaded. That's all there is to it.

However, if you're delivering a vessel from Manila in the Philippines to Darwin in northern Australia, things can be more sticky. If the vessel has no firearms aboard and you feel it should, due to the threat of piracy, then you'll need to carry them to Manila with you on the airplane. If you want to keep the guns after the delivery, that means you'll need to fly them back with you from Australia.

Most countries don't want foreigners walking around armed. Call or write the consulates of the countries where the boat delivery begins and ends, and check with the airlines you're using. Tell them exactly what you want to do, why and when. You may find out it's better to throw the gun overboard rather than enter with it or try to sell it in that country. You may find out you can save yourself enormous hassle by simply carrying a different type firearm or weapon, which still would offer you the protection you need.

In most cases involving foreign travel, it simply isn't worth the hassle.

When carrying a gun on deliveries through dangerous waters, our personal choice is one 12-gauge pump-action shotgun, period. A shotgun is often categorized as a sport

Secure navigation. A 12-gauge, short-barreled, five-shot, pump-action shotgun is a good weapon for protection at close range.

weapon, which in some countries is perfectly legal to keep on board. A shotgun can be a devastating weapon at close range, where most violent confrontations occur. Boarding by stealth at night is a good example. We carry a 12-gauge, 5-shot pump with a short barrel. The first round is 00 buckshot, and the second is a hollow-point slug sufficient to penetrate a pilothouse or hull. The remaining rounds are buckshot, slug, buckshot.

The Audie Murphy types who go armed to the teeth usually carry three basic types of firearms: shotguns, sidearms and rifles. Sidearms are designed for close range, and rifles for longer range.

People choose sidearms for two reasons: concealment and portability. Where does concealment fit into the yachtsman's scheme? Nowhere, legitimately. Portability is another story. In hostile waters, he might wish to carry a sidearm in a holster while on deck, mostly to keep his hands free for other work. Or, he might sleep with it under his pillow; in a surprise night attack, a pistol is much easier and quicker to bring to bear than a shotgun. Quicker, but less accurate.

Automatic pistols are more dangerous to innocents than is any other weapon. Not only are they wildly inaccurate, but well trained soldiers accidentally shoot themselves and innocent bystanders because of all the "safeties" found on these guns. Accident or not, .45 slugs are very destructive to human flesh and bone.

Pistols are also highly susceptible to illegal confiscation. If any official in a foreign boarding party takes a fancy to your pistol, even if it is legal, it may be taken away for unofficial examination. Latin American machismo involving sidearms far exceeds our own U.S. frontier-bred attachment to them. This infatuation with guns is heightened in countries where private citizens are forbidden to own them. Pistols are hot black-market items, so if you insist on carrying one on board in foreign waters, be prepared for the consequences, the least of which is to have it taken away from you.

Rifles are meant to eliminate or neutralize the opposition at long range, before they get too close. At first that sounds reasonable, but at such distances, it's very difficult to evaluate whether someone is about to be hostile to you or not. In fact, it's nearly impossible to ascertain hostile intent unless someone opens fire on you from that distance. If one or more do, they are also apt to be heavily armed and organized, and are fully prepared to win. A rifle encourages you to shoot too soon, which would be to your opponent's advantage and would just make things worse for you. For this reason, I don't think rifles have much practical value on board. The best tactic is to avoid areas known for such attacks.

In most of our world, local authorities take a very dim view of high-power rifles aboard small vessels. Even semi-automatic rifles are highly suspect, because of their usefulness as military weapons. Fully automatic weapons are sure to land you in deep yoghurt, even in the U.S. Arms smuggling is rampant along the waterfronts of many nations, and all governments are sensitive to it.

The captain is totally responsible for the

control, care, and use of weapons onboard, and for training the crew. Unstable crew members could cause problems in this department, as John illustrates:

We were delivering a large motor yacht from Florida to California, and as we departed Cozumel heading south, we headed well offshore to stay away from political problems that were reported along the coast of Nicaragua. This route took us about 100 miles offshore of Honduras and right by tiny Swan Island, which is close to absolutely nothing but more sea and sky.

We had passed Swan Island many times and always wanted to check it out, but it had never fit into our schedule. This time, however, an overnight stop at Swan would give us a perfect landfall at our next stop, Isla San Andres, where we could arrive and fuel in daylight.

Swan Island was a U.S. possession, uninhabited for decades except for a tiny, U.S.-manned meteorological station. In 1979 the island was given to Honduras, and the weather station was phased out to the point where, after a few years, only two or three U.S. citizens were left to maintain the building.

The Mexican deckhand we had aboard on

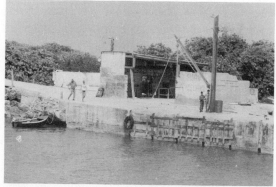

Only a few minutes before this photo was taken, we were fired on at close range by the men on this pier on Swan Island in the western Caribbean.

this delivery had paid a visit to the island six months earlier, and he had been warmly received by the lonely American meteorologists. We were looking forward to our stop and a peaceful night's sleep.

As we neared the tiny, barren island, I made a slow approach to the only anchorage, because it is not well-charted and has many coral heads around it. As I inched further into the cove, I could see someone riding a bicycle down a hill toward the water and what might have been a crude cement seawall.

I carried on to the south to look at our departure route amid the coral heads while it was still daylight, because we intended to leave before dawn the next morning. At a distance of several hundred yards I heard gunfire—several equally spaced shots.

Thinking that it was a distress signal, I turned and headed back in. One of our crewmembers was a paramedic, and we thought that if somebody were in medical trouble way out here in the middle of nowhere, we could be of help.

Steering from the tall flybridge, I slowly approached the lowest point of land where the seawall was. When we were within 100 yards of it, I could see several more figures running in all directions. Looking through the binoculars, I saw about a half-dozen men dressed in combat fatigue pants, cut-off shorts, either bare-chested or wearing T-shirts of various colors. They were carrying M-16 rifles and one had an M-60 machine gun.

I stopped the boat. Whatever medical or political problem was happening on Swan Island, I decided, they could take care of themselves; I wanted no part of it. Slowly, I turned the boat in on its length and headed back out to sea.

Just then, I heard the unmistakable sound of a bullet whizzing very close to my head and then the sound of the gun that had fired it. This is because bullets travel faster than the speed of sound. I'd been shot at before, and I had no doubt I was being shot at again. Then two more bullets passed very close in rapid succession.

Pat was standing right next to me, and we were both highly silhouetted on the open bridge. At a range of 100 yards, I knew we were both dead if the rifleman wanted us that way. I stopped the boat completely. Whatever they wanted, there was no point in trying to run, because Pat and I were sitting ducks.

Just then, the boat lunged forward and started moving toward the exit. I tried grabbing the throttles but someone down on the lower bridge was also trying to take control. While Pat tried to hold back the throttles, I ran down below.

I found my engineer at the throttles, but to make matters worse, the deckhand had broken out our weapons (a 16-gauge shotgun and a .22 pistol) and was getting ready to return fire! In their panic, they thought I had been hit by the gunfire, and they were trying to run away.

I was furious and got them to leave the controls alone and put the guns back in the screw-top compartment. Considering our range and the type of firepower that was leveled against us, if my crewmembers had returned fire or just kept the boat moving, the whole boat might have been blown to smoking splinters and all of us killed.

Two men circled us in a launch, one dressed in a dungaree jumpsuit, carrying a .45 pistol. He was ordering us to come to their "pier" to be boarded by the Honduran Navy. This was our first indication that these scruffy-looking men were not pirates. But we still weren't sure. I said I would rather anchor off for the boarding, because their "pier" had a dilapidated face and because the water alongside it looked too shallow. He waved the pistol and kept repeating that I must go to the pier.

Pat went down to the pilothouse and immediately got on the ham radio, which was set, as usual, on 14.313 MHz, for the maritime mobile net. If we were about to disappear, we wanted the whole world to know where. The net control immediately patched her through to the U.S. Coast Guard in Miami, and moved the normal net off to another frequency. She related exactly what had happened and then stayed on the air, keeping the contact open by describing what was occurring.

Two soldiers boarded us from the launch while we were still making our way to the pier. With the pistol and two M-16s drawn, they quickly ran through the entire boat, counting people, opening doors and poking gun barrels into closets. As we docked, soldiers swarmed out of the bushes and climbed on board. Several soldiers then moved the machine gun down to the pier so it was facing right through the pilothouse windows, trained at Pat on the radio right next to the lower helm station. A squad of infantry fanned out in the low hills around the pier with their M-16s trained on us.

A small but freshly painted sign near the pier read "Armada de Honduras," and standing beneath it was the young man in the bright red T-shirt who had fired at us.

When I got off the boat the man in the dungarees asked in patois English, "Who are you? Where are you going? What are you doing here?" Spanish is the common language of Honduras, so I thought this man was probably from Roatan, Honduras, which has a large, native English-speaking population, and that he was going to act as interpreter.

I was angry and insisted on using Spanish. "Who are you and what the hell did you fire on us for? Who's in charge here?"

The kid in the red T-shirt came over and said, "I'm the *sargento* and I'm in charge. And I fired on you because I didn't like your attitude."

I suspected we were in trouble then. That's not much of a reason to shoot at somebody.

"Why did you turn around and leave?"

"I saw your men in fatigue pants and T-shirts, and you looked like bandidos or drug smugglers or revolutionaries. There are a lot of those around this part of the world, you know. You aren't wearing any recognizable uniform."

I could tell from the look in his eyes that I had hit a nerve and he hesitated a moment.

"We are going to search your vessel."

For the next few minutes, the armed soldiers made a very thorough search of the boat. One stood guard over Pat as she continued to talk to the U.S. Coast Guard in English.

Feelings were tense when they first boarded, but when they saw we weren't carrying a big load of firearms or drugs, they began to relax. Pat gave the microphone to our engineer, then she opened three six-packs of ice-cold Coca-Colas and passed them around to the soldiers. It must have been the universal peace offering, because from that minute on, they did an about-face.

"OK, we see you're clean. Do you want to disembark and walk around the island? How many days do you plan to stay here? We don't get many visitors."

"No thanks. If you will please just untie the dock lines we will be on our way."

I didn't want to give them the chance to change their minds, so five minutes later we were out of range of their guns. So what if we arrived at our fuel stop a little early?

I protested this action by letter to the U.S. Consulate in Honduras and to the Honduran Consulate in the U.S. At that time, Honduras was supposed to be the U.S.'s staunchest ally in Central America, so I also sent a letter of protest to my senator. I never received a reply from any of them.

The moral to our story is this: Hollywood theatrics with guns tend to be fatal in the real world.

If you do decide to carry arms aboard, the captain must be totally responsible for them. Fom the start of the trip, all guns should be kept in one location, and they should be locked up by the captain with orders that they are not to be unlocked or loaded without his explicit order. It is also the captain's responsibility to familiarize crewmembers with the use of the guns on board.

Some shooting ranges offer very good training sessions in the use, safety, and maintenance of various firearms. The classes are taught by firearms specialists, who pass on healthy attitudes about when to use or not use a gun.

Whenever you point a loaded gun at someone, be prepared to take his life with it. Why? Because he may try to end your life before you can end his. If you're not sure you're capable of killing another human being, don't take guns on board. If you do take guns on board, use them responsibly.

CHAPTER 19
COOKING AT SEA

We left our seafaring heroine in Chapter 8, chained in one corner of the boat, obscured behind boxes, bags, and stalks of bananas, muttering quietly to herself while stuffing pancake mix into small, neat packets.

As we rejoin her now, she's being encircled by hungry native sailors whose stomachs growl like hollow drums. "How about some *grub!!* Something simple," they implore her, "like toasted BLT sandwiches."

Woefully, she casts her eyes about, hoping to find even one open stretch of counter space that measures four by four inches. "I'd wanted to make something really special for our first day out," she laments. "At this rate I'll be lucky to come up with hot dogs."

Once underway, the galley must be transformed into the ocean-going epitome of the kind of synchronicity found in McDonald's. Just like the bridge, the galley is a vortex of life at sea. As cook on duty, your galley becomes the central dispensary of all sustenance, both edible and moral. How you're going to pull off this herculean transformation, I have no idea. But on every successful passage, this magic does happen during the first few hours underway.

You might choose an open galley, or a closed galley. An open galley means each crewmember helps himself to whatever is available on board, perhaps cooks for himself, and lets the cook handle the cleanup. In one variation of the open galley, each crewmember also cleans up after himself.

A closed galley means the cook chooses, prepares, serves and cleans up the meals. This virtually puts the galley off limits to the rest of the crew.

Over the years we've tried it both ways, and what we think works best for yacht delivery, as opposed to cruising, is a modified closed galley. That means the cook keeps certain areas open to wandering crewmembers who need a little something between meals.

When we were cruising and would run low on money for food, we would tap into a savings account, or stop the boat and work for awhile, or just eliminate some of the pleasant side trips.

Because of the stringent budget imposed on each delivery, and because of the critical planning of provisions, food must be rationed over the length of the delivery. The idea of allowing hard-working crewmembers only so much food is ridiculous. It brings to mind the infamous slave galleons of the 15th century.

This is why you need to plan well: so each crewmember is well fed for the entire length of the trip. Stingy cooks can create disharmony on board. I've never had crew complain about not getting enough to eat, and after much practice, there isn't an abundance of food left over at trip's end. Reprovisioning enroute for some food items is a common practice (see Chapter 8, page 58 on reprovisioning underway), but on a delivery it won't compensate for not having enough on board in the first place.

Meal preparation gets easier as the rhythm of the voyage grows more regular. Port stops are wonderful adventures, great chances to reprovision, eat out, meet new people, but I find that they interrupt my efficient rhythm in the galley, and it takes me a few meals at sea to get back on track.

USING THE MASTER MEAL PLANNER

Pull out your handy master meal planner (see Appendix II) and start crossing off lunch and dinner entrées as you serve them. Mark the date next to each meal menu as you serve it, especially if you plan to repeat the list. This will also help you avoid redundancies, like serving chicken every other night.

During the first few days you'll find out how much new crewmembers usually consume. Prepare enough for second helpings of main entrées and desserts for everyone onboard. Someone who never ate a spoonful of applesauce before may discover halfway through the trip that he loves the stuff. When you're deciding how much to make, be sensitive to the fact that sailors are generally independent animals, and most of us like to decide for ourselves how much we're going to eat. If you can't seem to get the amounts to work out perfectly, it's better to have leftovers than to have a crew who thinks you're starving them.

MEALTIME

My version of the closed galley works like this. Using my master meal planner, I decide what to serve for dinner. I usually tell the crew

ahead of time what's on the menu, because surprises don't always generate the reaction you hope they will. Besides, this gives them a chance to savor the thought of food for awhile. When possible, I ask crewmembers to decide between—say, chicken cacciatore or chicken parmesan. But since I have an exact amount of chicken to use up, they can't always choose roast beef instead.

As the meal is coming together, I set out the plates and silverware on a counter top or somewhere just outside the galley's normal work area. Use the rubber mesh to keep them from sliding away. In normal sea conditions, it's best to leave hot food on the stove. In glassy seas or when in port, I may also set out the serving dishes.

When it's time, I call the first round of eaters—those who are about to go on watch next. If you choose a closed galley, it's up to you to have meals on the table early enough so they can be done eating in plenty of time to relieve the previous watch. Everyone eating grabs their plates and utensils and comes to the stove to dish up for themselves. This way they can see how much mashed potatoes and gravy is available for everyone, and determine for themselves exactly what constitutes their fair share.

Food must either be kept hot for the second shift, who will come to the table directly from watch, or you'll have to serve it to them where they are. Each delivery is different, but if someone is hand-steering in heavy seas, they'll prefer to wait to eat until they're relieved by the next watch. I try not to let the food get overcooked for the next round.

Only during the first few meals should you need to remind the first round of eaters to save enough food for the second round.

If people want to wander off, that's fine. On the other hand, sometimes the meal is the only time a large and busy crew gets to see one another for a chat. This is one of the routines the cook should let develop as it may.

We had one crewmember who was an interesting fellow and was great at his job, but he had this obnoxious habit of stuffing his mouth and then talking. Partially chewed food dropped out all around him, yet he remained oblivious to it, halting neither his monologue nor his fork. At first, it was all I could do not to burst out laughing, which would have been rude. I had to take my plate into another cabin. But as the delivery went on, other crewmembers grew increasingly angry with him for this habit. Even when people mentioned it to him in a nice, polite way, he persisted. We weren't about to change the bad habits he had developed over a half-century.

Crewmembers' habits will surface around the dinner table, so we just let people work them out for themselves. We don't sign on problem people more than once.

When the crewmembers are finished eating, they tear up their paper plates and dispose of them in the biodegradable trash, along with all paper napkins and organic refuse, meaning the beans they didn't finish, etc. Later, if we're well out to sea, we'll put organics overboard. Any plastics go into the "bag of higher consciousness," which stores nondegradable trash until I can dispose of it properly in port.

The crew brings all washable plates, mugs, and silverware back to the galley so I can wash them. Very seldom do crewmembers dawdle over their plates for hours, but if I've already got the dishes done and put away, I let them wash their own.

Coffee cups like to wander around all over the boat in the twilight hours of dawn and sunset. That's fine. As mentioned in Chapter 8, I buy each crewmember his own mug, label it with his name, and make him responsible for bringing it back to the galley and washing it

sometime before I get busy with the next meal.

Some of those mugs would be incredibly grotty by the end of the delivery if I didn't give them a good washing every once in awhile. With some crewmembers, having their own mug is an opportunity to show their utter responsibility; never is it cruddy or absent from its rack between meals. Others never can seem to remember where they left it. Buy spare mugs.

A common exception to this meal routine is the short-handed delivery. If the cook is standing full night and day watches (see below), we occasionally let each crewmember fix his own breakfast of, say, Granola and bananas or Instant Breakfast or coffee, toast and orange juice, which the cook can simply set out before retiring. Breakfast seems to be the easiest meal to handle this way, since most of our crewmembers prefer to skip it and sleep in anyway.

Cook's Watch

If you're not already an experienced galley hand, you will be by the end of your first long passage. But until that time, it's best for everyone on board if you sleep during the normal nighttime hours and stay awake during the day. This way you can make and serve three daytime meals and make up one "mid-rats" snack (midnight rations), for the night watches.

Or, depending on your seagoing experience, Cook's Watch may mean that you also stand one or more helm watches during daylight hours, while other crewmembers are roaming about but not actually on duty.

Whichever way you set it up, Cook's Watch is the most desirable watch ever devised, and it's the envy of everyone else on board. They, after all, must hurry up to sleep for three or four hours, roust themselves at unnatural hours of the darkness to take the helm, and then try to sleep in while the sun is shining.

Seasoned cooks long for the days before they became so adept that they could do both jobs: prepare all the regular meals plus stand regular helm watches around the clock like the rest of the crew. Don't be too impatient to give up your Cook's Watch.

While I'm standing my regular "four-on, eight-off" (no more Cook's Watch), I plan out the next two days' meals in between steering the boat, updating the fix, doing engine room checks, changing sails or filters, or whatever must be done. It sounds something like this:

Thaw today's lunch meat in the sink, but tomorrow night's pot roast can thaw slowly in the ice box. If I use the big roast this time, I can use its leftovers for lunch the day after tomorrow, when we'll be bashing up Buzzards Bay and I won't want to be hanging out in the galley. I'll save the small pot roast for that first day after our next port call, because it will be calm in the lee of Cape Cod.

THE GALLEY IN MOTION

You may find that some adjustments are necessary before you can get in full swing. If the pots-and-pans cupboard is right near someone's bunk and they rattle excessively when you're underway, you'll have to find another place for the pans. Maybe dry staples could go in the pots-and-pans cupboard, and vice versa.

Invariably, now's when you learn of all the foods that the crew absolutely can't stand, but forgot to tell you about when you first asked them at shopping time.

Drawers and doors that fly open when the boat heels, the pitcher of juice that tips over inside the fridge, the microwave dish that sloshes over—all the little nuisances that de-

fied detection during the sea trial will start sneaking out during these first days underway.

My first resort for solving motion-induced problems is the all-purpose homemade wedge, described in Chapter 8. Cardboard and duct tape go a long way to secure those flight-prone drawers and doors. Fold up some cardboard, wedge it in above the drawer to make sure it's the proper size, and then tape the loose folds closed. Tape the wedge in place so that the drawer can still close and the wedge stays stationary. Door fasteners usually can be adjusted with a screwdriver to clamp closed and stay there. If that fails, a duct tape closure may look sloppy and need to be replaced often, but it beats having the cupboards spill their contents.

We were delivering a large fishing vessel through some heavy seas, when the huge top-loading freezer toward the bow began to flip its lid open each time we dropped off a wave. I strapped the lid closed with duct tape and limited the number of times I needed to get into it by pulling out a day's worth of food at a time. Every third day or so I had to replace the dried-up tape. But soon the seas overpowered even my widest duct tape, and I had to resort to a wedge. Our Panama Canal fenders are about three feet in diameter and have a nice bail and painter on them. One of these huge dayglow-orange fenders fit perfectly between the freezer and a deep shelf above it. The line on the fender helped me pull it out whenever I needed to get into the freezer, and stuffing it back in was a cinch, as long as I waited for a rising wave.

Extra rolls of paper towels and toilet paper make excellent wedges in the galley, even inside the fridge, to keep the juice pitcher from falling over. Extra paper plates wedged between glass plates will keep them from rattling and shattering.

That spool of bungee cord we put onboard

during the boat prep comes in handy now. Cut off what you need and tie a knot in both ends. Bungee stoppers are ideal to tie cupboard doors shut and to immobilize things like the coffee maker, small furniture, tool boxes, produce bins, camera bags, tubes of charts, overhead fishing rods, and even cabin doors.

Once underway, you may want to leave the pan holders attached to the stove rail (see Chapter 8, page 68) and just adjust them to different sizes as you change pans. I sometimes leave pans stored on the stove, held in place by holders even when they're not being used.

If the boat's motion has an extra jerk or snap to it, modify the pan holders by adding bailing wire from the engineer's tool box to hold pots in place. In a pinch, I once used a wire coat hanger to keep our Thanksgiving turkey in its roasting pan and to secure the pan to the oven rack. The paint or varnish has to be removed before putting coat hanger wire in contact with food or heat, because it flakes off and also is flammable.

You'll discover many galley uses for wire, bungee cords, duct tape, cardboard, and all forms of wedges, but there is a limit to how secure you can make the galley or any living space on board a vessel underway. Even the best gimballed stove on the market can only swing so far before the soup launches itself across the cabin.

Heavy Weather Grabbers

These are re-heatable entrées that you prepare in fair weather or in port. Even in fair weather, a beam sea can make the galley uncomfortable and hazardous.

Ideally, before each leg of a long voyage, I cook up a batch of chicken pieces, ground turkey, steak cubes, hamburger patties, and other principal ingredients for dinner entrées in anticipation of bad weather. I freeze them in Ziploc freezer bags or Tupperware canisters so I can defrost them quickly in the microwave or in a sink of warm water. This reduces the amount of time I must spend in the galley by more than half, yet my crew gets a hot, hearty meal despite the weather.

Cooked pasta freezes well, thaws quickly and it even microwaves nicely. Boil up a batch and freeze some alone in baggies. If you can, make up a few complete pasta dishes with ground beef or chicken or tuna, tomato sauce, veggies and spices. Cheese sauces tend to granulate after thawing, but you could plan to add grated cheese while reheating the otherwise-complete entrée.

Canned and frozen entrées are also handy grabbers for foul weather, but don't overstock with whole boned chickens and La Menus.

When it's too rough to cook, but you can still heat water, make everyone a large mug of rich bouillon. Pass out trail mix, graham crackers or soda crackers in baggies so they can tuck them in their pockets and munch as weather permits. Unfortunately, leftover sandwiches seldom make good foul-weather grabbers. I can't count how many dozen dried up or soggy sandwich halves I've saved, only to toss.

When To Get Out Of The Galley

Even after strapping yourself into the cook's sling, you may encounter sea conditions in which you're no longer able to work in the galley. After almost 10 years of cooking on boats and more than 70,000 sea miles, I don't look proudly on my many scars as battle medals, but rather as mementos of all the times I knew better.

When your route calls for 48-hours of beating around Punta Ventosa, try to make up a few good meals ahead of time that can be reheated easily or eaten cold. Consider that no one may feel like eating in rough seas, and that what little they can eat should be as nutritious as possible. Avoid dairy products or other ingredients that tend to sour the already-queazy stomach. Whip up a few and then get out of the galley. Rough weather often means all hands are needed on deck anyway. The world won't stop if you postpone a meal or two. That's what snacks and grabbers are designed for.

Each of us has to decide when it's time to get out of the galley and when to dive back in. If unforseen bad weather persists, you may run out of nutritious grabbers. In sustained storm conditions, what the crew really needs is one good, hot meal each day. It's not only mandatory for their physical well-being, it's also an important morale booster, a welcome comfort in hours of stress.

RECYCLING AT SEA

Plastic is a convenience at sea, yet it endangers life in the sea. Lightweight, washable, durable, there are many seagoing advantages in using plastic bags, bowls, wraps and utensils. The problem with plastic is that it virtually never disintegrates, whether plowed into landfills or tossed overboard at sea. At the end of 1988 the U.S. Congress joined other nations in ratifying Annex V of the International Convention For Prevention of Pollution From Ships. Worldwide, it is no longer legal to dump any form of plastic from any vessel in any body of water.

Plastic is not just an eyesore; it upsets the ecological balance and can kill marine life indiscriminately. My heart is sickened by the hundreds of styrofoam coffee cups I've seen floating two hundred miles from shore, the dozens of fish and sea birds I've seen drowned or strangling slowly inside a collar of plastic that once held someone's six-pack. Remember the old adage: If you're not part of the solution, you must be part of the problem.

The only solution is to keep all your plastics on board until you reach your next port. Designate one plastic bag as your plastics saver, your "bag of higher consciousness."

I normally start off each trip with a small plastic grocery bag hanging handy in the galley, next to the other garbage bag or the trash compactor. When I can no longer wash and re-use Ziplocs or baggies, I rinse out any remaining food debris to prevent odors from growing before I scrunch them down into my bag of higher consciousness. When this first bag is filled, I squeeze all the air out of it, tie it down small and store it in a burlap bag stashed in a shady spot. If burlap is unavailable, designate one of those large lawn and leaf bags.

Even when you're making ocean passage, odor and space aren't problematic if you treat your plastic trash like this. Normally, you can take it all to shore when you arrive in the next port. I try to make sure the locals don't just dump their trash cans back into the water, as I've seen in some Latin American ports. We have sometimes buried our own trash, just as we do while camping.

We all make jokes about giving the "Float Test," or "Deep Six-ing" things, but seriously, make every effort to compress your remaining trash and to keep it on board until you can dispose of it wisely onshore. Food, paper, tin cans, and glass jars can go overboard only in certain locations and only with many reservations. Don't throw anything overboard within sight of land or where current could carry it shoreward. Don't throw anything overboard in deep trenches where lack of oxygen inhibits disintegration. Don't throw things overboard near shallows or seamounts that scuba divers frequent. The ocean is not a featureless desert; be aware of where you are before your throw biodegradables over the rail.

Food scraps should be torn small and jettisoned in small quantities, not in big batches.

If paper plates have plastic backing or if paper towels have plastic mesh, add them to your bag of plastics and avoid buying those brands for your next trip. Otherwise, paper and cardboard should be torn into small scraps before getting the toss.

Aluminum and steel oxidize quickly in salt water, and even Jacques Cousteau says that they make fine temporary houses for small sea creatures, but if you don't sink your cans, they can float for months without rusting through and often end up on the beach. Squeeze the middle of each aluminum soda can and tear a big hole in its side before tossing it. Remove at least one end of each food can and either start another hole in the other end or fill it with salt water before tossing it.

Glass jars and bottles can be recycled in almost every major U.S. port. Otherwise, large glass containers are best smashed in the trash compactor, if you have one. Eventually all glass objects can return to silica sand, but they must be shattered as soon as possible to start them on their long journey back to that natural state. If there is no trash compactor aboard, put a few jars and bottles into a large bucket, cover them with newspaper or some other disposable cover, and carefully break them up

with a hammer or winch handle. Wash splinters out of the bucket and off the deck.

Since most trash compactor bags are made of sturdy plastic-coated paper, keep the broken glass in these bags along with your bag of plastics. If you can't break up your glass jars and bottles, at least remove the lids, fill them with water and sink them. By not smashing them, I fear you are adding hundreds of years to their life as part of the pollution problem.

During my first year cruising the Sea of Cortez, I was anchored in 35 feet of crystal-clear water over white sand and coral in a pristine cove on the north end of Isla Carmen. We'd been scuba diving all morning and were returning under water to the three boats, checking our anchors, when two Campbell's soup cans fluttered down from above. Still awed by the cove's natural loveliness, we all froze and just gaped at the rude red cans until they settled onto the sand bottom. Then, without comment, we swam forward and retrieved the offensive cans. The incident left an indelible image in my mind, and for days it inspired a thoughtful discussion among many boats about our responsibility for the environment we enjoy so much.

CHAPTER 20
KEEPING HEALTHY

Don't believe for a minute the myth that going off to sea will whip you into peak physical condition, or that a nice long voyage with plenty of fresh salt air and exercise will cure any case of the blues. It's a lovely notion, but coastal hopping and passagemaking do not necessarily provide adequate exercise for the entire body.

If you are vacation cruising on your own vessel, you can set your own itinerary and take time for physical fitness. Yacht delivery, on the other hand, makes stringent demands on your time, your body, and your mental state. Physical strain and mental stress are very real parts of the job. They're not insurmountable, but you should learn how to deal with them. In fact, anyone contemplating an arduous sea voyage should first take a close look at his physical and mental fitness.

THE STRESS OF SAILING

If you go off to sea with a paunchy belly, hoping to work it off underway, you're very likely to injure your back while hauling on lines or lifting things as the boat rolls. Weak abdominal muscles contribute directly to weak back muscles. And once you've suffered a back injury, how much exercise will you get lying flat in your bunk for the remainder of the trip?

If your agility level has ebbed a bit since the last time you got out on the water, you're likely to injure yourself and others by tripping over lines, missing as you grab a handhold, not being able to dodge moving objects fast enough, or careening into bulkheads. Cuts, bruises and sprains are common complaints that follow a drop in overall physical agility.

Short voyage or long, a delivery schedule is strenuous. Round-the-clock watches immediately disrupt the mechanism of your internal clock. Overnight port stops confuse it even more, and your reserves of vitality are soon drained away. If you start off with a little flu, lack of normal sleep could aggravate it into pneumonia. Food and water are different from your normal routine, sometimes genuinely foreign to your body.

The myth that the constant roll of a boat provides good physical conditioning should be clarified. True, there's some isotonic value to clenching your leg muscles, but not in keeping them clenched or in keeping your knees locked. To do this hour after hour, day after day without frequent stretching and relaxing of those muscles leaves a toxic residue of lactic acid to build up in your muscles. This isn't healthy.

If you're the captain, not only do you get the constant mental stress of being responsible for everything and everyone, but you carry all the decision-making burden. You're the one they call at the last minute before the freighter runs you down.

For any crewmember, those monotonous

hours of watch standing are punctuated by un-expected, short bursts of action, blasting your languid system with an adrenaline rush that makes some people nauseous. And then as quickly as it sprang up, the crisis is past, hope-fully, and the metronome ticks away for the rest of your solitary watch. That kind of jerking around of the sympathetic nervous system does not contribute to anyone's health.

Good heavens, what a dismal picture! You might think from all this that we're trying to scare people away from going to sea or enter-ing the yacht delivery profession. On the con-trary. We're trying to be painfully honest about the real demands, to help you be better pre-pared before going to sea.

Getting Into Shape

We suggest that anyone contemplating an extended voyage get into shape, physically and mentally, long before they plan to leave. We believe there's a significant correlation be-tween regular physical exercise and mental health. If you go into the yacht delivery busi-ness, you may find you spend much of your time between trips recovering from the last one and getting yourself prepared for the next, as we do. Establishing a healthful routine is the best medicine.

Proper rest and moderation in the use of alcohol are important to staying in shape. Al-ways rest when you can, so you can hold up when sleep isn't possible. Historically sailors have a bad reputation for alcohol abuse. Make sure you don't damage your health and repu-tation with alcohol. When arriving at an inter-mediate port after a difficult passage, don't be seen boozing it up at the yacht club bar. You should be taking it easy so you'll be ready for the next leg. We feel so strongly about this that we don't allow alcohol consumption on board. Airplane pilots don't drink on the job and neither do we.

SEAGOING EXERCISES

Some familiar exercises can actually harm you when they're done onboard a small boat underway, because your center of gravity shifts as the boat moves. The most common result is that you put a vertebrae out of line or strain a major ligament while trying to keep in shape.

Here are some simple adaptations of famil-iar exercises that we've tailored for our sea-going world. They're intended to be done underway only as a last-ditch effort to keep you in good condition to avoid injury on the job.

First, to keep your agility honed, this famil-iar series of yoga stretches, called Salutation to the Sun, can be done in a companionway that's narrow enough for you to brace your arms against bulkheads. Also, by staying close to the boat's own center of gravity you'll lessen your chance of injury due to unex-pected motion.

1 With an elbow and forearm braced on each wall, stand as tall as possible without arch-ing your back. Inhale deeply and lift your stomach up and out of your hip enclosure a bit. Hold arms as high as possible while still braced on the bulkheads. Place feet as far apart as your shoulders. If possible, breathe deeply 12 times with each posture, but tailor this to your situation.

2 Tighten your tummy muscles, and while al-lowing your knees to bend slightly and your arms to slide down the bulkheads, ex-hale and bend over as far as comfortable. Keep your elbows and hands parallel to the horizon so you don't pitch forward or aft.

3 Carefully, bring your fanny down to make a squat over your feet, trying to keep your heels on the cabin sole. This should feel good to your ankles, calves, thighs, fanny,

Figure 20-1 through 20-3. Exercising at sea can help ease the stress of a long voyage, but only if it's done carefully.

and lower back. If you have no back problems, and only if sea conditions permit, continue bringing your shoulders and head down, arching your upper back slightly. Don't push out or curve your lower back.

4 Bring your hands down to the cabin sole as far apart as the narrow passageway permits, about a foot ahead of you, so you're well balanced athwartship. Stretch one leg behind you as far as possible with that knee and toes braced on the sole. The knee of the leg that doesn't move should be directly below your shoulder and directly above its foot. This should feel good to both inner thighs and to the top of the thigh behind you. Alternately flex and point the foot of the extended leg. Take a couple of deep

breaths and feel both leg muscles relax. If you're limber enough, let the bent knee move outboard of your shoulder and let both thighs stretch a bit more. Breathe some more. Try to look at the ceiling on the exhale, but don't force anything.

5 Bring the extended leg back under you, tucked into the squat position, breathe, and repeat slowly with the other leg, keeping both hands braced on the cabin sole. Then return to the squat position.

6 You'll be loosened up more now, and able to curl down into a smaller ball, but again don't push out on the lower back.

7 Bring your forearms and hands more to the bulkheads. With your shoulders low and

your weight centered over your feet, raise your fanny as far as comfortable without completely straightening your knees. In other words, keep your knees flexed, head low and fanny high. This should feel good to the back of your thighs. Breathe.

8 Knees still bent, tighten your tummy muscles and straighten up, *not* by lifting your head, but by tucking your hips back in line under your shoulders. Slide hands up

the bulkheads with you to keep yourself braced.

9 Raise your hands on the bulkheads as high as possible and stand tall without arching or hyperextending your back. Lift your tummy muscles up from your hip socket again, breathing in and out slowly.

Numbers four and five are great for releasing the toxic buildup of lactic acid from your

legs, caused by long hours of standing at the wheel.

Stress builds up in your shoulders from extended periods of steering, too. Try our version of the shoulder roll:

Brace your torso against the binnacle or something large and stationary. Face into the boat's primary direction of pitch so that any unexpected motion will be fore-and-aft to your body, not side to side. Imagine you're a puppet with the strings attached to the outside edge of each shoulder, and let your arms hang limply by your sides. Slowly lift both shoulders up and roll them forward, down, back and up again, circumscribing as large a circle as possible. Your arms simply hang down, letting your shoulders have all the fun. Roll 12 forward circles and 12 backward circles. Alternating circles feel good, too.

To clear the gravel from your weary neck,

find a solid place to sit and face into the boat's motion as above. Sit up straight with your head and back in a tall line. Slowly turn your chin "hard over" to starboard until it's directly over your shoulder. Don't force anything or twist your neck. Breathe a couple deep ones, and then slowly turn your chin hard to port, again no farther. Breathe again, and this time as you turn to starboard, raise your chin an inch higher than last time. Then to port a little higher. Each time you're drawing a higher horizon line with your chin. You can repeat this one often if you don't strain your neck the first few times you do it. It's normal to hear some gravelly sounds.

We actually do these exercises and some others underway. But in heavy seas or on a boat with a jerking motion, you face the possibility of harming yourself in the midst of an otherwise healthy workout.

CHAPTER 21
MORALE

Perhaps the main contributing factor to high morale on board is confidence in the captain.

If the captain shows his crew he is capable of prepping the boat well, navigating it across stormy seas, keeping their tummies full, showing consideration, and assuring them of further delivery work, then morale is bound to be good.

This book may not provide a lot of laughs, but we do believe that humor and levity are essential ingredients of high shipboard morale. Nowhere is it written that a capable delivery crew can't have a good time while doing their jobs well.

It's up to the captain to establish the level of humor and levity he expects underway. He has to open the first lines of communication between himself and crew and then keep them open for healthy input from the crew. If unhealthy tendencies develop during the voyage, the captain must recognize them and quickly redirect them back into healthy avenues.

If new crewmembers don't know from experience how much joshing around or relaxed behavior the captain thinks is appropriate, he should let them know early in the trip. Example is the best instructor. Tell a few sea stories and jokes. Allow people's natural personality to come out and show them it's okay.

If humor isn't appropriate, such as when you're in the middle of a DEA boarding, or if the crew gets out of hand and starts ignoring its responsibilities, put the cap on it. You may have to come right out and confront crewmembers by saying, "Hey, Fred, I said no backgammon playing while you two are on watch."

Morale and discipline are highly personal matters. Every person must handle them differently. Whatever is to be the level of camaraderie and familiarity on board, establish it clearly and early on, so misunderstandings don't have room to develop.

The two most common demoralizers at sea are boredom and fear.

BOREDOM

If crewmembers are bored, it's usually because they aren't used to providing their own mental and physical activities without the aid of a TV or car. They may not have the foggiest idea of how to make good use of their time between watches.

We do a lot of reading underway. In fact, between deliveries we save up books we want to read, which amounts to a tiny library of paperbacks for each trip. These are fun to share among the crew. The conversation on one delivery with a particularly literate crew roster sounded like a college class called "Analysis of Current American Novelists." It was great.

Remind everyone that a port stop is coming up soon so they'd better get those cards and letters written if they want to impress their friends with exotic postmarks and such.

Let crewmembers know when and where they'll most likely get a chance for shore leave. A boat is a small space, and they may be relieved just to know when they'll have a chance to get away from everybody. Or to get with somebody, if that's the case. We had one fine engineer who, on each delivery, was a cranky old bear to live with until he could get ashore in Panama and visit one of its famous houses of ill repute. For the rest of the long trip, he was a lamb. Well, relatively speaking.

Many crewmembers ask us to teach them coastal or celestial navigation. For this purpose, we take along at least one extra spiral notebook for each crewmember. Spiral notebooks also are good to give to crew for writing their own journals of the voyage.

FEAR

If new crewmembers aren't sure about their own ability to do their jobs on board, fear usually lurks just below the surface. And before they ask for help or advice from the captain or other crewmembers, what may pop up is a little case of hypersensitivity or "ouchiness." They may become disgruntled about things totally unrelated to the source of the fears they're harboring.

A good captain picks up on such underlying fears before they jeopardize the whole crew's morale. Clearly define their jobs and what you expect of them. Offer to show the new crewmember how you usually work out running fixes, or how you like to set up the complicated fuel transfer operation. Do it in such a way that no one's dignity gets slammed.

How do you open those proverbial but ephemeral lines of communication? Get into the habit of expanding the catch phrase, "How's it going?"

Instead try, "How do you like using the plot mode on that radar with this much traffic?" or, "Maybe it's time to start keeping a radar log." Or, "Yah, the dog watch is a real dog. I'll show you a set of calisthenics you can do at the wheel." Or, "Maybe it's time to start keeping a radio log. Have you heard from anybody tonight? Let's see if anyone else is out there."

It seems that once we learn what each of us needs to make us smile, compassion and camaraderie come easier. And we all tend to smile more.

A good captain will spot stress developing between crewmembers and will step in to ease the situation before it turns to hostility directed at other crewmembers or toward him.

If it's appropriate, warn others of someone's temporary personal problems. "Say, Joe. I don't know if you know it, but Pete seems to be having a pretty hard time of it getting through the death of his kid brother. I guess that's why he doesn't feel much like yukking it up with us. We shouldn't press him. He doesn't mean to be unfriendly, and I know he'd give you your space if you needed it." Or whatever.

Don't go telling everyone's personal problems just for the sake of juicy gossip, or you'll really stir yourself up a hornet's nest. But if you can ease hostilities, do so as soon as possible.

A little snappiness is common whenever people change their sleep patterns, so talk about it openly and make jokes about it.

But when unwarranted hostility develops, the captain must make haste to redirect that energy into harmless or helpful avenues. If you can help it, don't team up people on the watch schedule who obviously don't get along. Talk to each crewmember privately about how important it is that they get along reasonably, at least until the trip is finished. Remind them that nobody is perfect and it's important for the welfare of everyone onboard that they all be pulling on the same end of the rope.

Assign special projects to crewmembers with too much misdirected energy, but design the tasks to make the best use of whatever they consider to be their unique talents. Otherwise the projects may look like punishment.

Although brightwork maintenance is not normally part of our delivery contract, there are times when just such a project would serve as a morale builder.

TIDINESS ON BOARD

If the boat's interior starts looking untidy, crewmembers' habits tend to grow equally slovenly. Keep the main salon, helm area or bridge, nav station, galley and any common areas tidy.

If the muslin furniture covers creep down onto the salon floor right where everyone needs to walk, take responsibility and do something about it. Either ask crewmembers to help straighten them when they get up, or if they slip down due to the motion of the boat, then tie them up. If someone repeatedly leaves magazines on the sole where others could slip on them, ask the whole crew to put magazines away when they're done.

A crewmember's private berth should remain his domain, except if you suspect contraband. Make it clear from the beginning that bunks are to be kept neat. If someone's personal area starts looking like the aftermath of a knockdown, ask yourself whether that person is just a natural-born slob, or if he may be getting despondent. If asking him outright to please clean up his bunk doesn't seem appropriate, then organize a general cleanup every few days that involves the whole crew. They'll either get the hint or they won't.

Knocking down the salt crystals, deglazing the windshield, cleaning the transom, and bathing are all good projects for just before you enter a port.

BAD APPLES

Way back when you first interviewed these prospective crewmembers you should have sensed any personality quirks that might cause conflict underway. Every human being has personality quirks, good and bad, and sailors probably have more than their share of both. You took them on board for their seamanship qualifications, not for their smiles, it is true. And you are developing your own crew screening qualifications at the same time. And if you'd only bothered to keep the batteries charged in your crystal ball, you wouldn't be in this predicament.

But too late, here you are, far at sea with a rotten apple.

If one crewmember is obviously unbearable to everyone else on board, if he won't heed the gentle or not-so-gentle warnings from the captain, then you may have to "fire" him or replace him.

Our rule has always been that we won't actually fire anyone while underway. We may make the decision to fire him while we're in mid-passage, but for the sake of harmony and safety underway, we wait until we make port.

On a delivery, the captain has the obligation to pay off that crewmember in cash to date. If you can't pay him off, he has the right to put a lien on the vessel. All governments take this matter absolutely seriously.

Since you also have an obligation to pay for the return of crewmembers to their home port, firing them in Costa Rica or Hawaii could be very expensive. And if their absence leaves you too short-handed, then you must find a replacement for the duration of the delivery and no doubt return them to Costa Rica or Hawaii as well.

Weigh the consequences thoughtfully.

Sometimes ridding yourself of a truly dangerous person is worth great expense. Safety and harmony onboard are precious commodities, too. We've been lucky and have never had to fire anybody in mid-trip, but there have been times when we would have had it not been so expensive.

Let's hope it doesn't come to that. If you or your crewmembers have beefs, save them until you're in port and everyone is more relaxed, or write them down in a personal journal and consider the matter shelved until the delivery is completed. If Martin can't rise above Jose's shortcomings for at least 30 days—be it talking with his mouth full or being an inane braggart—the problem is partly Martin's.

If you have problems underway that simply cannot wait, problems that concern how people are doing their jobs, then the captain must step in and use his prerogative to solve the dispute.

The captain's word is law at sea. Lack of swift and appropriate action on the part of a wishy-washy captain can foment even more crew stress.

If you need to, use words like, "I don't allow arguments on my ships that disrupt anyone's ability to do their job. From now on, this is how we're going to do it. Period. If either of you think you need to express another word about it, can it 'till we reach Hong Kong and we'll straighten out this matter there. Is that clear?"

PART IV
THE YACHT DELIVERY BUSINESS

CHAPTER 22
DO YOU HAVE WHAT IT TAKES?

Whether you're a solo captain, a couple team, or a family business, yacht delivery is an exciting profession, no doubt about it. But in order to make a success of it, you need certain attributes, both physical and mental.

Chapter 20 on staying healthy pretty well describes the rigorous physical demands put upon the yacht delivery crew. Next, at the risk of sounding like a troop leader at a Boy Scout swearing-in ceremony, let's examine the personality traits required in the everyday life of a yacht delivery professional.

Business Aptitude: In addition to being a fine seaman, you must be a good business person, but unfortunately, some people find it hard to reconcile being both. Couples who work together well often can make up for slight shortcomings in their other half, but because of the nature of the work, each partner must have at least average business sense. Contracts and decisions must be made en route or when the other partner is unavailable.

Financial Flexibility: With self-employment comes financial insecurity. There's no guaranteed paycheck every two weeks. Unless you make it happen by sheer hard work and determination, nothing happens. And, it helps to have a cushion of savings to carry you through lean times.

Ultimate Sense of Responsibility: Being captain of a ship is like no other job in the world. The person in charge, the master, is completely responsible for the safety of the vessel and its crew, and for every act that occurs on board. If you are the kind of person who whines after losing your charge in heavy weather, "But it wasn't my fault; the owner told me to deliver this boat in the middle of hurricane season," then being a captain is not for you. There is no shifting of blame. You must make your own decisions and take responsibility for their results.

Self-Motivation and Self-Discipline: You are your own boss. Nobody makes you punch a time clock. To many, this is the primary attraction of self-employment. But others thrive on externally imposed structure that eliminates their decision of when to go to work and what to do next. They are simply told and therefore they have no doubts.

In yacht delivery, you have to clearly determine your own goals and then keep your nose to the grindstone while pursuing them. If you have no history of self-initiation or no self-imposed schedules for discipline, this may not be the place to begin.

Organization: Because of the expedient nature of yacht delivery, you must get things done much more quickly than the Corinthian cruiser. Time is more than just money, sometimes it means safety, too. If you waste time through disorganization you won't last in the business. In preparing a vessel for a trip you will be juggling hundreds of projects, big and small, and delegating tasks to perhaps a dozen workers. Everything must be accomplished within its own shortest possible time frame and so that all the project schedules dovetail with each other. At the same time, you may be lining up delivery trips to coincide with the finish of the present one, and therefore dealing with another complete set of projects. Are you good at keeping it all straight and on time?

Punctuality: If you have a mañana attitude or habitually arrive late for appointments, then you may as well forget this business, too. The captain can't be late, ever. That means you have to be habitually *early,* just to leave enough time for all the little things that could go wrong.

Assertiveness: You can't be wishy-washy. You must know what you want and be willing to go for it. This is true both on board and in your office. However, you don't want to be overbearing or deaf to the needs of others. That behavior is self-defeating.

Persistence: When making contacts with prospective clients you must follow through without hesitation. If you are shy about follow-ups or have an I-hate-to-keep-bothering-him attitude, you will lose business.

Communication: You will be dealing with very successful business people as your clients, so you must be articulate, have excellent communication skills, and be able to present yourself well. If you are easily tongue-tied, or give an impression of someone who's not too bright, you won't make it. Working against you is the notion many have that sailors are a bunch of transient low-lifers.

Composure: If you blow up in anger when things don't go the way you need them to, or if you become panic stricken when a fire breaks out on your ship, then yacht delivery is probably not for you. As captain, you must be very much in control of the situation during emergencies. You must direct and inspire the crew. Internally you may be scared to death, but you can learn to control your fear so that it doesn't control you. Never can you panic or transmit disabling fear to your crew.

If you were born with all these necessary attributes, you're a natural captain. If you weren't, don't give up. All of these characteristics can be developed through dedicated commitment to the task. Most of us must spend our lives learning and improving our leadership skills, but it's one of life's most rewarding tasks.

CHAPTER 23
SETTING UP SHOP

LOCATION

To launch yourself into the yacht delivery business you must locate yourself near one of the major yachting centers of the world. Starting this full-time business while living in some remote location is next to impossible. Just having a phone is not enough.

Later, after you are well established, you may move farther from the scene, but still you must live within range of instant communication (not just a once-a-day message desk or VHF radio), a large airport, preferably an international airport, and be available for a face-to-face interview tomorrow morning.

Let's look at these prime locations:

Ft. Lauderdale, Florida. This is the center of the U.S. yachting scene because it is located on the populous East Coast with a heavy concentration of wealth. Yachtsmen along the Eastern Seaboard gravitate toward the year-round warmth of this "Venice of America." All of the big-name yacht brokerages and yards are there, and it is the jumping-off place for the vast cruising and charter region of the Bahamas and the Caribbean. Ft. Lauderdale is the hub of the whole South Florida yachting region—which includes Miami, only a few miles away—extending all along the coast north to Palm Beach and beyond, and across the peninsula to Tampa Bay. This is the place to start in the yacht business, in the heart of all the action. Jobs are much more abundant and so is the competition. But to succeed you have to be a better hustler than the rest of the crowd, and Ft. Lauderdale is where it is happening.

Newport Beach, California. This is the trendy vortex of activity for the megamillion Southern California population center that extends 200 miles from Santa Barbara to San Diego. All the big name brokerages are concentrated in one small area of Newport Beach. Though the action is not as heavy or intense as Ft. Lauderdale, it's more than enough to get started in the business.

We mention other yachting centers in passing. The entire megalopolis of the Northeast is delightful cruising for small boats and has much commercial boat traffic, both conducive to delivery jobs. But the work here is too seasonal to support many deliverers without supplemental income.

San Francisco. The Bay area's yacht brokerages and marina areas are scattered, making it difficult for you to be highly visible. Tiny clusters of brokers and marinas tend to rely on their own in-house people for their infrequent delivery work. If you already live in the Bay Area, one of these small clusters may be a place to start, but generally speaking, San Francisco's yachting population isn't large enough to support many full-time professionals.

Seattle, Washington. Seattle is also very spread out, less densely populated, and you have to like the climate. Seattle-based deliveries tend to remain quite regional, the most distant being the highly seasonal Alaskan commercial vessels.

Hawaii. It's a great destination, but to base yourself there means being too isolated from where the long-range contracts are signed. Competition for local deliveries is high enough to keep the price sadly low. The cost of living in Paradise is exorbitant, and the number of passagemaking boats and brokers based there is quite small.

St. Thomas, U.S. Virgin Islands. This is the center of one of the world's largest charter sailing fleets and is part of a large cruising circuit that includes Europe. Despite the glamour here, it is really just a small and distant satellite of Ft. Lauderdale, where the contracts to deliver all these lovely boats are really negotiated. Chartering and delivering are not the same. Like most tourist paradises, St. Thomas has an outrageous cost of living.

Especially while building a reputation, you must start out where the business action is, not the glamour. Building a local reputation is the basis for building a worldwide one.

Telephones are essential, but your clients will not move to where you happen to like to hang out. We know of no successful, full-time delivery skippers who are not located within at least an easy commute of either South Florida or Southern California. They might exist; we've just never heard of them.

If you own a boat and live aboard, move yourself to one of these centers. In fact, try to find the center of the centers. Get on a waiting list for a liveaboard slip at one of the major yacht brokerages, yards, or marinas in Newport Beach or Ft. Lauderdale. Granted this is not always possible, but get as close as you can. Once there, you'll be so surrounded by business opportunities that you'll have to play blind not to see them. If you're inquisitive, omnipresent, and articulate about your business, you'll come up with many leads.

Only by comparing many leads will you become qualified to recognize a good delivery situation from the many potentially disastrous ones that will come your way. The more delivery possibilities you have to choose from, the less likely you are to grab the first job dangled in front of your nose.

If you live ashore, live as close to the yachting hub as possible, and develop waterfront business contacts. Spend as much constructive time on the docks as possible, not just standing around with your hands in your pockets.

TELEPHONES AND ANSWERING SERVICES

Before you begin making a systematic round of sales contacts, you should have your own telephone with its own answering machine (business announcement, not personal) or a 24-hour answering service, business cards, and a current resume. Without them, you're wasting everyone's time, because your contacts will have no reliable way of getting back in touch with you and no information on hand to review your background should they need your services in the future.

You cannot succeed without immediate access to your own telephone. This may be obvious to most people, but beginning yacht deliverers living on boats often do not have telephones. Many live on the hook and can't get a phone or don't wish to go to the expense of installing a telephone in the marina. To get around this they may use the telephone number of an answering service to which they are assigned an extension. This means that they can only be reached via phone message. This is better than nothing, but only slightly.

When a delivery client makes the initial call for information about a delivery, he is very excited about the prospect of having it done. The project is foremost in his mind and he has gone to the trouble of tracking down your phone number and placing the call. If you are there to answer the call when it comes in, the chances of that call resulting in a delivery are much higher than if you were to return the call via a message service. You will be able to instantly answer his questions, ask him relevant questions, and sell yourself while he is hot.

Returning calls relayed by message is difficult. The time delay involved depends on how often you pick up your messages. When you finally get his message, which might be the next day or later, you return the client's call. But by now he is out and you can only leave a brief message; thus a round of "telephone tag" follows. If and when you finally do get back in touch with him, he may not even remember your name or why he called you. Meanwhile, he very likely has dealt with some other skipper who answered his phone on the first ring.

If you live aboard and absolutely can't get a hard-line phone, get a cellular telephone. Slightly expensive perhaps, but you can't start a business without a phone. With a portable unit, you can move from cell to cell and remain accessible to your clients. Hard-line phones are the best.

Of course you can't always be sitting around waiting for the phone to ring, so get an answering service or a phone answering/recording device. The answering service with a live human being picking up your phone is normally far superior to the recording device. It gives your clients the impression of permanence and professionalism, and the operators are supposed to be trained to get the correct information: name, phone number, message, and time of call. Such services cost about $60 a month.

Finding a good answering service in some areas may be difficult. Ask other successful professionals for recommendations. We've gone through several companies over the years before finding a good one. The bad ones can drive your clients away.

Whenever both of us have to be away from the telephones, we use a 24-hour professional answering service on our highly advertised business phone number, plus an answering machine attached to our "back line." Even the answering machine has the capability of taping a 30-minute message, so clients don't feel rushed. We can take 15 two-minute calls before we pick up messages from a remote phone and clear them off.

The only problem with phone answering recorders is that some people still don't like them. In fact, some folks hate to leave an extemporaneous message on them, so instead they just hang up. Fortunately, they've become so popular and inexpensive that it's now impractical for anyone involved in the business world to avoid using them, like them or not.

As long as you're buying a phone-answering/recording machine, buy a good one. Check out those with remote message pickup capabilities, so that you can retrieve your messages from out of town, without running home. Ours also allows us to change our outgoing message from afar. Good ones cost about $100, which is considerably cheaper than a live answering service. Most machines begin to wear out within a year. As soon as it starts misbehaving, it could start losing business for you, so replace it immediately. You can't afford to miss clients' telephone calls.

Good business sense dictates that you show your reliability by returning calls as quickly as possible. Changing your phone number will also lose business for you, since is gives potential clients the impression that you're unstable. Furthermore, the phone company doesn't continue redirecting your callers for very long—especially after you move twice.

Don't change your phone number unless there is absolutely no way around it. Any contacts you made in the past probably have your old phone number and address, so it may be impossible or too much trouble to track you down. This negative effect carries over for years, losing you much business, unless you make an effort to track down all those former contacts and keep them advised of your new phone number and location.

We've moved twice in the past four years, but have stayed in the same San Diego waterfront neighborhood, partly to be able to retain the same phone number we've used for 10 years.

MINDING THE STORE

You will have to find someone to take care of your business while you're out on a delivery, otherwise business will grind to a halt each time you are gone. Pat can mind the store perfectly well, and occasionally she stays behind to do so, but normally she is an indispensible part of the seagoing crew. Delivery teams have this decision to make.

Whoever stays behind should at least be able to return phone calls that are delivery inquiries, relay messages via radio, give quotes, send out delivery proposals and your resumés, pay bills, and keep simple books. An obvious solution is to hire a secretary to sit at your desk while you are gone. However, we know of no individual in the yacht delivery business whose volume justifies hiring a full-time secretary.

You could try to get by picking up your messages from your own answering service every few days. However, high seas and foreign phone calls are prohibitively expensive. Also, the delay of a few days will cost you jobs.

Try to find someone to pick up your messages and screen your calls for you. Then you can be in touch with them every few days. Two problems with this arrangement are: the delay involved in returning calls; and finding someone who knows enough about boating and

yacht delivery to intelligently answer questions and ask for the appropriate information from the caller.

We struggled with this problem for years. We finally found a very acceptable solution. When we leave town, we call forward to our "secretary" who has an active, waterfront mail order business and is always at the phone during business hours. We simply call forward to her back line, and when a call comes in on this line, she knows it is for us and she answers it professionally with a cheery "Captain Rains' office."

She is a very knowledgeable boat person who has been involved with deliveries before and can answer and ask the right questions. She talks directly to customers the first time they call, while they are "hot." It's obvious to them that our secretary knows what she is talking about.

We leave her with a list of questions to ask (printed on a tablet of paper), our price list, and a list of names of clients we had been dealing with before we left.

We stay in touch with her via telephone—either land line or high-seas radio hookup. We call collect, so if she has nothing of any importance, she rejects the call. This is important, because high-seas calls cost approximately $5 per minute with a 3-minute minimum. You can say plenty in three minutes.

Learning what is worth the price of a high-seas call takes experience, but we leave her with a good idea. Many phone inquiries that we get are from customers who are thinking about buying a boat and want to know how much it would cost to deliver it. We are always interested in such calls, and occasionally they result in a delivery. But between thinking about buying a boat and actually buying it, there lies a long, rough road fraught with many side exits, detours, stop signs, and dead ends. Such a call would hardly be worth a high-seas call.

If we or our secretary already has discussed price with a particular client, they've thought it over and still are interested, then we're getting warmer. If they also have a good boat and need a captain to deliver it long-range immediately, then it's definitely worth the expensive call via high-seas operators. We've lined up some good trips while out at sea, exactly in this manner.

We pay the secretary a reasonable amount per day while we are gone, but have no need for her services while we're in town. We also pay her a commission on any trips that are lined up as the result of any phone calls that come to her while we're gone. This is good incentive for her to keep following up on any leads. She also picks up our mail and pays the bills while we are out of town.

If you're going to be successful, you must find someone to mind the store. The right person is worth his or her weight in gold.

STATIONERY AND RESUMÉ

Before beginning your calls, have business cards printed, so you have something to leave with your sales contact to make an impression of permanence. These can range from very simple cards printed in a few days, to very elaborate cards with your own logo designed by a graphic artist.

You might choose to use a company name, which can leave an initial impression of an office and staff, rather than of one individual. This must be legalized by obtaining a business license and whatever local rules call for. The process is quite simple and speedy. We didn't realize the value of establishing a company name until we had already established a large clientele using simply John Rains Yacht Delivery, after which it would have been foolish to change to a company name. Pat's freelance writing business, Good Words Editorial Consulting, and her yacht maintenance company,

Bucket Brigade, both portrayed a solid company image.

The card should show your name (preceded by Capt., your license level, and license number, if you have one), address and phone number. There's nothing wrong with listing both your work number and home number. However, don't use more phone numbers than this; it means you are difficult to find, and it clutters the card.

Also put on the card simply "Yacht Delivery." Many people put everything they do on the card like, Yacht Maintenance, Carpentry, Mechanical Work, Electrical Engineering, Chartering, Nautical Photographer. This really clutters up the card and gives the impression that you haven't yet figured out what you want to do when you grow up.

Remember that your small business card is only a reminder of your name, business, and how to contact you. It's not a thumbnail resumé.

You should also have a resume to give to your sales contacts during these personal calls. Resumés for yacht delivery should be totally oriented towards your nautical background, touching only briefly on other areas of your life that don't have anything to do with yacht delivery. List your name, date of birth, and citizenship, license levels and numbers, languages, education and accredited classes, particularly as they pertain to yacht delivery.

Then the resumé should list significant voyages you have made, delivery or otherwise. List them either chronologically or by size, starting with the biggest or most recent first. Data should include: type of boat, boat name, length or gross tonnage, your position on board, departure and destination ports, and dates.

Brief, one-page resumés are best for sales contacts. If this means you have to select only the most significant voyages to list, so be it. If your resumé arrives unsolicited, your contacts might just barely peruse a one-pager, but it is unlikely they will get past the first page of a resumé as thick as the *Random House Dictionary*.

We like to use a professionally printed resumé with our logo and a small photograph, with room at the bottom to add recent trips by typing them in.

If you must use two pages, try to keep your list of voyages entirely on the second page. Your name at the top is helpful, in case the two pages get separated.

You can have two resumés, one to present to sales contacts and one to show to prospective clients. This second one can be more extensive and contain your references.

RESERVE FUNDS

From the previous discussions it may have occurred to you that you'll need money in the bank to start down the path of yacht delivery. Money to buy your own boat, to take an extended cruise, or to crew on a boat while paying your own expenses. This is very true.

You need money to start any business and yacht delivery is no exception. Assuming you already have enough experience to land that first delivery job, you'll need enough capital to cover your own living expenses. Minimally, we'd say you need a least a year's income in the bank to get started. Ideally, you should have two years' income because that's how long it takes to make any business pay for itself, if it ever will. In other words, be willing to gamble one or two years' worth of your savings, because by the end of two years, you may have nothing left but a wonderful adventure and a lifetime's worth of sea stories.

If you're still with us, the good news is that yacht delivery doesn't demand a heavy capital outlay as do most other business. Aside from your normal cruising gear, you need only a telephone, an answering service and a post office box or some constant address. If you keep your living expenses low and budget your savings, you can probably get by just fine as the work starts coming in.

If you are saddled with a large mortgage and high car payments, installment loans and credit card debt, it is wise to postpone launching this career until these are paid off. There never will be a *regular* pay check in the mail to make these payments. (Even when you're a raging success, you will pay yourself from the business account *when you can.*)

It's best to begin with no major bills, with minimal rent or mortgage payments for your boat or home, and with a couple years' living expenses in the bank.

Having backup money is crucial for a second reason. It allows you to make rational decisions about whether to take certain trips. In the beginning you will be asked to make trips on unsafe vessels, during hurricane season, to politically dangerous destinations, or possibly even to deliver contraband. If you are hurting for money you may make a fatal decision.

How much can you expect to make in a year? If your goal in life is to become rich, then go back to school and become a lawyer or a doctor, achieve your goal, buy a boat and hire your own captain.

We euphemistically call yacht delivery "an alternative life style," since it is not a regularly categorized box to check along with mainstream American livelihoods. But if your goal is vocational independence and the excitement of a life at sea while making enough to maintain a roof over your head, put clothes on your back and food on your table, then yacht delivery is a truly viable occupation.

If you have all the attributes of an excellent *capitan par capitan* and are an aggressive and efficient businessperson, after five successful years in the business you should be netting about what full-time yacht captains make, about $36,000 annually.

Still here? This financial profile is actually better than that of the full-time yacht captain, because you will make that in six to eight months each year. That's the maximum time you will be delivering, because you'll need administrative time between deliveries to find other deliveries, or to nail down the ones the secretary worked on. Much more sea time than that approaches "burn-out" level.

You need time off from the sea, and it should be quality time with good shelter and relaxing living. Remember you will be working and traveling hard and fast, and that's physically and emotionally demanding.

During the six to eight months at sea you are living on the delivery's expenses, which cover your food, ground transportation, and naturally, your sea travel. Only your personal purchases or entertainment come out of your pocket.

Running your own business brings with it those tax advantages, and you won't have to pay nearly the taxes that the full-time yacht captain does. Much of what you do is tax deductible.

The big plus is that you are your own boss. The big minus is the insecurity of wondering if and when the next delivery will arrive.

SUPPLEMENTAL INCOME

While getting started in the delivery business you could certainly use supplemental income from other jobs. Many beginning deliverers are self-employed mechanics and boat maintainers. The problem is that you must keep yourself free of entanglements that prevent you from leaving on a delivery at a moment's notice. If you take off in the middle of a maintenance job for a delivery, you'll have unhappy maintenance customers—not good advertising for yourself as a reliable delivery captain. And soon, there goes your supplemental income, too.

Another factor is image. If you develop the personal image of being a boat maintainer, you get stuck in that occupation in everybody's mind. Potential delivery customers think of you as a maintainer (sort of a nautical janitor or jack of all trades) rather than a serious captain. Because of this, they'll neglect to contact you for deliveries. However, such jobs do keep you on the waterfront making contacts which can lead to deliveries, and they do keep the phone bill paid. If you do have a supplemental job, don't let it be known to regular sources of yacht delivery business.

Overall it is better to have enough savings to devote yourself full-time to seeking yacht delivery jobs than trying to do maintenance. Just as any yacht salesman will tell you, you'll never succeed as a part-timer. However there are some sources of extra income that are more compatible with deliveries than others.

Some yacht delivery captains also are surveyors. This occupation goes hand-in-hand with deliveries, because you must be able to be your own surveyor anyway, each time you get on a boat to deliver. However, to be a really successful surveyor, you must be available at all times to do surveys. The best a yacht deliverer can do is to pick up an occasional survey to supplement his income.

Consulting is another income source. As you become more of an expert on boat preparation and certain routes, some people just getting ready for a trip may be willing to pay you for your opinions and advice. We charge $75 dollars per hour for this service. It's good work if you can get it. We wish we had more.

Seminars, speaking, and writing are other means of generating income. Pat's writing business even goes to sea with us, and our laptop computers are part of our regular sea gear.

CHAPTER 24
PRICING A DELIVERY

How much should you charge customers for delivering boats? You are limited by market conditions, i.e. what others are charging. You must constantly ask around to find out the going rate. Some deliverers resort to unscrupulous methods to do this, a form of industrial espionage.

In the beginning you will have to charge less to get the jobs. No one is going to hire an unknown unless there is a financial incentive for them to do so. As you gain more experience and credibility you can slowly raise your prices. If you reach the peak of the profession you can nearly name your own price. This might take several decades.

Here are several ways of slicing the "price pie," and the wage range inherent in each:

PRICE PER DAY

Experienced captains charge $150 to $200 or more per day.

This is the easiest pricing method for the deliverer. He simply charges an owner by the day for his time and that of the crew. All expenses, including air fares, food, fuel, port charges, spare parts and repairs are paid by the owner. The per-day method is most commonly used on the U.S. East Coast.

A delivery captain may be able to earn more than that if he can provide a qualified crew for less than prevailing crew wages. Suppose he provides a crew of four for $325 per day. He pays a mate/engineer $50 per day, when the prevailing wage is $100, a cook and deckhand $25 per day when the prevailing wage is $50. The captain is now making $225 per day, but still charging the owner a reasonable daily rate for the total crew. This is fine if the crew is qualified. We are able to find very good people who are willing to work for lower wages as a means of gaining sea time.

Captains who serve as their own engineers can make even more, but we find that on larger vessels this is not a good practice. Especially when things start going wrong, it is difficult to run a ship from the engine room. The captain's primary position is on the bridge.

We could get crew to go for nothing, but this is another bad practice. You aren't able to completely control someone who isn't being paid. They probably won't be well qualified and they might start acting more like guests of the owner rather than working crew.

In the beginning, you may have to start working for $100 per day or less to get the jobs. When you have become an experienced captain you should develop your bottom line. We have found that owners who are always looking for a deal are difficult to work for. Once you start a business relationship by cutting your price below your standard, you set the tone for the rest of the delivery. Everything becomes negotiable. The owner may accuse you of taking too long to get the job done, of spending too much for spare parts that he really doesn't need, etc.

PRICE PER MILE, PLUS EXPENSES

If you quote a delivery per mile, the standard is $2.00 to $2.25 per mile for a crew of three. For vessels requiring additional crew-members, add $.25 per mile.

This pricing method is more commonly used on the U.S. West Coast. How does that stack up against the daily rate? Let's use the example of a 1,000-mile trip on a 10-knot boat with non-stop range capability, requiring a crew of three. The charge at $2.00 per mile is $2,000. The vessel takes one day to prepare for the trip. That means that the total time spent should be 1,000 miles ÷ 240 miles per day = 4.2 + 1 day preparation = 5.2. Let's round that off to 6 days to take care of the unexpected and give a realistic view of the figures. The skipper's daily crew wages amount to $25 for the cook, $50 for the engineer; or $75/per day x 6. To figure his daily profit, take his gross for the trip ($2,000), minus total crew salaries ($450), which comes to $1,550. Divide this by 6 days, and he nets $258.33 profit each day.

Notice that the bottom line is still, "How much do I make per day?" That's much better than the $200 per day average daily rate. However, this method is fraught with uncertainties. What happens if it takes more than a day to prep the boat, or the boat breaks down en route, or it isn't a 10-knot boat after all, or it doesn't have a 1,000-mile range and you have to stop frequently, or you have bad weather and have to lay over? All these factors can cut into your profit to the point that the trip is not worth making. Thus you will have to make certain contingencies.

First is a contingency for vessel preparation. It is difficult to gauge beforehand how long a boat is going to take to prepare, espe-cially from one phone call. The owner often will insist that it is ready, or nearly so. You can't really tell until you are on board, and even then it is impossible to tell exactly. We've delivered vessels that took only a day to prep, while others took as long as three weeks in a shipyard.

For short trips, like the 1,000-mile example, we include one day of preparation in the per-mile figure. Our reasoning is that a vessel that's in good condition and well outfitted would take only one day to go on board, check out the conditions and systems, provision, and then depart.

For long-range deliveries of thousands of miles, ocean crossings, and foreign voyages, we include two days of preparation because it takes longer to prepare for a longer trip. For any preparation longer than the initial allow-ance, we charge $300 per day plus expenses.

The second contingency is for mechanical breakdowns en route that could require a lay-over. Again we charge $300 per day. Don't be overly optimistic and exclude this provision with the attitude, *that will never happen to me,* because if you stay in the profession long enough, it is bound to happen, no matter how good or how careful you are. Machinery, es-pecially its internal components, does not last forever, and it may decide to pack it in on you. Major breakdowns can take weeks.

It is customary on the mileage basis not to charge for weather layovers. Pray for good weather. Or make other contingency arrange-ments on a route known for bad weather dur-ing a bad season.

For instance, take Los Angeles to Seattle in the wintertime. This is not an impossible trip, provided the vessel has good speed and range. But you might have to wait many days for a proper "weather window" and then scoot between ports before it closes, and then wait again. You could charge by the day for weather layovers in such a case. However, by then you've made so many contingencies that you might as well just charge by the day for the whole trip. If an owner wants his boat delivered in such a season badly enough, he'll have to agree to such contingencies.

The third contingency is range, which can limit your profit. It's extremely time-consuming to stop for fuel several times during a trip. If you can do it safely, carrying deck fuel can help solve this problem. The variable of speed is controllable only to a certain extent, and no price contingencies are made for it. If you run too fast you will burn too much fuel and may make the delivery too costly for the owner. Cutting back to 10 knots on the faster powerboats is a reasonable speed for economical consumption. Of course, some powerboats aren't capable of that, and fewer sailboats are. That's why sailboat deliveries on a mileage basis are not very profitable.

Look at your daily profit on the 1000-mile example for a sailboat, using a 5-knot average. It will take 8.33 days plus one day prep, rounded off to 9 days. Total crew wages of $675 subtracted from $2,000 equal $1,325 net for the trip, or $147 per day. That's slightly below the $150 bottom-line daily figure for experienced captains. The economics of this explain why most beginning delivery captains start in sailboats and graduate to power after a long period of paying their dues and suffering in cold, open-cockpit "rag boats."

It might occur to some of you that the crewmembers are the ones who make out on this deal, since they get paid by the day no matter what the delay. Why not pay them by the trip? Our reasoning for not doing this is that their wages are low enough as it is. They need some guarantees of how much they will make. Paying them by the trip could lead to dissention if unpaid delays occur.

The per-mile method is advantageous to an owner because he doesn't have to worry about whether the captain is taking his own sweet time making a delivery in order to make as much money as possible.

FLAT-RATE PRICE

The final pricing method is a flat rate. The delivery captain gives the boat owner one price for the delivery, which includes crew wages, preparation charges, air fares, food, fuel, lubricating oil, and port charges—in effect, all expenses involved except spare parts, outfitting expenses, and insurance.

This represents a big gamble for the delivery skipper. He must know the route well in order to be able to quote a price that will leave him enough margin for profit. This is usually the most expensive method for the owner, because the skipper must build enough cushion in the price to absorb unpredictable occurrences such as fuel increases en route, excessive preparation time, and breakdown. Across the board we have found that skippers who use this method charge at least 25 percent more than what the prevailing total costs would be by other methods. On a long-range trip, that additional sum amounts to several thousand dollars. If the deliverer has estimated correctly and nothing goes wrong enroute, that means his profit is about 75% higher than if he charged per mile or per day.

We find the flat-rate method is good to use for shorter trips of up to 1,500 miles. The advantage to the owner is that he knows what his total costs are going to be from the very beginning. This might make a neat, clean package for a delivery skipper to sell. However, when you get into trips of several thousand miles, the flat-rate charge exceeds the per-mile or per-day rate by several thousand dollars. We feel that the owner is better off to participate in the financial uncertainty of the unexpected happening, by going with the per-mile or per-day rates. He can do this much less expensively if he is dealing with an experienced captain with a well established reputation and has thoroughly checked out his references.

The biggest problem for the deliverer using the flat-rate method is the possibility of mechanical breakdown. Most flat-rate delivery contracts state that breakdowns are considered part of the fee (expenses such as parts are extra), unless the crew has to call in outside help. In that case the owner will have to pay the outside help, but the delivery crew stands by without additional pay until repairs are made. Major breakdowns can sometimes take many days, and this is why "flat raters" charge more.

Preparation is another uncertainty. Generally, the flat-rate captain will look at the boat before giving his quote. He will have to build a big cushion in the price for this one.

The cost of fuel can vary greatly between trips. Consumption is different with each vessel. On foreign voyages the price of fuel can change suddenly. More than once we have seen the cost of Mexican fuel suddenly double. Anyone doing a long-range delivery involving several stops in Mexico at that time would have found his fuel bill hundreds, if not thousands, of dollars higher than what he built into his flat rate.

For the owner, the flat-rate method amounts to paying an expensive form of insurance premium. It insures that he will not have to pay extra to the crew in case of major breakdown. We doubt that the 25 percent extra charge is worth it.

Flat rate plus fuel expenses is a modification of this plan. For the skipper this reduces the uncertainty of fuel consumption and per-gallon cost. This is a popular pricing method. Other variations are a *flat-rate-plus-preparation contingency,* and a *breakdown contingency.* In fact, there are as many variations of these basic pricing methods as you need, based on the variables of each delivery.

CHAPTER 25
CONTRACTS AND PAPERWORK

Good faith is the basis of any agreement. Regretfully, the days of doing business on a handshake are long past. Broken promises, unpaid bills, rubber checks, and attorneys have become a regular way of life in the business world. Written delivery agreements in the form of contracts are a must. People who make their living delivering yachts are not wealthy people. On the other hand, their clients are wealthy, in some cases extremely wealthy. Often they are self-made millionaires who have made their money by being very shrewd businessmen. The delivery skipper must be just as shrewd or he might find himself a "newborn lamb among a pack of wolves."

Likewise, owners need to protect themselves from unscrupulous, flaky, and incompetent delivery skippers—and yes, there are a few of those around, too. Written agreements protect both parties by spelling out the major points in detail, in black and white, so there are no questions or disputes later.

Your contract should cover as many details as possible, because you want to protect yourself. However, some contingencies are very difficult to sell and may appear paranoid. In the final analysis, not everything can be covered by a contract. Here we are, back to good faith.

The following are three contracts we have used: per mile, per day, and per trip. They were not written by attorneys, but rather by ourselves. We've made modifications over the years as we learned. They have worked well for us, though we do not know how well they would hold up in court. We hope we never have to find out. We offer these contracts as examples of what has worked for us, with no guarantees they will work for you.

We'll analyze each one by paragraph and major provisions.

Contract Notes (Per Mile)

a) The date and place of the agreement are important in case of litigation to determine which court has jurisdiction. The vessel name and her gross tonnage are not only a means of identification but will come in handy later for documenting your sea time for the Coast Guard.

b) The delivery fee is noted along with the important statement "plus expenses" with expenses defined. Fifty percent of the funds are to be wired in advance. Wiring funds is much quicker than waiting for standard checks to clear. Cash or cashier's checks are an option. Don't start out on a trip until you know you have the funds in hand—real money, not an uncleared check. The remaining 50 percent is put in an *escrow account*. By so doing you have guaranteed that the owner has enough money to pay you and that you will get paid at the end. The funds are placed with a third

Per-Mile Contract
Vessel Delivery Agreement

(a) This agreement made and entered into in the

City of:

County:

State:

Date:

between:

Name:

Address:

Owner of the

Vessel Name:

Number:

Gross Tonnage:

hereinafter called Owner

and

Name:

Address:

Phone:

hereinafter called Captain.

(b) Owner agrees to engage Captain to deliver aforesaid vessel

from:

to:

for a delivery fee of: _____

plus expenses. Fifty percent of the delivery fee is to be wired to Account Number:

Bank:

Address:

prior to departure from captain's place of residence, the remaining fifty percent is to be deposited in trust with

Name:

Address:

Phone:

who shall become trustee of the funds, with instructions that the funds are to be paid to Captain upon completion of delivery of said vessel. The delivery fee of $_____ is compensation for the delivery only and is not intended to include monies for expenses such as foods, fuel, oils, supplies, or transportation of the Captain and/or crew. All expenses applicable to the delivery of said vessel will be paid by the owner.

(c) the delivery fee includes _____day(s) of wages to prepare said vessel for the voyage. If more days than that are needed then the Owner shall be charged $_____ per day plus expenses. The same charge will be applied for mechanical breakdown en route which requires a layover.

(d) If, upon initial inspection and preparation, any mechanical failure, loss, or damage occurs or has occurred to said vessel or its equipment which hinders its ability to make a safe journey and Owner refuses to correct, the voyage may be terminated by the Captain and he is to be paid: $_____ per day plus expenses (including return air fare)

Per-Mile Contract
Vessel Delivery Agreement *continued*

from point of departure to point of termination. If said failure or damage occurs en route and Owner refuses to pay for said corrections, then Owner is to pay Captain $_____ per mile plus expenses including return airfare. All remaining monies (if any) advanced to Captain and crew will be returned by Captain.

(e) Adequate expense monies will be made available in cash or cashier's check or wired to the above mentioned account to Captain by Owner prior to departure of said vessel, for the purchase of fuel, oil, food, fresh water, port and canal charges, repairs, telephone calls, and land transportation needed while en route. An itemized estimate of expense money for delivery of said vessel will be furnished to Owner by Captain. Captain will provide an itemized list of all expenses actually incurred at the journey's end, which shall serve as the basis for final accounting with Owner. If there are any remaining monies, they are to be returned to the Owner. If expenses exceed the amount advanced for expenses, then Owner will provide the additional funds when needed. If lay days were incurred, additional funds will be provided by the Owner to the Captain at journey's end.

(f) _____crewmembers in addition to the Captain will be required to assist in the delivery of said vessel. Captain will have the right, authority and responsibility for acquiring adequate, experienced crewmembers. Captain is to pay crew from the delivery fee.

(g) Marine Insurance will be provided by Owner with _____, with Captain as additional named insured to cover possible liabilities including but not limited to damages to the vessel or injuries to Captain , crew or others. Coverage shall include public liability and property damage.

(h) Captain is not responsible for normal wear and tear on said vessel. Captain is not responsible for acts of war, piracy, governments, insurgencies or counterinsurgencies nor for damage to vessel or injuries to captain or crew therefrom, nor for termination of voyage caused as a practical matter therefrom.

The parties hereby subscribe their names at the date and place first hereinabove set forth.

_____   _____
Owner   Captain

(i) Vessel has been delivered, inspected and Captain is hereby released from further liability. Trustee is hereby authorized to release funds to Captain.

_____   _____
Owner   Date

party with instructions to pay you upon completion of the delivery. We have set up an escrow account with an attorney, and this system has worked for many years without a single dispute.

c) Name the price for lay charges and the number of days included in the fee for preparation.

d) A bail-out provision ensures that you will be paid for your time and expenses, including your flight home, if the boat is not in good enough shape to make the trip. As stated in the boat-preparation section, you want to find out as much about the vessel as you can before you go see it. If it sounds like a bum boat, you shouldn't become involved with it. However, you can't always be sure until you've inspected the vessel and taken her for sea trials. If she is ill-prepared or in poor condition, you shouldn't proceed until her problems are remedied. This is a matter of safety for yourself, the crew, and the vessel itself. The insurance company would also take a dim view of you starting off on an ill-prepared vessel in poor condition.

e) An estimated expense list is to be provided along with the funds prior to departure. The captain is required to provide an itemized accounting, complete with each receipt. If lay days are incurred they will be paid upon delivery completion.

We consider it bad business practice to spend your own money for expenses. If you run out of expense money, as you might in the case of a breakdown, have more money transferred to you. We've known other delivery skippers who've gotten burned spending their own money.

Food is the most difficult item to account for, often involving dozens of small receipts. In foreign ports, it's often impossible to get receipts at all. An alternative method which is attractive to both deliverer and owner is to include food as a per diem item. State in this paragraph what the per diem figure is. For the owner, this means he knows what the bottom line on food will be and he won't have to worry about having to pay for extravagant meals in restaurants. You will still have to account for it for your own purposes.

f) Specify the number of crewmembers to be provided by the Captain. Sometimes owners will provide crew. This paragraph should list who provides whom, how many, and who pays them.

g) Insurance coverage. This assures you

that the owner is carrying insurance. From a personal liability stand point, especially in regards to your crew, it would be very unwise to deliver a vessel without insurance. Try to get on the policy as a named insured. Most insurance companies will go along with it, but you must ask. Demand a copy of the owner's insurance policy, not only to see that he has one, but to see that you are on as named insured and what some of the requirements and exclusions are.

h) Any trip, especially a long trip, will entail certain wear and tear on the boat. This is normal and this paragraph assures you that you are not responsible for it. It does not get you off the hook for negligent operation like slamming into the dock. Deliveries into foreign waters sometimes expose you to all kinds of unforseen political dangers. This statement excludes you from liability.

i) Contract completion. This releases the funds from escrow to you. Just as importantly, you are officially cutting the umbilical cord. Be sure to sign off every vessel. You could conceivably be liable for the actions of another operator until you do so.

Contract Notes (Per Day)

The per-day contract is a much cleaner contract, because it doesn't have to make so many provisions for laydays. The price per day is clearly stated in the beginning. Note that you must provide an estimated time in order to know how much money is to be set aside for an advance and escrow. A later clause indicates that if the trip takes longer than estimated, then the owner will pay for these extra days, or if the trip takes fewer days, then the captain will make a refund.

Contract Notes (Flat Rate)

In paragraph (b) the flat rate is given, as is the provision for transfer of funds. The amount advanced to you should be what you

Per-Day Contract
Vessel Delivery Agreement

This agreement made and entered into in the
City of:
County:
State:
Date:
between:

Name:
Address:
owner of the
Vessel Name:
Number:
Gross Tonnage:
hereinafter called Owner

and

Name:
Address:
Phone:
hereinafter called Captain.

(a) Owner agrees to engage Captain to deliver aforesaid vessel
from:
to:
for a delivery fee of $ _____ per day plus expenses. Estimated delivery time is _____days. Fifty percent of the estimated delivery fee is to be wired to
Account Number:
Bank:
Address:
prior to departure from his place of residence, the remaining fifty percent is to be deposited in trust with
Name:
Address:
Phone:
who shall become trustee of the funds, with instructions that the funds are to be paid to Captain upon completion of delivery of said vessel. The delivery fee of $_____ per day is compensation for the delivery only and is not intended to include monies for expenses such as foods, fuel, oils, supplies, or transportation of the Captain and/or crew. All expenses applicable to the delivery of said vessel will be paid by the Owner.
_____crewmembers in addition to the Captain will be required to assist in the delivery of said vessel. Captain

will have the right, authority and responsibility for acquiring adequate, experienced crewmembers. Captain to pay crew from the delivery fee.

If, upon initial inspection and preparation or en route, any mechanical failure, loss, or damage occurs or has occurred to said vessel or its equipment which hinders its ability to make a safe journey and Owner refuses to correct, the voyage may be terminated by the Captain and he is to be paid his daily wages plus expenses incurred (including return air fare) from point of departure to point of termination. All remaining monies (if any) advanced to Captain and crew will be returned by Captain.

Adequate expense monies will be made available in cash or cashier's check or wired to the above mentioned account to Captain by Owner prior to departure of said vessel, for the purchase of fuel, oil, food, fresh water, port and canal charges, repairs, telephone calls, and land transportation needed while en route. An itemized estimate of expense money for delivery of said vessel will be furnished to Owner by Captain. Captain will provide an itemized list of all expenses actually incurred at the journey's end, which shall serve as the basis for final accounting with Owner. If there are any remaining monies, they are to be returned to Owner. If expenses exceed the amount advanced for expenses, then Owner will provide the additional funds when needed. If the journey exceeds the estimated number of days, additional funds will be provided by the Owner to the Captain immediately at journey's end. If the journey takes less time than estimated, Captain will refund any monies due.

Marine Insurance will be provided by Owner with _____, with Captain as additional named insured to cover possible liabilities including but not limited to damages to the vessel or injuries to Captain, crew or others. Coverage shall include public liability and property damage.

Captain is not responsible for normal wear and tear on said vessel. Captain is not responsible for acts of war, piracy, governments, insurgencies or counterinsurgencies nor for damage to vessel or injuries to captain or crew therefrom, nor for termination of voyage caused as a practical matter therefrom.

The parties hereby subscribe their names at the date and place first hereinabove set forth.

_____
Owner

_____
Captain

Vessel has been delivered, inspected and Captain is hereby released from further liability. Trustee is hereby authorized to release funds to Captain.

_____
Owner

_____
Date

estimate to be one-half of your and the crew's wages, plus all expenses. The balance goes into the escrow account. The percentage of the advance is about 75 percent because it includes expenses; the remaining 25 percent is for escrow.

Paragraph (c) defines what is covered in the flat rate and what is not. In this example the

Flat-Rate Contract
Vessel Delivery Agreement

(a) This agreement made and entered into in the

City of:

County:

State:

Date:

between:

Name:

Address:

owner of the

Vessel Name:

Number:

Gross Tonnage:

hereinafter called Owner

and

Name:

Address:

Phone:

hereinafter called Captain.

(b) Owner agrees to engage Captain to deliver aforesaid vessel

from:

to:

for a delivery fee of: _____.

$_____ is to be wired to Account Number:

Bank:

Address:

prior to departure from his place of residence, the remaining $ _____is to be deposited in trust with

Name:

Address:

Phone:

who shall become trustee of the funds, with instructions that the funds are to be paid to Captain upon completion of delivery of said vessel.

(c) The delivery fee of $_____ includes payment for the Captain plus _____ crewmembers. Captain will have the right, authority and responsibility for acquiring adequate, experienced crew members. Captain to pay crew from the delivery fee. The delivery fee also includes: preparation of the vessel for said voyage; fuel, lubrication oils, air and land transportation of the crew; dockage, port and canal charges; food. It does not include spare parts, outfitting or insurance. It does not include spare parts and outside labor for mechanical breakdown en route. Owner will provide adequate money for spares and outfitting as needed. Owner will provide funds in case of breakdown if and when it occurs.

(d) If, upon initial inspection and preparation, any mechanical failure, loss, or damage occurs or has occurred to said vessel or its equipment which hinders its ability to make a safe journey and Owner refuses to correct, the voyage may be terminated by the Captain and he is to be paid: $_____ per day plus expenses (including return air fare) from point of departure to point of termination. If said failure or damage occurs en route and Owner refuses to pay for correction, then Owner is to pay Captain $_____ per mile plus expenses including return airfare. All remaining monies (if any) advanced to Captain and crew will be returned by Captain.

(e) Marine Insurance will be provided by Owner with _____, with Captain as additional named insured to cover possible liabilities including but not limited to damages to the vessel or injuries to Captain, crew or others. Coverage shall include public liability and property damage.

(f) Captain is not responsible for normal wear and tear on said vessel. Captain is not responsible for acts of war, piracy, governments, insurgencies or counterinsurgencies nor for damage to vessel or injuries to captain or crew therefrom, nor for termination of voyage caused as a practical matter therefrom.

The parties hereby subscribe their names at the date and place first hereinabove set forth.

_____   _____
Owner   Captain

(g) Vessel has been delivered, inspected and Captain is hereby released from further liability. Trustee is hereby authorized to release funds to Captain.

_____   _____
Owner   Date

deliverer has estimated how much preparation the trip will take and included it in his price. A modification of this is to give the owner a certain amount of preparation time included in the flat rate, with any amount over to be paid by the owner by the day. Provision for mechanical breakdown is included. No extra wages are to be paid for breakdown, but the owner is to pay for any outside labor charges and parts.

Accounting

When you work on a wages-plus-expenses basis, you are obliged contractually to provide an accurate accounting to the owner. Much of your reputation for future references and business is riding on your honesty and ability to justify these expenditures. On long-range deliveries this can mount to tens of thousands of dollars. Even if you work on a flat-rate basis you must make an accurate accounting of expenditures for the IRS, since these are all legitimate deductions. You have to do this for yourself in order to know how much money you made and for reference when quoting future jobs.

The accounting need not be some complicated, double-entry system. Just a simple listing of funds received minus expenditures will do. You must have receipts to justify the expenditures. In many places, especially foreign countries, receipts may not be furnished. We both carry a receipt book to shore with us, especially in foreign countries, but also in the U.S. Don't forget to have the various merchants sign your receipts.

We number each receipt back on the boat and file it along with an explanation of the expenditure, date, and location where it was spent. Do your accounting daily and don't get behind. This is especially important when preparing a boat for the trip, because money will be changing hands at a prodigious rate. It is also important in foreign ports for fuel stops and reprovisioning. One of the many joys of being at sea is that there is no place to spend money, and therefore no accounting to do. As part of your daily log, include explanations for any large or out-of-the-ordinary expenditures.

We do our accounting on our small, portable computers. This is far less time-consuming, much more accurate, and produces a very professional-looking printout to present to the owner.

Legal Documents

The contract can serve as a legal document to show port authorities or government boarding parties that you have official permission from the vessel's owner to be the captain, and that you have not stolen the boat.

Many of the yachts you will deliver are documented, with the owner listed as a corporation. You must have a notarized letter from an officer of the corporation, giving you permission to be the captain. If your voyage is into non-English-speaking areas, then have this letter translated and have the translated version notarized, too.

Since a large number of deliveries are of vessels that have recently changed ownership, redocumentation creates a problem. The U.S. Coast Guard, because of budget cutbacks, can take months to redocument a vessel. Technically, you are not supposed to move a boat without the new document. However, by using the following paperwork that traces legal ownership, we have had only minor problems. Most documentation firms will provide you with this, but inspect all the papers before you leave.

You need the following:

1 The old document or copy.
2 Bill of sale or copy.
3 If the owner is a corporation, the articles of incorporation, listing the corporation officers.
4 Notarized and translated permission from an officer of the corporation giving you permission to be captain.
5 A cover letter from the documentation service explaining that the document is in progress.

CHAPTER 26
THE DELIVERY MARKET

Why is it that certain types of boats seem to pop up easily as delivery jobs? Who do you need to know, and what do you need to do to drum up the good delivery work? Where do most boats need to be delivered to and from, and when? Here's a brief survey of the market situation for yacht delivers

WHERE TO FIND WORK

Cruising Boats

First delivery jobs often come to cruisers who encounter other cruising boats along the way that need to be moved or returned to a home port. If the cruiser-turned-deliverer has demonstrated the necessary skills and has a good association with the boat's owners, then it's just a matter of being in the right place at the right time.

Long-distance cruising boats are potentially the most seaworthy, most efficiently designed boats that ever come over the horizon in the yacht delivery business, simply because of the demanding nature of cruising. A solid, well-designed, well-equipped cruising boat can be a delight to deliver.

Of course, each boat must stand on its own merits. Don't forget that there's some reason why the owner isn't moving his boat, so there could be some inherent problem with the boat. The sluggish, downwind-only hull with the mouse-fart engine is not a delight. And

certainly pocket cruisers and trailerable gunkholers fall into another category. If you're already cruising, your awareness of cruising vessel characteristics should be good enough to guide you clear of the disasters.

Cruising boats become delivery boats for many good reasons. Older owners frequently run out of steam in foreign ports (such as Jamaica, Costa Rica, and other inexpensive tropical paradises) and they decide to sell the boat (usually back up in Bellingham or Boston where it will bring a better price) and retire to a *palapa* on the beach.

Many cruisers, regardless of age, tire of the constant diet of the dream life. Once they realize the party is over for them, they don't want to make the long, hard push homeward. It may be hundreds or thousands of miles to windward, and since they're heading back to the world of paychecks, they'd rather pay someone else to do it.

The sad reasons include a serious illness or death on board or at home. The most common reason is that too many of the crew have jumped ship. The happiest cruising boat deliveries are those wise folks who plan to cruise the various circuits for several years and *plan* to have their boat returned for them from their final destination by cruising buddies they know they'll meet along the way.

Whatever the reason, there you are—Captain Ready Willing and Able to the rescue.

We don't recommend that anyone embark

on a cruising adventure with the mistaken idea they can support themselves solely with cash attained by doing cruising boat deliveries. They simply don't happen that often. This is just one possible way to break into the business, and a delightful, potential means of replenishing the cruising kitty.

Race Boats

First deliveries often come out of the ocean-racing circuit. These races are primarily run downwind. For instance the famous TransPac starts just offshore from Los Angeles and ends in Honolulu. This route is entirely downwind in the northeast trades. Because "gentlemen don't sail to weather," the owners will have their boats delivered back home for them after the race is over.

The best way to get involved in this business is to find a crew slot for the race. Crew slots aren't always easy to come by and are often reserved for cronies of the owner. However, if you offer special skills such as superb navigation, sail trimming, or, more likely, much muscle to crank on coffee-grinder winches, you can find a position. Race boat deliveries also come from the hired help who maintain these boats in their home slips. Contacts for these deliveries are made through local yacht clubs and their social events.

This is a highly competitive aspect of the yacht delivery profession. Often the owner will have his boat returned by members of the crew who are repaid only for their expenses. That may mean only their food, not even a plane ticket, since they raced one-way on the boat to begin with. Unfortunately, as long as there are qualified people willing to do race boat deliveries for free, it's discouraging for someone who is competing for the job, trying to make a living.

Fortunately, a sufficient number of owners want a professional to do the delivery for them and are willing to pay a reasonable fee

for it. Here is where a beginning yacht delivery captain starts.

Race boat delivery is, generally speaking, more physically demanding than delivering a cruising boat. It means pounding hundreds or thousands of miles in a lightly built hull, standing watches in an open cockpit, and being underpowered the whole way. Race boat galleys are notoriously spartan, and some have only an ice cooler, and minimal stoves. Mesh hammocks slung between open frames might be the only sleeping quarters. The most macho racing sleds were designed for one thing only—to go fast downwind. But it is a good training ground.

Recently Purchased Boats

Boats that recently have been bought by owners in distant locations constitute the largest segment of the delivery market.

Why doesn't the new owner move it himself? For many reasons. Often the owner realizes that making the trip is beyond his expertise and wants to pay a professional to move it for him. Perhaps he realizes that it is a long trip involving rough weather and he would rather pay someone else to do his suffering for him. Insurance companies may not insure the owner to skipper his own boat on the trip because of his inexperience, and may require him to hire an experienced professional. Many boats, especially the larger ones, are owned by people who are so busy making money to pay for the boat they don't have time to make the trip themselves.

Recently purchased boats fit into one of two categories: used boats and new boats. Used boats are the majority. Old boats are the most difficult to deliver, as it is the nature of boats to be falling apart continually. The more years they have had to fall apart, the more difficult it is to hold them together long enough to make a delivery. However, new boats are a problem in themselves. By their very newness, they haven't been shaken down properly. This is especially true of custom boats or "hull-number-one" production boats. A number of our new-boat deliveries would be more accurately described "Research and Development." The best boat to deliver is a two-year-old boat that has been cruised and maintained by a professional.

Charter Boats

Charter boats that are offered "bare boat" often move seasonally. Charter companies hire captains to transport their fleets for them. These are generally small sailboats in the 40-foot range. The main bulk of this business is between Florida, the Virgin Islands, and the northeast United States.

Large Yachts

Most yachts 60 feet and over have full-time captains. However, many of these captains do not have the experience to make long range trips in unfamiliar waters. The captain and the owner may realize this, or the insurance company may not let them forget it. If a boat is to be delivered long-range, they may look for help. This help can take two forms, either with

One yacht delivery market is comprised of charter boats relocating to a new charter area. We moved this Peterson 44 from San Diego to charter in Tahiti.

the experienced delivery captain coming on as captain or with the delivery captain joining the crew as a "second license" or, in effect, as the mate/navigator/guide.

Both situations can be awkward and difficult for both parties. In the first case, the full-time captain may find it difficult to play second string on his own boat. In the second case, the "second license" has little control over his situation if the captain resents being forced to take him on, and he may not listen to his advice.

However, if all these problems are talked out and roles agreed upon in advance, the delivery can be a good one. The full-time captain certainly ought to know his boat well, so there are far fewer of the "mechanical and electrical mysteries" to sort out. And the delivery captain should know the route well. That makes for a good combination.

Popular Routes

U.S. East Coast. This constitutes the largest market in the U.S. as boats move seasonally back and forth and as various people hire professionals to do the moving for them. Owners in the Northeast have their boats delivered south, to Florida or to the Caribbean. This movement corresponds to the onset of cold weather in the Northeast and the end of hurricane season in the South, usually about November. They return to pleasant weather in the North in about May with the onset of hot weather in the South.

Much of this migration takes place in the protected Intracoastal Waterway, called the ICW. However it is difficult to make good time in the waterway, since you can't safely run at night. Most delivery skippers like to run outside during good weather, so they can run day and night. However, during heavy weather, you can still make some miles in the ICW.

Larger vessels are restrained by draft and mast height, making it impossible to go under fixed bridges. These vessels are forced to move outside.

Trans-Atlantic.   Some larger vessels move seasonally across the Atlantic. They spend the winter in the Caribbean and the summer in the Mediterranean. Occasionally owners will purchase a vessel in Europe and have it moved to the U.S. East Coast or to the U.S. West Coast via the Panama Canal.

U.S. West Coast.   Most movement is to Mexico in the winter and back to the U.S. in the summer. All seasons see some movement between Pacific ports of Southern California, San Francisco, and Seattle, but it peaks in the summer. The summer also brings seasonal activity to Alaska and back.

Hawaii and South Pacific.   Most deliveries are from Hawaii to the mainland because it is a difficult trip beating back against the northeast trades. Occasionally a cruising boat needs to be delivered from the South Pacific back to the U.S.

The Far East.   Taiwan is a huge yacht-building center whose major market is the U.S. We mention this as a warning to skippers and owners alike. Some owners think that they can purchase a boat in Taiwan, have it delivered on its own bottom to the U.S., and thus save money. We suggest that you don't do it for the following reasons. The Taiwanese boatbuilders have it set up so they deliver these vessels quite inexpensively to the U.S. on Taiwan flagships. That cost is much less than flying in a crew, outfitting the boat, and delivering it across the Pacific on its own bottom. Also, Taiwan boats often are shipped to the U.S. for commissioning. Trying to commission a vessel in Taiwan is a nightmare, because parts are often inferior or unavailable. Unless you have vast experience dealing with the Chinese, you will likely come out a big-time loser.

U.S. East Coast to West Coast via Panama.   While there are not a great many boats moving between coasts, each trip represents a major job for the delivery skipper. Most of the movement is from east to west, since West Coast buyers often turn to Florida to find larger boats. The East Coast has more larger vessels to choose from, because it has a larger population, a greater concentration of wealth, and consequently more big-boat builders.

Generally speaking, vessels under 50 feet can be trucked much less expensively than having them delivered on their own bottoms. Vessels larger than that have no other alternative. There are no regularly scheduled shipping companies that can ship vessels between coasts as deck cargo. Many owners have tried to arrange this, but the vast majority fail. The vessel must come on its own bottom. Movement is primarily seasonal. The best season is between November and June to avoid the summer hurricane months. Large motor vessels in good condition, with long ranges and good speeds, and operated by a knowledgeable and cautious captain, can make the trip in the summer.

SELLING YOURSELF

To succeed in the yacht delivery business, you are going to have to become a salesman selling yourself. Unlike opening a retail storefront, you can't hang a sign and wait for customers to walk in the door to browse through your wares. Your service is your only product, and you are its first representative. You're going to have to go out and find those customers.

Disdainful as some people are of salesmen,

it is they who make our economic world go round. If you have this disdainful attitude, you had better change it because you are going to have to become a superior salesman.

The most difficult part of the yacht delivery business for some of us is not navigation, weather, boat handling, or even securing customer satisfaction. It is finding the jobs in the first place. This is where salesmanship comes into play.

Your first step will be getting ready to make personal calls on key people: boat brokers, insurance representatives, boatyard owners and managers and foremen, marine management companies, and crew placement firms. These are the people to whom boat owners turn for skipper recommendations. Make a list of all these key people.

Before you make any personal calls, you need to do some homework. Put together a neat little package to leave with each call so they don't forget you as soon as you walk out the front door. On the tab of several file folders, write your name followed by "yacht delivery." Inside put a copy of your resumé, one or two of your business cards, and a cover letter explaining your specialty and your prices.

Before you go, find out the name and title of the person you should contact in each office. If the company's ads in yachting publications fail to give the name of the contact, call the front receptionist and ask who handles skipper referrals. A large brokerage may have one or two brokers who specialize in finding skippers and crews, while others may not know a thing about it. Seeing the wrong people may be interesting, but it wastes your time and energy. Generally you'll want to see the owner of the business, the broker, or the sales manager.

We question the value of trying to make advance appointments with busy people who don't know you. If you try to make an appointment, you may not be granted one. If you just show up, on the other hand, and the person you want is not busy, you stand a better chance of seeing him. However if there is someone you have tried to see without success, you may try an appointment.

Boat shows are an excellent way of contacting people, because they are all concentrated in one area at one time.

Be conscious of your personal appearance. People in the yachting business are conservative in attitude and appearance, and you should follow suit. Those who follow the sea often have a "drop-out" attitude, which they display to the world with their dress. Long hair, scruffy beards, earrings, red bandanna kerchiefs, and eye patches will only alienate the clientele you are trying to connect with. Be casual but well dressed. No one expects you to wear a suit, in fact you wouldn't want to project the image of a dandy. Look as if you're ready to go to work as a captain, but not as if you just climbed out of a bilge. Look as if you wouldn't mind crawling around a well maintained engine room for an inspection.

Think about what you are going to say before you speak. Open with something like, "Hello, I'm John Miller and I'm in the yacht delivery business. I want to introduce myself to you and leave a copy of my resumé to keep on file. Do you need a yacht delivered? Do you know anyone who does?"

Be prepared to quote prices if necessary. It seems as though every yacht salesman is always just putting together a proposed deal on some boat or another, and they need to know how much a delivery would cost their client. You can be helpful to them in this way, and they'll be glad you knocked on their door.

Don't ignore receptionists. When you call, don't just think of them as fixtures, they hold the door to see "Mr. Big Shot." Be friendly and courteous and remember, it is often the receptionist who runs the office. They often are the ones who know what is happening in each broker's region. Equally important, they answer the phone. One of their clients might ask, "I'm looking for somebody to deliver my yacht. Can you or anybody there recommend somebody?"

"Why sure, we recommend Captain John Miller. I have his number right here."

Where to Look

Yacht brokers. Yacht brokers are the single biggest source of referrals for yacht deliveries. Two of the biggest markets are delivering new boats to new owners, and delivering used boats to new owners after the broker closes the deal.

In the used-boat market, the broker serves as an agent for the boat's owner, and he wants the sale to go as smoothly as possible. The sale usually includes the delivery to the new owner, so the broker has a vested interest in seeing that the delivery goes well, too. For larger, more expensive vessels, the yacht broker may continue to serve both the former owner and new owner as agent and/or advisor long after the actual sale. The larger and more expensive the yacht, the more often this is the case. Owners of very large yachts are generally very busy people who don't want to be bothered with such mundane matters as choosing a yacht delivery skipper. They will trust this decision to their yacht broker.

The reputable broker provides this service free to his customers. He knows that good service to his clients will pay off in repeat sales and favorable word-of-mouth recommendations. However, in certain regions, a few brokers will recommend only yacht delivery skippers who agree to pay the broker a "referral fee."

This kickback system is deplorable, because it is an injustice to boat owners. A skip-

per's willingness to participate doesn't bespeak his worthiness; it merely demonstrates his lack of integrity. In the long run, such brokers rack up a history of dissatisfied boat owners and ruin their own chances for repeat business and good referrals.

Contact as many brokers as you can in your region. When you make deliveries into other areas, make sales calls there, too. The more key people you know, the more referrals you will get, the more jobs you will get, the more money you will earn.

This kind of selling is called "cold calling." It is the most difficult kind of selling. None of these people have asked to see you. Your reception will be varied. Sometimes your contact will be busy and unable to see you or spend much time with you.

Most often he will be bored, just sitting in his office, waiting and hoping that a big Rolls Royce will pull into the parking lot and a customer wearing a gold Rolex will get out, come in, specifically ask for him by name, and say that he wants to buy such-and-such a million-dollar yacht. And he needs to buy it quickly; he doesn't have much time.

But no, instead it is you who comes strolling in unannounced, trying to sell him something. You probably parked your heap right where the Rolls was supposed to park.

You must be able to handle rejection easily and not take it personally. If someone won't see you this time, just keep plugging away at it another time. It will pay off in the end. If they're not especially receptive when they do see you, don't get intimidated, don't grovel for forgiveness, don't let their coldness affect you.

If you can't see the licensed broker or sales manager, at least try to sit down and talk with one of the salespeople. Make and then maintain at least one good contact in each brokerage office. Just because you become good buddies with one salesman at Fantail Yacht

Sales doesn't guarantee that he will refer you to his associates in the same office. The nature of yacht sales is highly competitive, and brokers are often secretive about their boat deals, even within their own companies.

Try to meet as many salespeople in each office as you can. Ask your good buddy if he will walk you around and introduce you to others in his company.

Even though we painted a grim picture of "cold calls," your reception fortunately is not always that grim. When making the rounds like this, you will meet some nice people. Some salespeople love to chat and swap sea stories and who better to do it with than a yacht delivery captain or team.

Always ask your contacts if they have any potential deliveries pending, or if they have heard of anyone who has. Such networking has a snowball effect. If they don't have one, they may refer you to a broker friend who does, giving you a reason to contact him. He, in turn, may know somebody else you should talk to. Waterfront business communities are like small towns where everybody knows everyone else's business, in spite of their attempts at secrecy.

After you've polished your cold-calling technique and feel comfortable with it, go for the big guys. Only a very few brokers control the cream of the yacht delivery trade. They are the ones who sell the largest yachts. It may take years for you to get any business from them, because you need to prove yourself to them by staying in the yacht delivery business with an untarnished reputation. Persistence will pay off.

Strive to maintain your initial contacts through follow-ups, whether an occasional face-to-face visit or just phone calls. In time, you'll undoubtedly make many genuine friends within the world of yacht sales—social friends, not just business acquaintances.

Some of the most successful yacht deliverers who have been at it for decades have old friends who are successful yacht brokers who've also been at it for decades. They're what's known as the "old-boy" network. There are social/business networks operating on local, national, and international levels.

Insurance companies. Making contacts with boat insurance agents is as important as contacting yacht sales people. Though yacht brokers refer the greatest quantity of delivery jobs, marine insurance companies can provide the best quality ones.

Insurance agents also recommend skippers for boats they insure as a service to their clients. In major boating communities, they keep lists of skippers for full-time jobs and for occasional skippering. But more important, insurance underwriters demand that highly qualified, licensed captains be hired by their clients to move their larger, more delicate boats whenever they leave the waters of their normal insurance range. And that's what deliveries are all about.

Because of increasing losses over the past few years, "trip insurance" is getting harder to come by. Marine insurance companies are increasingly concerned with the qualifications of the skippers running their insured boats. This is especially true on long trips through foreign waters, in politically turbulent regions and during hurricane or gale seasons.

Yacht insurers now demand resumés from all skippers and crews, so they can evaluate their qualifications and decide whether to let the boats go on proposed trips.

Owners who have proposed delivering their own boats may be informed that they need to hire a licensed captain and professional crew who have experience on the proposed route before they can get insurance. Gone are the days when an unlicensed skipper or boat owner can obtain insurance based on his experience alone.

Some boat owners may be shopping price. They want to find the cheapest skipper to do the job, as long as he qualifies for insurance. But more than likely, the cheapest skipper is not the most qualified. His resumé will bear this out to the insurance company. And the owner may be forced to get someone else to do the job. Owners should be aware that even though they found a cheap skipper to do the job and they do get insurance coverage, it may cost them more in the end. Because of the large deductibles involved ($10,000 is not uncommon), a less experienced, cheaper captain may cause damage that the owner will have to dig into his own pocket to cover. The moral of the story is that you get what you pay for.

This insurance company trend of insisting on qualified captains and crew will help experienced professionals find work, and at the same time prevent losses.

Introducing yourself to insurance brokers can get you business and bring them business, too.

We sometimes are contacted by boat owners who already have run into insurance problems. Either their insurer won't give them trip insurance for a particular place at a particular time of the year, or the cost of the trip insurance they can get is prohibitive. Because we already have insurance friends who are aware of our capabilities, and who can find insurance coverage during some seasons when other brokers cannot or will not, we can put the boat owner in touch with our insurance friends. They may be willing to shop around with various underwriters to find the best deal for the boat owner. This brings them business and assures us of business.

Boat yards. Foremen of boat yards are a good source of yacht delivery referrals. They work closely with boat owners, frequently developing a trusted rapport. Owners sometimes ask them for referrals. Contact the larger yards that deal with larger boats.

Yacht management firms and crew placement firms. Both of these groups are relatively minor sources of business, but they're worth mentioning. Yacht management and crew placement are mostly an East Coast phenomenon, located primarily in the Ft. Lauderdale area.

Yacht management firms handle the maintenance, staffing, and paperwork of large, private yachts and charter boats. The boats may have absentee owners, or owners who are too busy making money and prefer to pay someone else to do it for them. Thus, these firms like to maintain a pool of qualified crew they can call on. Mostly it's for full-time work, but occasionally a delivery position comes up.

The same is true with crew placement firms. They normally charge a fee to the yacht deliverer for arranging a job for them.

Both of these types of firms are worth a call, as it pays to have as many contacts in the industry as possible. However, do not rely on them, as they are not a constant source of referrals. Don't sit around waiting for a phone call from them hoping you will get enough business out of them to survive. You must go out and pound on doors, finding your own business.

Advertising

Making sales calls is by far the best means of drumming up yacht delivery business. Advertising ranks next, not as a substitute but in conjunction with sales calls. Advertising introduces you to new customers and in many cases serves as a backup to your sales calls.

Perhaps the person you called on forgot about you until he needed a delivery crew, but he misplaced your name and phone number.

He sees your ad and suddenly remembers you and gives you a call.

"It pays to advertise" is an old business maxim and it is very true. But it also costs to advertise. How much should you spend and where?

You should spend as much as your budget allows. Advertising properly done is an investment in the future, because it rarely pays off immediately. Its effect is cumulative and long term. Many yacht delivery people are operating on such a limited budget that they can't afford to advertise. Our philosophy is, if we can't afford to advertise, we can't afford to be in the yacht delivery business.

We spend about 10% of our gross income a year on advertising. We didn't start by spending that much, but as business increased, we reinvested more in our future through advertising. Beginning yacht deliverers should start with at least one good advertisement in a useful publication. Well-funded beginners, very committed to making a go of it, should advertise in several publications.

The classified sections of waterfront magazines and newspapers are the best places to advertise. Check out several of these publications. If they don't already have a section called Yacht Delivery, then they are probably not worth spending your money on. The more ads there are, the more successful the advertisers have found this publication. Delivery customers are used to turning to this publication to look for delivery skippers.

Magazines with large national circulations catering to the most affluent segment of the boating market are the best; their ad rates are also the most expensive. However, if you are going to have only one ad, it should be in such a magazine.

The classified sections of local waterfront newspapers can be effective also. They are inexpensive compared to the glossy magazines, but their circulation is limited. Regional marine directories, the nautical equivalent of the yellow pages, are another possibility.

Careful wording is important when you advertise in a publication in order to distinguish yourself from other delivery skippers. Since you will be paying by the word and yacht delivery is the heading of the section, don't waste your money by including yacht delivery in your ad. "Have sextant, will travel" and "Ready, willing, and able to go anywhere, anytime" will not do you any good, because that's what they all say.

Specialize in a particular route, but make sure it is one that has a lot of business. Don't specialize in only power or only sail unless your are unqualified to do both. This is much too restrictive to your market. We hear many skippers say "you'd never catch me on one of those stink potters," or the opposite, "the only way I'd ever deliver a sailboat is if you chop down the mast." Being able and willing to do both makes you a much better rounded seaman and opens up far more jobs to you.

In order to know how effective your ads are, get in the habit of asking each customer who calls how he heard about you. If you are not getting responses after several months of advertising, try different wording or a different publication. Experiment to find what suits you best. After you have been advertising for awhile, ad salespeople from other publications will be calling you to advertise in their publications. You can easily go overboard on advertising and spend money that does you no good. Make sure the publication is oriented to the right market for you.

Publicity. Try to get your name in front of the public as much as possible. As you gain more experience you will find that cruising people want to hear about your experiences. Public speaking is a good way to distinguish yourself from the crowd of aspiring yacht deliverers. Yacht clubs are always looking for guest speakers to address their meetings for free. If you are a photographer, slide shows of your travels make a good venue. You can make good business contacts this way. We both do speaking engagements at yacht clubs and regional colleges. We also present our slide shows for business and personal friends at home and in public.

After you establish a reputation as a speaker, you may be able to earn supplemental income from speaking and cruising seminars. We've done a few speaking engagements this way, and would do more if time permitted.

If you have an aptitude for writing, you can write about your delivery experiences. Pat has volumes of sea stories for magazines articles. This generates supplemental income. And the publicity you generate pays off in increased yacht deliveries.

Client lists and phone contacts. Once you begin to generate leads, either from direct sales calls or incoming phone inquiries, you must keep track of them or they can become a bewildering array. Of roughly 20 possible delivery contacts you make, only one may become an actual job. Until you've sorted the wheat from the chaff, you must have a means of organizing all this information.

Upon making an initial contact with a customer, we take hand-written notes based roughly on the format shown in Chapter 4, page 19. We keep these hand-written notes in a file. We then take the following essential information and enter it into a custom-made data base on our computer.

1 Name
2 Address
3 Phone numbers
4 Date of initial contact
5 Source of referral

6 Kind of boat, details
7 From where to where, when
8 Price quoted
9 Correspondence sent and computer file names
10 Dates of followups and notes
11 When should we contact again
12 Classify lead as hot, mediocre, dead

You should review this list often for followups and to reclassify your leads. If a lead becomes dead, give the reasons why, such as: hired another captain for less money, didn't buy the boat, or decided it was too expensive and didn't move the boat.

During the initial contact on phone inquiries, we can easily give a price for a familiar route and boat. However if the client is asking for something unusual and the quote requires some research, we ask to call him back in 30 minutes or so. Even if he's asking for a ballpark figure, we don't want to anger the client by later having to revise an estimate upwards. If the delivery inquiry has the potential of becoming reality (determining this is an art that takes years to develop), we send along the following: a written copy of our quote, a recap of our phone discussion, our resumés, and copies of our licenses. If it is a hot lead we also enclose a sample copy of our contract.

Keep your correspondence as neat and professional-looking as possible so the customer will know he is dealing with professionals, not some fly-by-nighters.

As a lead moves toward the contract stage, we keep a separate file folder on each vessel containing all jotted notes, hard copies of all computer-written notes, correspondence sent, received, any references, and contracts.

Expanding your business. Once you have become well established in the yacht delivery business, you may find yourself in the enviable position of having more business than you can handle. What do you do about that?

One of the benefits of too much business is that you can afford to be choosier about which deliveries you will do and which you will turn down. One of the first categories you will want to turn down is old derelict boats. Second are small and open-cockpit sailboats. It is extremely tiresome and uncomfortable to constantly be out in the weather, trying to slug to windward at four knots. It is so much better to be inside, nice and dry traveling at 10 knots. You may get to the point where you don't even have to pack your foul-weather gear any more!

Another benefit is that you can begin to raise your rates. You can experiment with this a little at a time. You are still limited by the rates charged by the competition. When you find that you are losing good jobs to the competition because your rates are too high, then back off again.

Some skippers dream of having a company in which they turn over their excess business to other skippers in return for a fee. There are some delivery skippers who advertise themselves as a firm capable of placing several skippers. In fact they are just one-man operations who take most of the jobs themselves and occasionally pass along a delivery possibility to another.

One of the problems of referring business to other skippers is that you are putting your business reputation on the line each time you do it. If the skipper you have referred doesn't do a good job, his incompetence reflects back on you. By and large we have found that it is better to concentrate on securing the quality deliveries than to moonlight in the referral business.

CHAPTER 27
LICENSING

The United States Coast Guard (U.S.C.G.) reorganized its entire licensing structure in November, 1987, so that the requirements and authorizations inherent with each level of license were altered greatly. One year later, the U.S.C.G. was still in the process of smoothing out thousands of wrinkles for mariners licensed under the old system who were then upgrading within the new system. This merger was expected to take several years, but since the U.S.C.G. doesn't foresee any alterations to its new system, we've decided to pass along our brief description of the license levels pertinent to you.

TYPES OF LICENSES

- **OPERATOR OF UNINSPECTED PASSENGER VESSEL (OUPV)**—Requirements: 18 years of age; 360 days of experience in operation of vessel; 90 of those days in waters called Close Coastal (100 miles offshore or less) or Ocean (100 to 200 miles offshore), to prevent possible limitation of license to Inland only. License authorization is limited to vessels of less than 100 gross tons operating not farther than 100 miles offshore with six passengers or fewer onboard.

- **MATE, CLOSE COASTAL**—Requirements: 18 years of age; 180 days of experience in operation of vessel. Authorization is limited to rivers, lakes, bays, and sounds. Allows holder to work as Captain aboard "Six-Pack" vessels (OUPV above), or to work as Mate or Second in Command aboard Inspected Charter Vessels carrying more than six passengers.

- **MATE, OFFSHORE**—Requirements: 18 years of age; 360 days of experience in operation of vessel, 180 of those days must be outside jetties. Authorizes holder to work as Captain aboard "Six-Pack" vessels (OUPV above) up to 200 miles offshore, or work as Mate or Second in Command aboard Inspected Charter Vessels carrying more than six passengers.

- **MASTER, CLOSE COASTAL**—Requirements: 19 years of age; 360 days of experience in operation of vessel. Authorization limited to rivers, lakes, bays, and sounds. Allows holder to work as Captain aboard Inspected Charter Vessels carrying more than six passengers.

- **MASTER, OFFSHORE**—Requirements: 19 years of age; 720 days of experience in operation of vessel, 360 of those days must be outside jetties. Authorizes holder to work as Captain aboard Inspected Charter Vessels up to 100 gross tons, carrying more than six passengers in waters up to 200 miles offshore.

All the above licenses require passing a set of lengthy U.S.C.G. exams, including seamanship skills, navigation and chart problems, safety, fire fighting and first aid, and Rules of the Road.

All these licenses require completion of courses in CPR, first aid, and fire fighting, plus a physician's routine exam within the last 12 months. Vision must be 20/200 uncorrected in each eye, or correctable to 20/40. Color sense must be satisfactory. You must have been free of drug or felony convictions for the past three years, or past 10 years depending on the severity of any offenses. In all but the OUPV, 90 of your sea days must have occurred during the past three years. A U.S. passport is required, but foreign citizens may hold restricted OUPV licenses.

Larger licenses for Mate and Master are for vessels up to 200 gross tons, up to 500 gross tons, and up to 1600 gross tons. They require more sea time on larger vessels as Mate or Master, plus passing more difficult exams in coastal and celestial navigation, ship stability, radar, and lifeboat launching.

No longer are differentiations made between Mineral and Oil licenses or between Freight and Towing licenses. With the exception of the entry-level OUPV ticket, these U.S.C.G. licenses transfer into the U.S. Merchant Marine as various deck licenses.

One day of sea time now means four hours of work, as opposed to the old system's requirement for 12 hours of work to equal one day of sea time.

HOW TO GET LICENSED

Start by going to any U.S.C.G. office to get the avalanche of forms.

Get all your sea time documented, because this step can take many months to complete, and you can be fulfilling other requirements while getting sea time documented. That means locating former captains or fellow crewmembers with whom you worked. Each must go to a notary public and swear to the fact that you actually worked onboard the specific vessel on the specific days that you claim you did. It's far better to get this documentation from the captain than from a crewmember.

Anyone even remotely considering going for a license should ask the captain for documentation of sea time immediately following each job at sea. We always volunteer to do this for our crewmembers.

It often takes six months to track down some people, let alone to get them to go see a notary, sign the form and mail it back to you. There also are forms to sign yourself to claim a limited number of days you actually sailed your own boat with no one else to confirm the fact, but the U.S.C.G. evaluations officer doesn't have to accept any such undocumentable sea time. It's better if you can locate a neighboring boat owner who can swear to the fact that you actually took your boat out, or that you sailed it beyond the jetty for offshore time.

Once you've turned in all your sea time to the U.S.C.G. and it is being evaluated, find out when the next exams are scheduled for the license level you seek.

We highly recommend that everyone take a good license preparation class. They are designed primarily to beat into your short-term memory all the minute details you'll have to know to pass the various tests for each specific license level. They certainly are no substitute for long-term, deep-memory learning, but at least they'll help you get the license, which in turn allows you to gain further experience.

Prices and methods vary from school to school, so call around and compare. Most use *Dutton's, Chapman's* and *Navigation Rules for International and Inland*. The mass of information you'll be expected to know lends itself extremely well to computer learning, so many schools have developed their own software tools. Most license-preparation schools rely on feedback from successful graduates to keep their question information current. This does not guarantee you'll get every question right, but it certainly increases your chances over someone who has no idea of what to expect.

Many people do pass their U.S.C.G. exams without classroom study, but they spend significantly more time engaged in formal self-study. Such people have a long history of rigid self-discipline.

Why do you need to be licensed? For several reasons. First, because all your competition will be licensed. Second, because you'll never get an insurance company to give the boat owners their "trip binder" unless they see your license. Third, because until you actually can demonstrate your working knowledge of Rules of the Road and your seamanship skills in navigation and boat handling, you shouldn't be running other people's boats.

CHAPTER 28
SELECTING CREW

We think we have the ideal crew balance. John is the captain and engineer; Pat is the first mate and cook. We are the only permanent crewmembers. We fill every other crew position on a temporary or a one-time basis. Crewmembers are independent subcontractors. For 90 percent of our deliveries, we hire a third or fourth crewmember who is either the engineer or the deckhand. Everyone stands his or her own watch. On large vessels, we may have seven or more crewmembers. In those cases we need two people to a watch, because the engine room is so far from the bridge.

Choosing crew is one of the most important decisions you must make, so we recommend that you hire crew based on your own pool of talents and preferences. Insurance companies are beginning to require that a crew roster contain at least two licensed personnel, especially on larger vessels. If you are operating as a couple, it's best if both of you have some form of U.S.C.G. license. Otherwise, you may want to have to hire a third crewmember who has the desirable "second ticket."

THE INS AND OUTS

When to Hire

Since no delivery is certain until you cast off the dock lines, it's wise not to hire crew until you know it's a "go." If you get several people all revved up without really having a job for them, they may not want to be available for you the next time.

However awkward it may be, we still frequently call prospective crewmembers with a "would-you-could-you" proposal, just to see if they are occupied for the proposed delivery period or not. If they are available we put them on standby. Likewise it's not uncommon for a former crewmember to check in with us before he makes a commitment to hire on for some other work, just to see if we have anything better on a back burner.

We actually hire people only when the client's deposit check has been wired to us.

Where to Look

After several deliveries, you will have developed a cadre of trusted crewmembers. Not all of them are suited for all deliveries, nor will they all be available exactly when you need them. That's why you should assemble a file of crew resumés. But for the first few deliveries, your best chance of finding good crew personnel will come from personal referrals from knowledgeable, trusted people in the industry.

Personal referrals. A personal referral in this case is a personal evaluation of someone's professional and personal qualifications for the particular job. Person A tells Person B that he knows that Person C is a decent navigator, gets along well with other crewmembers on long voyages, and can be trusted to do his job in an emergency. Or it could be that Person A says that Person C frequently arrives late for work, occasionally with beer on his breath, and can't seem to keep a boat clean and seaworthy.

For this job, the most valuable personal referrals will come from other captains. "I need a good cook who also can stand watches, and I need an engineer who's familiar with 8V92TIs and Westerbekes. Can you recommend anyone?"

Captains who are friends frequently pass good crew recommendations around. We all need to keep our stable of valued, part-time crewmembers from starving during the periods we can't supply them with work. Since we don't keep anyone on retainer, it's only fair to help them when we can. If they are good enough for us to be interested in their welfare, they're good enough to "loan out" once in awhile.

Personal referrals ought to be from people who know what the delivery business is all about, not from people dazzled by the glamour of it. They need to be able to state truthfully that they know how this person performs while working at sea, preferably for extended periods.

When you let the word out that you may need to hire some crew, be prepared to receive some personal referrals that are well intentioned but rather dubious: Your next-door neighbor wants you to take along his teenage nephew, teach him about the sea and all that. . . . Your sister's brother-in-law has always wanted to do something like this. . . . Your mother's Uncle Jake used to be in the navy, and he's got plenty of time on his hands these days.

Don't hesitate to question the person giving the personal referral. How long have they known him, and in what capacity? How long were they offshore together? Does he have any drinking or drug problems? Any trouble with the law? Does he function well as a team member? Is he a self-starter?

If people say, "Well, she's supposed to be a good sailor and a good cook, and we've always heard good things about her," then ask who they've heard good things from. Or call her and ask her for some personal references.

Advertisements. While you're checking out personal referrals, look through "Crew-Position-Wanted" advertisements. These will be your second most reliable source of crew. At least these aspirants don't sit on their duffs, they get out there and advertise their qualifications and their availability.

Look in the classified sections of all nautical publications under "Crew" or "Positions Wanted." Look on bulletin boards in marinas, boat yards, and chandleries. Sometimes a business card stapled in the corner or an index card wedged into the molding can yield a very worthy crewmember.

Crew placement services. These businesses maintain files of resumés from aspiring crewmembers. We've never had to use them, but they are a source. Again, these are aspirants who've taken the initial step in your direction by listing themselves with a professional service. Some services charge the crew hopefuls a monthly fee to list them and some charge either the crew or the hiring party a fee. Some charge both, and some are free.

Those that charge both are fairly common. Crew place themselves on a list of available persons on a monthly or yearly basis, and pay a monthly or yearly fee, depending on whether they prefer permanent or temporary work. Crewmembers decide what position they are qualified for.

One of the larger international services has

almost 400 resumés on file. All services have their own application forms, and most ask the aspirants for a current resumé, phone number and address of personal and professional references, letters of recommendation, and sometimes a photo. Whether the service actually checks out references and recommendations or not, we can't say, but we always re-check them before we hire. Captains and owners hiring temporary crew pay a flat rate based on the size of the boat. You don't need to pay any fee until you actually hire someone.

Schools. We've been quite happy with a free crew-finding service offered as a sideline by a U.S.C.G. license-preparation school. Anyone enrolled for training in the school is striving to be a professional, so they fulfill one important prerequisite for top-notch crew. Because we feel confident in the quality of education these people are getting, we have some basis for trusting qualifications of people the school recommends. At night, we know they know the difference between two freighters coming at us head-on and one vessel crossing our bow. They aren't likely to try to cut between a tug and his tow.

Many who enroll in the "captains' schools" are long-time licensed captains, who've come back to study for endorsements to their licenses, such as radar plotting, lifeboat launching, and fire fighting. Since the U.S.C.G. reorganized its licensing structure, many captains have come back to school to brush up on Rules of the Road and coastal navigation before getting "recency time" prior to upgrading their tickets. If your upcoming delivery is to Hong Kong, Monte Carlo or Mombassa, they might be willing to work as crewmembers, as opposed to being the person in charge, just for the chance to expand their range of known waters.

The inherent drawback to hiring licensed captains as crewmembers of lesser rank is that they could have a tendency to take on too much responsibility, sometimes overstepping the bounds of their particular job on board. We often hire licensed crewmembers, but we always ask such questions as, "Would you have a hard time accepting orders from another captain? What if you didn't agree with the captain's decisions?" Since captains who are used to their own command are very aware of the importance of having orders followed, such problems are mostly a matter of individual personality. There are lots of good captains who can follow orders from other captains well enough to make good crew.

By now, you will be accumulating a bulging file drawer of potential crewmembers from which to select the perfect complement of mariners for each delivery. As jobs start lining up, leaf through your crew files to evaluate afresh who is best suited for which positions on which boats on which routes.

Advertising for crew. If your files of available crewmembers fail to turn up the exact right people, just place your own ad in local waterfront newspapers. These ads are inexpensive and very effective if properly written. Crew wanted ads will net you dozens of phone calls, so to eliminate inappropriate calls, be as specific as possible about what you need. "Deckhand wanted" should convey that you want someone with a strong back who knows how to work on the deck of a moving boat, but don't count on it. It's best to describe exactly what a deckhand must be capable of doing. Under the newspaper want-ad classification "Crew" or "Crew Wanted," try something like this:

DECKHAND WANTED for delivery of luxury motor yacht Florida to Hawaii. Need strong back, passport, previous experience.

Figure 28-1. It pays to be careful when selecting a crew.

Minimal salary plus all expenses paid. Call John Rains 999–555–1111.

After speaking to each applicant, you want to come away with a resumé of his qualifications. Only by comparing experience levels and qualifications can you narrow down the field. The resumé is the first concrete step in screening. It also may be necessary to give a copy to the insurance company after he or she is hired.

We like to see clear, concise resumés tailored to maritime experience. Resumés are most often typed, and nowadays we get many that are laser-printed with attractive typefaces. This says to us that the person values his image enough to hire a professional resumé writer.

But we often get handwritten resumes, too. These occasionally are from highly competent crew who thrive on temporary work. Image is less important to them, to be sure, and they seldom find the time or need to keep their resumés updated. Such resumés may consist of a handwritten list of boats and positions held on board, on lined notebook paper.

Pat calls this a distinction between style and content. What we look for in any crewmember is content, whether their resumé displays style or not.

Interviewing Crew

Once you've gathered a few suitable resumés, you have the nucleus for your crew file. Once you have a delivery scheduled, set up a personal interview with two or three of the best candidates.

We usually invite prospective crewmembers to come to our office. We set up an appointment for 15 to 30 minutes. If they haven't yet submitted copies of their licenses, passports or letters of recommendation, we'll ask them to bring them to the interview.

When you first meet prospective crew, notice a few things about them. How do they present themselves to you? With comfortable confidence or with awkward bashfulness? Do they look you directly in the eye? Avoiding direct eye contact can mean anything from their general fear of interviews to fear of discovery, as if they were misrepresenting themselves. In the other extreme, do they lock eyes with you and never relent? This is a common offense/defense mechanism.

People who show up too casually dressed, or who practically put their feet up on your desk, might be overcompensating for the feeling that they're expected to put their best foot forward. It's a common passive/aggressive mechanism. As crewmembers, these people might routinely resist your authority or resent having to follow orders.

Instead of asking them if they would resent following your orders, because they will never say "yes," ask them about other jobs listed on their resume, about why they aren't still there, about how they felt about their previous bosses, about their co-workers. Did they get along well with them? Were they asked to do too much? Ask if they mind if you contact those former bosses or co-workers.

Instead of asking them if they've misrepresented themselves to be more highly qualified than they really are, ask them which jobs they liked the best. If it was one of the less demanding jobs, ask why they liked it, but then go on to ask which one they felt was the most challenging or the most instructional. What about it was especially challenging (like having to do coastal navigation with a hand-bearing compass, or having to replace injectors on a Perkins while underway). Then ask if they now feel as if they've mastered whatever it was from that job. Could they take responsibility for doing it by themselves next time?

If this sounds like the Spanish Inquisition, it's not meant to be. Certainly, the interviewee may be under slight stress of being interviewed, but he very likely may encounter some stress while performing his duties onboard once he's hired. Besides, an interview for a temporary job just isn't that stressful.

Fifteen minutes should do it, unless you discover things you'd like to delve into more deeply. Common courtesy says you should give applicants a date when you'll let them know if they're hired or not. Perhaps tomorrow.

Checking references.
Next, check their references. Call the people they've listed as references, but don't be surprised if they're all best buddies. Also track down former employers they haven't necessarily listed as good references. We've been surprised many times by fictitious or bad references. The most common surprise is that they were not Master of Vessel but only a crewmember. Second to this is that they were not paid crew, but only a passenger or guest. We frequently learn from former employers that the reason for leaving is not flattering to the prospective crewmember. We've also had letters of recommendation that were complete fictions.

Check all you can, because whatever serious faults you fail to uncover now, you may have to live with at sea for several weeks.

Once you have checked all the references, use your two best employer tools—common sense and intuition—to make your choice.

If you're interviewing crew for a delivery that's tentatively scheduled for one or two weeks away, it's not unusual to let someone know you plan to hire him contingent on the delivery coming through. That means, as soon as the owner wires you money. That way you're not leaving people hanging longer than need be.

Barring any unforseen disaster, your new crew can begin making arrangements to be off at sea for the duration of the delivery. This usually includes giving notice on some other temporary job, paying bills in advance, finding a pet sitter, and buying new deck shoes or foul weather gear.

From a day's worth of interviewing, you may come up with several great crewmembers, and you'll have to save all but one for future deliveries. Be sure to call back each interviewee, even if it's just to say, "Thanks for your interest, but not this trip. However, can we keep your resumé on file and call you about some other delivery?"

Salaries

How much do you pay crew? Over the years, certain wage ranges have become standard throughout the boating industry. However, the yacht delivery business often falls on the low end of those ranges. Why? Because so many people want to travel to exotic places and be paid for it. Or, they want to go to sea with a delivery captain to learn. In all crew categories we find plenty of qualified crewmembers who would work for nothing. However, we insist on paying them something, because we feel that when the chips are down they may develop a bad attitude. When you pay them you gain some control.

We pay crew as follows:

Engineer—$50 per day. The industry standard is as high as $100 per day for full-time positions aboard large motor yachts. However, we have found highly qualified engineers who are more than happy to work for our wages, sometimes coming on several trips in a row.

Cook—$25 per day. The industry standard is $50 or higher. For this kind of wage you will not find a *cordon bleu* chef. However, you don't need or want one. Meals for delivery crew should be simple yet wholesome.

Deckhand—$20 per day. Industry standard is $40 per day. This is the easiest category to fill, yet we frequently have deckhands with captain's licenses who will work for this wage.

We pay crew 50 percent in advance and the remainder upon completion of the delivery. This conforms with the way we are paid. If they haven't worked with us before, we pay them when they show up at the airport or the first day on the boat. We caution them all not to spend it right away, because if for some reason the delivery washes out, they will have to pay us back the wages for those days they didn't work.

CHAPTER 29
HANDING OVER THE KEYS

Your success in any business depends on customer satisfaction, repeat business, and recommendations. Consequently you want each delivery to end with a happy customer and you'll want to keep him happy by following up.

NEVER HAND OVER A DIRTY BOAT

How good should it look? It should probably look better than it did when you stepped on board.

Here you are, just entering the breakwater of your final destination. Sure you've come a long way and you're tired and just want to get off the boat as soon as you can. Sure you took all kinds of precautions during the preparation stages to protect the boat's interior. But what does it look like now?

If it has been a long delivery, it will take time to detail the boat out no matter how clean you kept it along the way. Try to convince the owner to allow you clean-up time from the very beginning. Otherwise, he'll be standing on the dock when you arrive. No matter how successful the trip has been up to that point, if you have just been slogging a thousand miles uphill in sloppy weather on the last leg of your trip, the boat is going to look rough. First impressions are the ones that last, and if that's the case he will not be pleased when you arrive.

When coming into port, the very first thing you should do is to wash off the boat's transom before you even enter the customs dock or slip. Just use some boat soap and salt water to knock off any exhaust grime. We try to do this before entering any port en route, but at the final destination it's mandatory.

The order in which you perform the remaining tasks and any extra cleaning now depends on the owner's (or broker's) immediate plans for the boat. Find out via VHF whether a prospective buyer needs to see the boat immediately, if the owner or his guests expect to come aboard and use the boat for a few days, or if someone has already ordered a total "buff job" to begin as soon as you can vacate.

Our preference is to have one full daylight day to ourselves on the boat to perform our own thorough cleaning job, which we consider included in the price of the delivery.

Here's what the final cleanup entails:

Interior Checklist
- Laundry: Bed linens, galley and bath towels, small rugs, anything else that got wet.
- Galley clean-out: Toss perishables, leave staples, reorganize messy cupboards, empty and immaculately clean refrigerator, wash floor, clean stove and oven, clean counters, remove seagoing adaptions.
- Head(s): Scrub sinks, counter tops, clean and deodorize toilets.
- Carpet and Upholstery: Vacuum and possi-

bly shampoo any spots, whether they were there before or not.

- Walls and Overhead: Wipe down with gentle oil soap to remove invisible salt spray.
- Windows and Ports: Wash glass and frames, note any leaks.
- Engine Room: Wipe down splattered oil, straighten up tools

Exterior Checklist

- Wash down entire boat, top to waterline including topsides.
- Wash teak decks and oil if required.
- Reassemble bosun's locker: Coil and stow extra lines and gear.

Start the laundry detail first. If you have an onboard washer/dryer, it may not be large enough to complete this big job before you need to vacate, so consider using a laundromat in the marina or a fluff-and-fold service in the vicinity. Leave neatly folded linens in appropriate lockers or make up beds, depending on owner's wishes.

If no one will be staying on board once you vacate, empty the refrigerator of all perishables and leftovers. If shore power is trusty, leave all frozen foods in the freezer. If not, make some other arrangements, but if the owner paid for provisions, they belong to him, not to you. If you didn't plan closely enough to use them all up, it's your loss, not the owner's. Leave all staples in the cupboards, but straighten them up and leave shelves clean.

The refrigerator, stove, and oven probably suffered spills that only got superficially cleaned underway. Remove sea rails from stove. Ammonia detergent helps deodorize the fridge and trash bin. Don't forget the oven racks when you use the foaming oven cleaner. Wash the galley floor with Simple Green, a mild detergent used also in the engine room and for exterior hull soap.

Remove the muslin covers and unsnap any carpet runners; vacuum all carpet, upholstery, draperies, nooks and crannies. Replace carpet runners.

Exterior

To clean the exterior, start at the top by rinsing down all the accumulated salt crystals. Then wash down the entire boat with Simple Green and a deck brush and soft mop. Pay special attention to the topsides. After a Panama Canal transit and many stops in commercial ports along the way, we invariably have skid marks and shadows of the black tires used as fenders. Be sure to get them off. Rinse down and chamois all varnish and any water spots. Clean all deck cushions and replace them when dry. Scrub the waterline if needed. Dry, fold and stow all sails.

Tough salt buildup on exterior glass may need to be rubbed with *soft* Scotch Brite pads before the final Windex and squeegee. Remove rust from all stainless steel, including rails and stanchions, ladders, fighting chairs, bimini struts, and davits.

Any fuel spots on teak decks must be removed completely. Beyond that, use gentle cleaner and oil if required. Don't forget the swim step.

Stow all deck gear, coil and stow all lines and fenders not in use, and generally reassemble all tools and gear that you used from the bosun's locker. Don't leave rags hanging out to dry. Button up biminis or dodgers, depending on weather.

When we leave a lone crewmember aboard for security reasons, we clean the entire boat and then close off all but the smallest area that is absolutely necessary for him to use. We usually insist that no more meals be made on board, no guests permitted, and that he clean up after himself.

Final Inspection

When the owner or owner's agent comes aboard, make sure he walks completely through the boat. We then give him an "Out-of-Commission, Work-To-Be-Done, and Recommendations List." This is very valuable to an owner. On a long delivery, you will become very intimate with every aspect of the vessel. It might take an owner years of occasional use to become as familiar.

Go over the final accounting and settle accounts. If the owner owes you money, make sure it is taken care of at this point. If you have any of his money, give it back.

Have the owner *sign you off the boat*. Take a look at the completion clause in our contracts (see Chapter 25). This is to make sure you get any money remaining in escrow. It also cuts the umbilical cord cleanly. It means that you are no longer responsible for any events that occur on or to the boat.

Ask the owner if you may use him as a reference, and get a letter of recommendation from him.

Follow-Up

Call the owner after a month or so to see if he is still happy. After poking around on the boat after you left, he might have come across something which leaves him puzzled or not too happy. A follow-up call provides a chance to straighten out any forgotten loose ends and it leaves you with a happier customer.

CHAPTER 30
ADVICE FOR OWNERS: HOW TO HIRE A YACHT DELIVERY CAPTAIN

You need your boat delivered. It's a big project and it's going to cost a lot of money. How do you go about finding the right person who is competent and honest? Because there is considerable expense involved, you need to spend some time on this project to ensure that you don't get burned. It's going to involve research in tracking down the right people to interview, negotiating a contract, conducting a thorough interview, and checking out references.

WHERE TO LOOK FOR A CAPTAIN

Yacht Brokers

Brokers are the chief source of referral. Since many deliveries are generated because a vessel has just changed ownership and needs to be moved to the new owner's location, it is logical to ask the broker who sold you the boat for a referral. After all, he probably is more attuned to the waterfront scene than you are. And, because of the commission he's due from the sale of the boat, he should be eager to please, if he wants repeat business.

Owners of large vessels often rely on their broker exclusively. The broker in effect becomes the agent and handles all aspects of the delivery for the owner. We have successfully worked with brokers acting as the owner's agent, and had little or no contact with the owner.

If a broker is from a large, well known firm with one or more branches and has been in business for many years, then he is very qualified to do this. If you are dealing with a relative newcomer from a small firm, you may have to analyze any skipper recommendations with more caution. Often brokers will recommend two or three skippers and let you do the choosing. That way, if you are unhappy with the captain you hired, you can't blame the broker for it.

Insurance Companies

Insurance brokers also are acquainted with yacht delivery skippers and are good sources of recommendations. Because they are sensitive to any insurance claims, you can bet that the skippers they recommend haven't driven boats on the bricks.

Advertising

Look in the classified section of any large, national yachting magazine for yacht deliverers.

Crew Placement Firms

There are crew-placement firms that also can provide you with a delivery captain and crew. However, you must pay them a fee. In addition, the crew is paying the firm a fee for being placed. Some owners we know feel that the placement firm does not adequately screen the crews. You may be better off finding a captain and crew on your own.

SCREENING A CAPTAIN

Your initial contact with a captain is likely to be on the telephone. Find out about his or her background, experience, and licenses. These are some questions you should ask:

1 How many trips has he made on this route and on what kinds of boats?

2 Navigation abilities: If it is an offshore trip, does he know celestial navigation?

3 Mechanical abilities: Can he handle troubleshooting and minor repairs? (The captain should know his way around an engine room, however he himself doesn't necessarily have to do the mechanical work.) If not, make sure he can supply a good engineer and ask to see his resumé.

4 Language ability: If it's a trip into a non-English-speaking area, at least one person on board should speak the language. English, Spanish, and French cover most of the yacht delivery world.

5 What kind of crew will he supply? Ask about their qualifications and check their resumés.

The captain should be asking you very specific questions about your boat, its condition and equipment. If not and he sounds overly eager, be skeptical of his capabilities.

Discuss his prices and terms. If you are still interested, ask him to send you a quote in writing, a sample contract, a resumé (with photograph), a copy of his license, and references. If the captain is local, arrange a personal interview before bothering to check out all his references. There may be something about his personal demeanor or mannerisms you don't like. However, if you live in Pocatella and he lives in Boston and the boat is going from San Francisco to Spain, a face-to-face interview may not be practical. In this case your phone interviews should be as thorough as possible.

Kinds of Captains

A captain's license is not legally required to deliver a vessel. However, as previously mentioned, insurance companies usually require that a paid delivery skipper be licensed as a prerequisite to trip insurance. A license does not guarantee that the captain knows anything, only that he has demonstrated a certain proficiency to a Coast Guard examiner. A license should be a minimum requirement for choosing a skipper.

Refer to Chapter 27 to learn the requirements for obtaining various classes of license. Check an applicant's license for expiration date, tonnage limits, and geographic limits. If he has a 50-ton limit on his license, and your vessel is 98 tons, you should perhaps look for someone else. If you are having a vessel delivered from Maine to Florida and his license is restricted to Florida waters, he's not qualified.

Captains come from a variety of backgrounds. Here are the general categories with some comments so you can better judge an applicant.

Merchant Marine. *Unlimited Masters:* These captains are graduates of four-year merchant marine academies from which they received a third mate's license. This license is not restricted to any tonnage or geographical range. This means they can work on a supertanker anywhere in the world. To qualify as an Unlimited Master they have gone to sea for several years aboard large ships and worked up the ladder from third mate to second mate to first mate and then master, documenting their sea time and being tested by the Coast Guard each step of the way.

Though the Unlimited Master is on the top of the maritime heap, if he has had no background in small craft, he probably is not qualified to run your boat. There is a vast difference between running a large ship and a small boat. Besides, Unlimited Masters make lots of money—what is he doing messing around in the yacht delivery profession? However, if he also has much small craft experience, he may be the most qualified of all.

The Merchant Marine category includes a variety of different types besides the Unlimited Master, right on down to 200 tons and under. The main criterion to look for is small-boat experience.

Ex-military. Some former Navy and Coast Guard officers do deliveries. The same advice about small-boat handling experience applies. Just because someone was a lieutenant commander in the Navy doesn't mean he's qualified to deliver your 40-foot ketch, unless he also has had extensive small-boat experience.

Former Coast Guardsmen with small-boat experience usually make good skippers because of their background in safety, lifesaving, and operating in adverse weather conditions.

Yachtsmen. Since it is a yacht that you want delivered, you are better off hiring someone with a yachting background as long as he or she has much experience on the route and in the kind of boat you have. Yachts are more delicate and are kept in a better state of cosmetic maintenance than are commercial and military craft.

Checking References

If you are still happy after looking over an applicant's resumé, check out his references thoroughly. Be cautious of letters of reference, since many are written by the skipper himself and the person making the recommendation simply signs the letter. Be especially skeptical of letters from famous people. For instance, if he has a letter of recommendation from Dan Rather, don't adopt the attitude, "Well, if he's okay with Dan, he's okay for me." Call Dan and ask him about it.

We know of one owner who hired a captain based on a letter of recommendation from a well-known senator without checking out any of his references. Two months later, the captain sank the boat off Cape Hatteras. In the subsequent investigation it was found that the letter was a fake.

Remember that no one is going to give you a reference that says bad things about him. References from well-known people in the boating industry are good, but still should be checked out. Of particular value are references from boat owners for whom the captain has delivered boats. Ask them the following:

1 What kind of boat did he deliver, from where to where, and when?

2 Was there any damage or unnecessary delay, and was the boat clean when it was handed over?

3 Was the captain honest and thorough in his accounting of expenses? Did the trip cost a great deal over his original estimate?

4 Is there anything unusual or excessive about the captain's personal habits? (Drinking? Drugs? Abusive personality?)

5 Do you know other people I might contact about the captain?

The deeper you dig in checking out references, the greater the likelihood you will choose a captain who will do the job well.

APPENDIX I
THE IDEAL BOAT

After spending many years and hundreds of thousands of sea miles on hundreds of different vessels, an ideal boat begins to evolve in our minds. Granted, a great boat for the canals of Europe might not do for major passagemaking in the Equatorial Pacific. It depends on what you want it to do.

What is our ideal world cruiser?

- Motor sailer, steel hull, 50–60 feet on deck
- Pilothouse
- Double-ended
- Shortened rig, but perfectly able to make port under sail alone
- Roller-furling jib; downwind pole arrangement
- Deep draft
- Engine: Single screw capable of powering at at least 8 knots; minimum of 1,000-mile cruising range; simple, roomy engine compartment
- 110 AC Generator (for refrigeration, power tools, but not overly dependent on 110. Designed to be used only occasionally)
- Proper full-sized chart table, handy to helm yet protected from spray
- Autopilot: simple Wood Freeman
- Ground tackle: 300 feet BBB chain, and good second system. Heavy anchors on

bow, electric windlass with good manual pickup ability, self-flaking chain locker
- Well-ventilated cabins; small lucite portlights. Fans and Dorades throughout. Air conditioning nice but difficult to maintain
- Refrigeration: combination engine-driven and 110 AC. Ten-cubic-foot top-loading compartment; some freezer ability
- Gimballed propane stove, 3-burner with sea rails; balanced oven door
- Water tankage: 250 gallons; low-maintenance watermaker; filtered raincatcher plumbed to reserve tank
- Bilge pumps: electric with warning lights at helm and elsewhere; engine-driven; manual, mounted and portable
- Proper sea berths with lee boards; no pipe berths

What do we look for in a sailboat?

- Adequate power matched to hull design
- Adequate fuel range for emergency
- Ability to sail to weather—modified fin keel
- Roller furling jib; slab-reef main; cruising spinnaker
- Good downwind sailing rig: Pole-out jib, wing-and-wing or double-head sail rig. Poles stowed on mast and ready to go
- Dodger or bimini protection for helmsman

- Full-size navigation table near companionway or helm, yet protected from spray
- Autopilot and windvane
- Stout rigging, easy to maintain and repair offshore

What do we dislike in a sailboat?

- Too-lightly-built fin-keel boats
- Lack of weather protection for helmsman
- Inadequate cockpit scuppers
- Too much rigging hardware mounted on foredeck
- Inefficient non-skid, both on deck and below
- Finicky spinnakers
- Underpowered sailboats
- Cramped engineering space
- Lack of dry storage space
- Too much varnish, especially in tropics

What do we look for in a powerboat?

- Good seakeeping ability: trawler design
- Twin screw, or get-me-home link from generator
- Ten-knot ability at medium RPMs
- 1,000-mile range minimum
- Diesel engines (NOT gasoline); low RPM, like Caterpillar or Gardner; good fuel consumption; dry exhausts (dirty but safe); ability to check oil while running, like Caterpillar or one equipped with murphy gauge; proper fuel filtration (dual filters) with built-in electric prime pump
- Autopilot, radar, Satnav, sounder

- Second steering station for docking
- Anti-roll device (but not built so that they're mandatory). Prefer stabilizers, steadying sail, paravanes
- Proper sea berths
- Gimballed stove with sea rails
- Hooks on upright refrigerator doors
- Through-bolted furnishings, or at least securable
- Night vision light over chart table

What do we dislike in a powerboat?

- Top-heavy, shallow-draft floating condominiums
- Large glass windows on front or sides of house
- Opening windows that invariably leak
- Bow rails that aren't through-bolted with backing plates
- Awkward access to back of power panels
- Souped-up engines with turbo chargers, exotic intercoolers
- Household beds that fling you out in a seaway
- Overdependence on auxiliary generator power
- Lack of manual bilge pumps
- Engine rooms so crammed with extra machinery and systems that proper maintenance is difficult
- Lack of chart table; reliance on table in main salon or on unprotected bridge
- Fixed electric stoves with no fiddle rails
- Fast boats, which generally are not good sea boats

APPENDIX II
PLANNING THOSE MEALS

MASTER MEAL PLANNER

Here's a simple example of a master meal planner—plus how to create and use your own master meal planner. By estimating the quantities of ingredients required for each meal, the difficult task of generating the enormous shopping list is simplified and 90 percent of the guesswork is eliminated. What follows was developed for the delivery of *Pasas*—five people at sea for six days. That's 90 individual meals.

Note that frozen meats are listed first, because you order them in advance of your real shopping trip. Ground sirloin appears three times, but each time it is packaged in different quantities, for use in different recipes, on different days.

Fortunately, I knew that three of my *Pasas* crew were heavy eaters, so I guestimated an extra third to one-half serving for them. For example, in estimating the size of the rump roast, I allowed a half-pound each for two of us and a whole pound each for the three heavy eaters.

Shopping List

Meats (frozen)
Beef, 2″ x 2″ chunks, 1 pkg. 2 lbs.
Ground sirloin, 2 pkgs., 2 lbs each
Ground sirloin, 1 pkg., 1½ lbs.
Ground sirloin, 1 pkg., ½ lb.

Rump Roast, 4 lbs.
Turkey Breast, sliced, 2 pkgs., 2 lbs each
Chicken Breasts, 1 pkg. of 8

Meats (unfrozen)
Chicken Breasts, 1 pkg. of 8
Tuna, 4 lg. cans
Smoked oysters, 3 cans
Bacon, lean, 2 lbs.
Eggs, brown, 5 doz.

Dairy
Swiss cheese, 2 lbs.
Sharp cheddar, 2 lbs.
Cream cheese, 1 lg. tub
Parmesan, 1 sm. can
Powdered milk for 5 gal.
Non-dairy coffee creamer, 1 lg. jar

Grains
Whole grain bread, 6 loaves ass't.
English muffins, 2 pkgs. of 12 each
French-garlic bread, 1 lg. loaf
Burger buns, egg-style, 8
Spaghetti noodles, med.
Pasta spirals, tri-color, 1 lg. pkg.
Quaker granola, 2 boxes
Instant oatmeal, ass't flavors, 2 boxes
Saltines, 1 lg. box
Minute rice, med. box
Popcorn, Orville's med. jar
Blueberry muffin mix, 2 pkgs.

Brownie mix, 1 lg. box
Triscuits, 2 boxes

Canned Veggies & Fruits
Stewed tomatoes w/herbs, 2 cans
Pineapple chunks, 2 cans
Spaghetti sauce w/meat, 1 lg. can
Asparagus spears, 3 tall cans
Green beans, French cut, 2 cans
Sweet corn, 4 vacuum-packed
Mushrooms, chopped, 2 med. pkgs.
Mushroom caps, marinated, 1 jar
Beets, sliced not marinated, 2 cans
Black olives, pitted, 2 cans

Soups & Condiments
Soups: 3 each: tomato bisque, chicken noodle, beef minestrone, split pea, cream of mushroom.
Mayonnaise, 3 med. jars
Mustard, grey poupon, 1 med.
Peanut butter, crunchy, 1-lb. jar
Jam, grape, 1 med.
Jello, Nutrasweet, large, 4 ass't. flavors
Tamari soy sauce, 1 small jar
A-1 steak sauce, 1 small bottle
Swedish meatball sauce package, double
Salted nuts, 2 med. cans
Ground ginger, 1 sm. can
Tarragon vinegar, 1 sm. bottle
Sesame oil, 1 sm. bottle

Beverages
Coffee, ground, 1 lb.
Coffee, instant, Tasters' Choice, large jar
Herb teas, ass't. box of 24
Grapefruit juice, 1 lg. can
Apple juice, 1 lg. bottle or can
V-8 juice, 5 med. cans
Sodas, diet varieties, 12 six-packs
Sodas, sugar varieties, 12 six-packs
Soda water, 12 five-liter jugs
CrystaLite diet drink powder, 2 pkgs. for 5 gals. each

Fresh Produce
Romaine, 2 heads
Iceberg, 2 heads
Green cabbage, 2 med. heads
Red cabbage, 1 sm. head
Green onions, 3 lg. bunches
Cucumbers, 4 lg.
Red sweet peppers, 2 lg.
Green sweet pepper, 2 lg.
Yellow sweet pepper, 2 lg.
Radishes, parsley, celantro, 1 bunch each
Snow peas, 2 selected handfuls
Jicama, 1 lg.
Carrots, 3 lbs.
White onions, 10–12 med.
Red Bermuda onion, 1 lg.
Zucchini, 6 sm.
White baking potatoes, 5 lg.
Red boiling potatoes, 10 sm.
Grapefruits, 10 or lg. bag
Oranges, 12 lg.
Bananas, 10 not too ripe
Pippin or Granny Smith apples, 12 or 15
Red delicious apples, 6 or 8
Various fruits for hand grabbers: peaches, plums, nectarines

This shopping list was derived directly from the six-day meal planner below. We were facing storm weather on the *Pasas* delivery, so I planned alternate meals for rough conditions in the galley, and an extra day's worth of food, in case the trip were to take longer. In fact, we had to hole up for two extra days for storms, never got to eat the cheeseburger dinner, and instead feasted two nights on fresh-caught mahi-mahi.

Six-Day Meal Planner

Breakfasts (Fair Weather)
Scrambled eggs (12 eggs, ¼ lb. grated cheddar cheese (may use leftovers from

previous dinner), bacon, toasted English muffins w/ jam, fresh grapefruits, oranges, juices, coffee, tea.

Breakfasts (Foul Weather)
Quaker granola w/ milk, instant oatmeal w/ bananas, fresh grapefruits, oranges, juices, coffee, tea.

Lunches
1 Tuna sandwiches (16 slices whole-grain bread, tuna, mayonnaise, pickle relish), sliced red and green apples. Beverages are self-service, sodas in separate ice chest outside galley.

2 Pasta salad (1 pkg. pasta spirals, tarragon vinegar, sesame oil, 1 can sliced black olives, slivered sweet peppers of red, yellow, green, marinated mushroom caps, sliced cucumbers, cubed tomatoes, cubed cream cheese, fine-chopped parsley, parmesan cheese). Self-serve drinks.

3 Grilled cheese sandwiches (16 slices sourdough or rye bread, 1½ lbs. grated or sliced cheddar and Swiss cheese, sliced tomatoes), chicken noodle soup, 3 cans.

4 Turkey sandwiches (16 slices whole-grain bread, 2 lbs sliced turkey, mayonnaise, mustard, lettuce, sliced tomatoes, Swiss cheese), coleslaw (shredded green and red cabbage, mayonnaise, green onions), and leftovers from previous dinner.

5 Pasta salad (as above), sliced red and green apples.

6 Peanut butter & jam sandwiches (16 slices whole-wheat bread, toasted if fair weather, peanut butter, jam), coleslaw (as above) or minestrone soup, 3 cans.

7 Turkey sandwiches (as above), Jello w/ cubed cream cheese.

Dinners
1 Hawaiian chicken (8 breasts, 1 can pineapple chunks, soy sauce, red, yellow, green sweet peppers, 2 white onions, snow peas, ground ginger, baked and served over ⅓ box Minute rice), green beans, Jello, green salad (iceberg, Romaine, green onion tops, sliced radishes, grated carrot, grated jicama, sliced cucumber, slivered sweet peppers, sectioned tomatoes), vinegar/oil dressing.

2 Cheeseburgers (2 lbs. ground sirloin, ¼ cup A-1 steak sauce formed into 8 patties, grilled and topped with ¼ lb. shredded cheddar cheese, 8 grilled egg buns, sliced Bermuda onions, lettuce, tomato slices, mustard & ketchup), buttered corn, Jello w/ creamed cheese.

3 Pot Roast (seared and roasted beef rump roast, soy sauce broth, ½ lb. carrots, 8 boiling potatoes, 3 white onions, 1 can corn), green salad as above, Jello.

4 Spaghetti (½ lb. ground sirloin, Ragu sauce, 1 onion, 1 can mushrooms, pasta noodles, parmesan cheese), garlic bread, green salad as above, lemon Jello.

5 Swedish meatballs (1½ lbs. ground sirloin, seasonings package, sauce mix w/ milk), French bean casserole (2 cans green beans, 1 can tomato bisque soup, 2 eggs), green salad as above, Jello, Brownies.

6 Chicken cacciatore (8 breasts, 2 cans tomato, 6 zucchinis, baked and topped with Swiss and parmesan cheese), baked potatoes, asparagus spears, green salad as above, Jello w/ banana slices.

7 Beef stroganoff (2 lbs. beef cubes, seared and sauteed in soy sauce, 2 white onions, 1 can mushrooms, 1 can cream of mushroom sauce, served over minute rice),

buttered beets, green salad as above, Jello w/ pineapple chuncks.

MID-RATS (Midnight rations for night watches)

Leftovers in individual Ziplocs ready for microwave re-heat.

Iced carrot sticks and hard-boiled eggs.

Popcorn w/ butter, sprinkled w/ parmesan cheese.

Popcorn w/ peanut butter and melted butter drizzled over.

Blueberry muffins in individual baggies.

Bite-size chocolate candy bars.

Crackersw/ sliced cheese and apples.

Crackers w/ smoked oysters.

Instant cocoa-coffee blend.

Longer Trips

For longer voyages follow the same basic procedure: Develop a menu and then determine the quantity to buy of each item by adding up the quantities for each ingredient needed for each mealtime. Use hash marks or whatever personal notations you need to add up all those half cans, thirds of bottles, quarter pounds, and half loaves. For shorter trips, round up; for longer voyages, round down. Consider repeating a menu. For example, for a thirty-day voyage you might simply develop a 15-day menu and repeat it.

There will always be things you forgot and things you bought but didn't use, but careful work now will make your job at sea a thousand times more enjoyable.

Now we're ready to go shopping!

APPENDIX III
WEATHER AND ROUTING:
Florida to California via Panama

Although hundreds of yachts pass between the East and West Coasts of the United States via the Panama Canal, remarkably little specific information is available about weather conditions and fuel stops along the entire route. Because this route has been our long-range specialty for 12 years, we've made the voyage more than 20 times, each time gathering more details on fuel stops, routes, distances, and weather en route.

We used a small-scale planning chart and a navigation calculator to determine distances between waypoints, so you may find small differences in latitude and longitude and distances, depending upon the charts you use. When the route between waypoints consists of many course changes close to shore we use the term "coasting" rather than give the courses. Be careful when making landfalls near some waypoints; other course changes are necessary to carry you into port. We give this information for planning purposes only; the prudent navigator will always double-check as in any navigation situation.

For a thorough description of the route see John's book, *Cruising Ports: California to Florida Via Panama.*

BEST TIME TO MAKE THE TRIP

May and November are the best months if you plan to cover this route as quickly and safely as possible. Both these 30-day periods are times of transition between two distinct seasons in the tropics—summer hurricanes and winter northerlies. Figures III-1 and III-2 show average conditions during these two contrasting seasons. Late May heralds the onset of hurricane season, which is by far the more dangerous. It peaks during September and fades during November. May is the best month. A few fast, long-range power boats do make this trip during the summer, but it's a high-risk venture and insurance companies

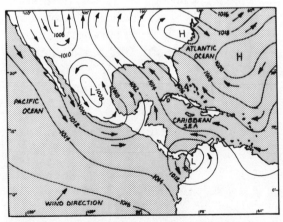

Figure III-1. Summer in the tropics, hurricane season.

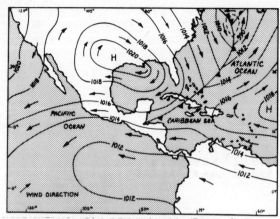

Figure III-2. Winter in the tropics, northerly winds.

normally won't permit it. Even though November is another good month, virtually free of the heavy northerly weather, it is not without risk of late hurricanes in the Caribbean and Gulf of Mexico. Your chance of encountering one of these killer storms is low but still possible, so pay close attention to weather reports.

KEY WEST TO PANAMA

The prevailing wind flow is easterly, called the tradewinds. In winter months, tradewind strengths are often around 20 knots. Passing cold fronts cause winds to shift to the north and increase, causing the dreaded northers in the Yucatan Channel between Cuba and Mexico. There, the cold wind opposes the northward flow of the warm Gulf Stream, and that causes wicked seas to stack up. No matter which direction you are sailing or powering,

do not enter the Yucatan Channel if these conditions are approaching.

In the spring, cold polar air quits invading this far south. Wind strengths drop off and any wind shifts tend to be more southeasterly. By June the first hurricanes are forming in the lower latitudes, but they don't usually get into full swing until late July. During summer the tradewinds often die for days on end. This makes it difficult for a slow sailboat to make passage or to get out of the area before a hurricane approaches. The chance of hurricanes drops dramatically in November, and the first strong northers begin at the end of the month.

See Table 1 for the specifics on waypoints for the nonstop route from Key West to Cristobal, Panama. From Key West to Waypoint #2 off Cabo San Antonio, Cuba, the wind will normally be astern. Heading in the other direction can be tough, but do not come closer to Cuba than the defined waypoint; Cuban coastal patrol boats have opened fire on yachts and seized them for coming within 12 miles of their coast. The Gulf Stream can easily carry you toward the Cuban coast, so pay close attention to your navigation. Loran coverage is very good on this stretch.

From Waypoint #2 to #3 the wind is usually on the beam, which can make for some very rolly going. Waypoint #3 keeps you well offshore of Nicaragua and its political problems, and takes you through a narrow strip of deep water between Cay Gorda Bank and the offshore Rosalind Bank.

From Waypoint #3 to Cristobal, the course

Table 1. *Key West to Panama, nonstop (1,075 nautical miles)*

	Coordinates	True Course	Distance
Key West:	24°28′N, 81°48′W		
Waypoint #1:	22°56′N, 84°28′W	238°	(173 nm)
Waypoint #2:	21°52′N, 85°16′W	214°	(78 nm)
Waypoint #3:	15°45′N, 81°00′W	146°	(440 nm)
Cristobal:	09°23′N, 79°55′W	170°	(384 nm)

is more southerly and usually the wind is astern.

For sailors north-bound from Panama to Key West, late spring gives the most advantageous winds. The trades shift more to the southeast and lend a more favorable slant than they would during winter. For fuel stops along the route, see Table 2.

From Key West to Cozumel, steer to Waypoint #1, then proceed directly to Cozumel. In winter, be sure there are no northers predicted before you leave Key West, because they might catch you in the Yucatan Channel. The Gulf Stream flows very strongly against you on the approaches to Cozumel. We've seen it as strong as six knots between Isla Mujeres and Cozumel.

From Cozumel, steer straight to the west end of Roatan, and then to Coxen's Hole for port clearance. Loran coverage normally fades out during this leg.

Table 3 covers the leg from Roatan to San

Table 2. *Fuel Stops En Route (1321 nautical miles)*

	Coordinates	Distance
Key West:	top off	
Cozumel:	20°30′N, 87°00′W	(377 nm)
Roatan:	16°18′N, 86°34′W	(253 nm)
San Andres:	12°32′N, 81°44′W	(483 nm)
Cristobal:	09°23′N, 79°55′W	(216 nm)

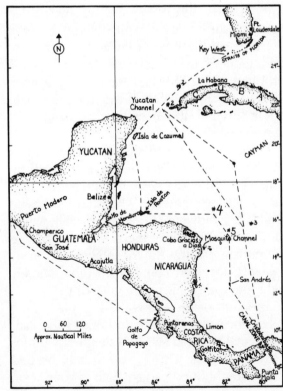

Figure III-3. Waypoints, Key West to Cristobal, Roatan to San Andres.

Andres. When leaving Roatan, steer to Waypoints #4 and #5, and then to San Andres. This course keeps you far enough away from Nicaragua and Honduras to avoid known war zones. Unfortunately, it is dead to windward for 235 miles and can be extremely rough in the shallow seas. Columbus was the first European to sail this coast, and he had a difficult time of it. From Waypoint #4 to #5 you can turn somewhat off the wind, and after #5 you're even more off the wind. Your direct course to San Andres should be more comfortable. Northbound is much easier with both the wind and current astern.

From San Andres steer directly for the Cristobal breakwater. Your wind should be anywhere from on the beam to abaft the beam. Northbound in winter, mariners may find the winds and seas contrary and violent on this leg.

Table 3. *Roatan to San Andres (483 nautical miles)*

	Coordinates	**Distance**
Waypoint #4:	16°20′N, 82°35′W	(230 nm)
Waypoint #5:	15°25′N, 81°38′W	(80 nm)

1600	same as 1130
2200	8765.4
	13113.2
	17307.3

ROUTES VIA GRAND CAYMAN (19°17′ North, 81° 26′ West)

Grand Cayman offers another possible routing option which keeps you to weather. Avoid working your way down into the Gulf of Honduras and then having to bash your way out of it. We would choose the Key West-Cayman-Panama Canal route for vessels with a minimum fuel range of 605 miles, which is needed for the Cayman-Canal leg.

From Key West, follow the route to Waypoints #1 and #2, rounding San Antonio well outside the 12-mile limit, and then straight on to Georgetown, Grand Cayman. Once around the cape of San Antonio, you'll generally have a long slog to windward. From Cayman to the Canal, winds will be on your beam.

An option for shorter-range boats is the Key West–Cozumel–Cayman–San Andres–Canal route. The longest leg is 395 miles, between Cayman and San Andres, but it's still shorter than the Roatan-San Andres leg. The bad news is that from Cozumel to Cayman is dead to weather.

Weather Broadcasts

Radio weather broadcasts for the Atlantic, Caribbean, and Gulf of Mexico:

Greenwich Mean Time	**Megahertz (MHZ)**
0400	4428.7
	6506.4
	8765.4
0530	same as above
1000	same as above
1130, 2330	6506.4
	8765.4
	13113.2

PACIFIC ROUTES

Because the next leg of our long-range route lies so close to the equator it is extremely vulnerable to any movements of the Intertropical Convergence Zone (ICTZ). The ICTZ, also known to sailors as the Doldrums, is an area of low pressure, rain, and light winds. In the summer the ICTZ moves north with the sun and covers the area we're discussing. Winds range from nothing to light, but they can become heavy and squally near the frequent thunderstorms. Lightning is a problem. Costa Rica and Panama are considered to be safely south of the hurricane belt, but in very rare instances, hurricanes have occurred here.

During winter months the ICTZ moves south of the area, which brings on the dry season, a period of dry weather with winds from the north through east. When the Caribbean Trades are blowing strongly, especially when they're coming out of the north, they bridge the narrow Central American landmass in its lowest places and continue to blow fiercely right into the Pacific (see Figure III-4).

The Gulf of Panama is the first place we'll experience this. Southbound out of the Panama Canal to Punta Mala is a sleigh ride under such conditions; a strong north tailwind and strong southbound current both in your favor. If you are going the other way, you will quickly discover why Punta Mala (Bad Point)

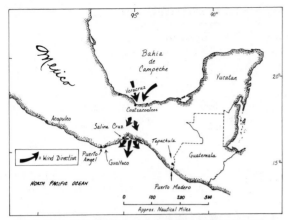

Figure III-4. The Caribbean Trades can bridge the narrow Central American landmass and blow fiercely into the Pacific.

summer months, the northern half of this stretch is exposed to hurricanes. They begin the last week of May and continue until the beginning of November.

In the winter the Caribbean Trades bridge the continent at the Rio San Juan valley, a low spot on the Nicaragua-Costa Rica border. They blow north through east, and especially from December through March, these winds reach gale force. This wind is strongest in the Gulf of Papagallo, but it can be felt from Cabo Velas to the Golfo de Fonseca.

Northbound during these months, monitor the weather in the Caribbean. If a strong cold front moves down into the Caribbean, we'd bet money the Papagallo will be hootin'. Don't leave Puntarenas until weather reports are favorable.

If you're southbound, don't depart Puerto Madero until the weather in the Caribbean moderates. This is the worst direction of travel, because if the wind is east you are heading into it. We were once blown 150 miles offshore in a gale in the Papagallo.

Other than Papagallo, wind conditions are generally light.

Table 6 takes you from Puerto Madero to

got its name. Both the wind and current will be on the nose. Generally, current flows in a counter-clockwise circle within the entire Gulf of Panama, but at Punta Mala it becomes erratic, occasionally causing eddies, rip tides, and choppy seas during the dry season. For the remainder of this leg, the current is generally moderate southbound alongshore, and the wind is light and variable. Table 4 gives routing information from Panama to Puntarenas, Costa Rica.

Table 4. *Panama to Puntarenas, Costa Rica (456.7 nautical miles)*

	Coordinates	True Course	Distance
Seabouy Panama:	8°53.5′N, 79°30.0′W		
Isla Taboguilla:	8°48.5′N 79°30.0′W	180	(3.5 nm)
Punta Mala:	7°28.0′N 79°58.0′W	199	(85.1 nm)
Morro Puercos:	7°09.2′N 80°20.0′W	229	(28.8 nm)
Isala Jicarita:	7°10.0′N 81°48.0′W	270	(87.3 nm)
Isla Montuosa:	7°25.0′N 82°16.5′W	298	(32.0 nm)
Isla Cano:	8°37.0′N 83°59.0′W	305	(124.4 nm)
Isla Herradura:	9°36.0′N 84°41.5′W	324	(72.4 nm)
Puntarenas:	9°58.0′N 84°49.0′W	341	(23.2 nm)

Note: Coordinates are carried out to tenths of minutes, not seconds.

Golfito in southern Costa Rica is also a possible fuel stop in case of emergency.

Table 5 covers the 567 nautical miles from Puntarenas to Puerto Madero. During the

Acapulco, 483 nautical miles. In the summer months this is a dangerous coast because of the threat of hurricanes. In the winter, the Gulf of Tehuantepec has the most notorious

Table 5. *Puntarenas to Puerto Madero (567.3 nautical miles)*

	Coordinates	True Course	Distance
Puntarenas:	9°58.0'N, 84°49.0'W		
Negritas:	9°49.0'N, 87°47.8'W	172	(9.1 nm)
Cape Blanco:	9°31.0'N, 85°06.7'W	226	(25.9 nm)
Guionos Pt.:	9°49.0'N, 85°44.0'W	296	(40.9 nm)
Guatemala:	14°04.0'N, 91°52.2'W	305	(441.5 nm)
Puerto Madero:	14°42.5'N, 92°25.0'W	320	(49.9 nm)

weather of the entire route from Florida to California. High pressure moving into the Gulf of Mexico behind a cold front creates strong northerly winds. These funnel through the narrow valley between two massive mountain ranges on the Isthmus of Tehuantepec and sweep out into the Pacific for several hundred miles. Though a "Tehuantepecer," as this wind is called, can occur in any month, December through April is the worst period, with gale force winds blowing almost continually.

Always transit the gulf of Tehuantepec close to shore. One mile or less. Because the wind blows off the land, there is no sea close to shore. As you move farther offshore seas build rapidly to monstrous proportions. Many stout yachts have been lost offshore here, as have several 2,000-ton tuna seiners. While in most other situations the prudent mariner wants lots of sea room, Tehuantepec is the exception to the rule.

Gale warnings for the Gulf of Tehuantepec are given on both NMC and WWV.

Leaving Puerto Madero stay close to shore. Abreast of the town of Solo Dios, the wind may begin to blow. You can safely stay within a few hundred yards of the beach in five fathoms of water and flat seas. At the lagoon entrances of Mar Muerto and Laguna Inferior move out past 10 fathoms to avoid the shoaling, and then move back close to shore. At Bahia Ventosa (Windy Bay) the wind will blow strongest, but you will then head to the southwest and the wind will shift aft and begin to dissipate. After Puerto Angel, the wind is frequently calm all the way to Acapulco.

Salina Cruz is an alternate fuel stop. We don't recommend it because it is a dirty, windy, industrial city.

Southbound from Acapulco toward the Canal is the most difficult direction to transit the Gulf of Tehuantepec. You turn north into the Gulf at Puerto Angel. Severe blows can be felt even this far out, and Puerto Angel can be used for refuge. However, the wind generally is not felt until north of the tiny port of Hualtuco. If the wind is blowing, stay here until

Table 6. *Puerto Madero to Acapulco (483 nautical miles)*

	Coordinates	True Course	Distance
Puerto Madero:	14°42.5'N, 92°25.0'W		
Salina Cruz:	16°09.0'N, 95°11.0'W	Coasting	(190 nm)
Hualtuco:	15°43.5'N, 96°08.0'W	CST	(60 nm)
Puerto Angel:	15°35.5'N, 96°30.0'W	CST	(23 nm)
Punta Galera:	15°53.0'N, 97°49.5'W	283	(78.5 nm)
Rio Papagayo:	16°34.5'N, 99°29.0'W	291	(104.2 nm)
Acapulco:	16°48.0'N, 99°53.5'W	314	(27.1 nm)

gale warnings are dropped. Then move north quickly, as close to shore as the rocky coastline safely permits. The wind will be on the nose. Once you have passed Salina Cruz you have it made. Stay close to the sandy, regular beach, and the wind will begin to shift aft.

Table 7 covers the 295 nautical miles from Acapulco to Manzanillo. In the summer

the northwest, though often the coastal waters remain calm. During night and early morning hours, a gentle breeze called the "Terral" blows offshore.

Zihuatanejo is an alternate fuel stop. However, fuel arrangements and conditions are inconvenient.

Table 8 will bring you from Manzanillo to

Table 7. *Acapulco to Manzanillo (295 nautical miles)*

	Coordinates	True Course	Distance
Acapulco:	16°48.0'N, 99°53.5'W		
Manzanillo:	19°03.0'N, 104°23.0'W	coasting	(295 nm)

months this coast is very exposed not only to hurricanes, but also to "chubascos." Chubascos are strong thunderstorms which build over the land and sweep out to sea in the late afternoon and evening hours. They are accompanied by strong winds and lightning but last only a few hours.

Winter conditions are very pleasant with light winds. Afternoon seabreezes blow from

Cabo San Lucas. The same summer conditions apply to this route as above.

Northbound during winter, you begin to feel the prevailing northwesterlies of the North Pacific. Strong north winds often line up in the Sea of Cortez and make themselves felt this far south. The best route from Manzanillo is to run the coast north to Frailes, and then jump off from there non-stop to Cabo San Lucas. Make sure you have a good weather report before you leave Frailes. The wind strengths increase as you close with Cabo San Lucas. Southbound you will rarely have trouble as the wind and seas are behind you.

You may shorten this open ocean crossing to 290 miles by continuing on from Manzanillo to Puerto Vallarta where you may also fuel.

Figure III-5. Puerto Madero to San Diego.

Table 9 will take you on the final 724 nautical mile leg to San Diego. Northbound from Cabo San Lucas to San Diego is one of the toughest legs of this entire trip. The prevailing wind is northwesterly and it can frequently blow 20 knots or more for days on end. The spring and summer months have the strongest and steadiest northwesterly flow. In the winter, invading cold fronts at times give a respite from the Northwesterlies.

Table 8.   *Manzanillo to Cabo San Lucas (390 nautical miles)*

	Coordinates	True Course	Distance
Mazanillo:	19°03.0'N, 104°23.0'W		
Frailes:	19°16.0'N, 105°00.0'W	coasting	(40 nm)
Cabo San Lucas:	22°53.0'N, 109°54.0'W	308	.(350 nm)

Table 9.   *Cabo San Lucas to San Diego (724 nautical miles)*

	Coordinates	True Course	Distance
Cabo San Lucas:	22°53.0'N, 109°54.0'W		
Cabo Falso:	22°51.0'N, 110°00.0'W	coasting	(7 nm)
Cabo San Lazaro:	24°49.0'N, 112°27.0'W	302	(178.9 nm)
Turtle Bay:	27°39.0'N 114°54.0'W	322	(215 nm)
N. End Cedros Is.:	28°23.0'N, 115°09.0'W	coasting	(48.0 nm)
Todo Santos Island:	31°47.0'N, 116°57.0'W	335	(224.4 nm)
San Diego Sea Buoy:	32°37.2'N, 117°14.6'W	343	(52.4 nm)

However on rare occasion these cold fronts can be preceded by south easterly gales.

Southbound is usually easy. If you are sailing it can be a fantastic passage.

You may also fuel at Puerto San Carlos in Bahia Magdalena, but it is 20 miles from the harbor entrance up a narrow, twisting channel. Fuel is also available at Ensenada, just 60 miles south of San Diego.

Weather Broadcasts
Radio weather broadcasts for the Pacific:

Greenwich Mean Time	Megahertz MZ
0430, 1030, 1230, 1630, 2230	4428.7
	8765.4
	13113.2
	17307.3
0230, 1460	2670

SUGGESTED READING LIST

NAVIGATION

Bowditch, Nathaniel, *American Practical Navigator*. Washington: U.S. Government Printing Office, 1984.

Shufeldt, Henry, *The Calculator Afloat*. Annapolis, Md: Naval Institute Press, 1980.

WEATHER AND ROUTING

Allen, Philip, ed., *The Atlantic Crossing Guide*, 2nd Ed. Camden, Maine: International Marine Publishing Company, 1988.

Cornell, Jimmy, *World Cruising Routes*. Camden, Maine: International Marine Publishing Company, 1987.

Kotsch, William, *Weather for the Mariner*. Annapolis, Md: Naval Institute Press, 1983.

PASSAGEMAKING

Beebe, Robert, *Voyaging Under Power*. Camden, Maine: Seven Seas Press, 1975. (out of print)

Hiscock, Eric C., *Cruising Under Sail*, 3rd Ed. London: Adlard Coles, Ltd., 1981.

Rains, John, *Cruising Ports: California to Florida Via Panama*. Ventura, California: Western Marine Enterprises, 1982.

MECHANICAL

Calder, Nigel, *Marine Diesel Engines*. Camden, Maine: International Marine Publishing Company, 1987.

SEAMANSHIP

Maloney, Elbert S., *Chapman's Piloting, Seamanship & Small Boat Handling*, 58th Ed. New York: Hearst Marine Books, Motor Boat and Sailing Book Division, 1987.

US Coast Guard, *Navigation Rules, International - Inland*. Washington, D.C.: U.S. Dept. of Transportation, 1986.

Silver, Jan, *Heavy Weather Cooking*. Camden, Maine: International Marine Publishing Company, 1980.

Colgate, Doris, *The Bareboat Gourmet*. City Island, New York: Offshore Sailing School, 1982.

EMERGENCIES AND MEDICAL

Hollander, Neil, *The Yachtsman's Emergency Handbook*. New York: Hearst Books, 1980.

McCasland, Truman, Dr., *The Ship's Medicine Chest and Medical Aid at Sea*. Washington D.C.: U.S. Public Health Service, 1978.

SECURITY

Mueller, G.O.W., *Outlaws of the Ocean*. New York: Hearst Marine Books, 1985.

SURVEYING

Nicolson, Ian. *Surveying Small Craft,* 2nd. Ed. Dobbs Ferry, New York: Sheridan House, 1984.

ELECTRONICS

West, Gordon and Freeman Pittman. *The Straightshooter's Guide to Marine Electronics,* 2nd Ed. Camden, Maine: International Marine Publishing, 1987.

Index